Approaches to Teaching Molière's
Tartuffe and Other Plays

Approaches to Teaching World Literature

Joseph Gibaldi, series editor

For a complete listing of titles,
see the last pages of this book.

Approaches to Teaching Molière's *Tartuffe* and Other Plays

Edited by

James F. Gaines

and

Michael S. Koppisch

The Modern Language Association of America
New York   1995

Library of Congress Cataloging-in-Publication Data

Approaches to teaching Molière's Tartuffe and other plays / edited by
    James F. Gaines and Michael S. Koppisch.
        p.   cm. — (Approaches to teaching world literature ; 54)
    Includes bibliographical references and index.
    ISBN 0-87352-731-3 (cloth). — ISBN 0-87352-732-1 (pbk.)
    1. Molière, 1622-1673. Tartuffe.   2. Molière, 1622-1673—Study
and teaching.   I. Gaines, James F.   II. Koppisch, Michael S.
III. Series.
PQ1842.A87   1995
842´.4—dc20   95-4721

Cover illustration of the paperback edition: Engraving by
François Chauveau for *Le Tartuffe ou l'imposteur*,
1669 and 1673 editions. Paris, Bibliothèque Nationale,
Département des Imprimés.

Published by The Modern Language Association of America
10 Astor Place, New York, New York 10003-6981

CONTENTS

Theatrical Approaches

PREFACE TO THE SERIES

In *The Art of Teaching* Gilbert Highet wrote, "Bad teaching wastes a great deal of effort, and spoils many lives which might have been full of energy and happiness." All too many teachers have failed in their work, Highet argued, simply "because they have not thought about it." We hope that the Approaches to Teaching World Literature series, sponsored by the Modern Language Association's Publications Committee, will not only improve the craft—as well as the art—of teaching but also encourage serious and continuing discussion of the aims and methods of teaching literature.

The principal objective of the series is to collect within each volume different points of view on teaching a specific literary work, a literary tradition, or a writer widely taught at the undergraduate level. The preparation of each volume begins with a wide-ranging survey of instructors, thus enabling us to include in the volume the philosophies and approaches, thoughts and methods of scores of experienced teachers. The result is a sourcebook of material, information, and ideas on teaching the subject of the volume to undergraduates.

The series is intended to serve nonspecialists as well as specialists, inexperienced as well as experienced teachers, graduate students who wish to learn effective ways of teaching as well as senior professors who wish to compare their own approaches with the approaches of colleagues in other schools. Of course, no volume in the series can ever substitute for erudition, intelligence, creativity, and sensitivity in teaching. We hope merely that each book will point readers in useful directions; at most each will offer only a first step in the long journey to successful teaching.

Joseph Gibaldi
Series Editor

PREFACE TO THE VOLUME

Molière has, almost since the moment he began writing, been a central—and controversial—figure in French culture. His plays have been written about, protested against, and, of course, staged in ways that reveal not only how different historical periods have viewed Molière and the seventeenth century in France but also what their own preoccupations are. As Laurence Romero has shown, there is a long tradition of Molière studies in a distinctly moralistic vein. The actor La Grange, a friend of Molière's, said that the dramatist's comedies were intended to "obliger les hommes à se corriger de leurs défauts" (Romero, "Molière's *Morale*" 706) ("to oblige men to correct their faults"). Later, in the nineteenth century, Molière was seen by Ferdinand Brunetière and others as a *libertin* (free-thinker). Ralph Albanese has discussed in great detail how the Third Republic treated Molière's theater in its schools. So varied have the responses to Molière been that over the years a substantial corpus of scholarly work about Molière criticism and theatrical productions has developed. What accounts for Molière's immense popularity is that his plays are immediately accessible despite their being firmly rooted in the French seventeenth-century tradition. It is impossible to read or to see a good production of *Le bourgeois gentilhomme* without laughing. No matter how much or how little one knows about *préciosité* as a literary movement, *Les précieuses ridicules* evokes laughter. Roger Planchon, the famous director who has both staged and acted in *Tartuffe*, says of that work: "It's a play that I can reread every year, that I can rework every year . . . . For me, it's an inspirational work. . . . I have never made a definitive mise en scène of it. . . . My relationship to this play is one of fascination" (Carmody 55). The literary and theatrical richness of *Tartuffe* is inexhaustible.

Tartuffe is also, not surprisingly, one of the most widely taught of Molière's plays. In one sense, it is an easy play to teach, for beginning high school students and advanced graduate students alike find it engaging. But every teacher who has ever taught Molière has confronted the question of how best to approach his theater. *Tartuffe* demonstrates what a good teacher faces. The play is about a phenomenon, religious hypocrisy, that students understand and condemn. So emphatically did Molière portray Tartuffe that the case against him is decided well before the character appears onstage. Yet as soon as we begin to read the play more critically, complications aplenty emerge. Is Orgon really just Tartuffe's dupe, or does he not play a more active role? Orgon may actually have something to gain by allowing himself to be victimized by the wily Tartuffe—control over the household into which the hypocrite has been welcomed. And what is the explanation of the play's resolution by a kind of deus ex machina that is, for many readers and viewers, problematic? Teachers must find ways to use these and other such thorny questions to focus discussion in their classes. The goal of this collection of essays by colleagues who have regularly taught Molière is to share with other teachers techniques and ideas for effectively doing just that.

Part 1 of our book provides bibliographic information and teaching materials that will be helpful to both those who teach Molière in the original and those who work in English. Responses to a questionnaire sent to teachers of Molière have been invaluable in our formulation of this information, and we appreciate the generosity of colleagues who took the time to respond so fully to our queries. It is not possible, in the context of a project like this one, to list all the fine scholarly and critical work on Molière, but we have tried to cull from that vast bibliography works that will, in our view, be of the greatest benefit to instructors who teach Molière to students at a variety of levels. Much of the finest writing about *Tartuffe* occurs as part of larger works that include discussions of other Molière plays as well. In the classroom, too, *Tartuffe* is often presented along with other Molière texts. Many teachers like to introduce their students to all three great masterpieces—*Tartuffe*, *Dom Juan*, and *Le misanthrope*—and the *comédies ballets*, such as *Le bourgeois gentilhomme* and *Le malade imaginaire*, have always been popular choices for students. Contemporary interest in the role of women in society and developments in feminist criticism have led to productive new ways of thinking about and teaching *Les précieuses ridicules*, *L'école des femmes*, and *Les femmes savantes*.

We have attempted, in the second part of this volume, to respond to the rich diversity of choices made by teachers in their selection of Molière plays for their classes. All the essays in the first section of part 2 focus on *Tartuffe*, for it remains the play most frequently taught in both French and English. What we want to offer here is a variety of critical perspectives that might help teachers direct classroom discussions of the play and develop their own individual readings. The second section of part 2 includes essays on other plays by Molière, once again written from substantially differing points of view. All the plays discussed figure regularly in the curricula of schools around the country, and each essay will suggest how we might engage our students in the study of Molière.

One aspect of Molière's work that is crucial but too little discussed is its theatricality. Even if we cannot always have students act out the plays they are studying, it is important to keep in mind as we teach Molière that he was, above all else, a complete man of the stage. The authors of chapters in the final section of part 2 broach this subject from several angles.

The edition of Molière that authors have consulted and cited throughout this volume is that of Georges Couton, published in the Bibliothèque de la Pléiade collection. Act, scene, and line numbers (or act and scene numbers only, for the prose plays) indicated in the text refer to this edition, even when an author gives only an English translation of a word or passage. Richard Wilbur has translated five of Molière's verse plays—*L'école des femmes*, *L'école des maris*, *Les femmes savantes*, *Le misanthrope*, and *Tartuffe*—and for these works, his translations have been provided in this volume. Unless otherwise indicated, translations of other plays by Molière and of passages from other works in French are the authors' own. In a few instances, the authors have substituted their own translations for Wilbur's to make a particular point; such translations are indicated by the phrase "my trans." To avoid unnecessary repetition, all the many other editions of Molière's plays mentioned in part 1 are not listed in the works-cited section at the end of the volume.

In the preparation of this volume, it has been a real pleasure to work with our contributors, who have been unfailingly thoughtful in responding to the exigencies of the task before us all. The referees chosen by the MLA to review the proposal and manuscript of the volume wrote carefully considered critiques that were of great assistance. We appreciate their concern and their efforts on our behalf. Joan Schroeder has helped enormously in the preparation of the volume and has our thanks for all her good work. We are particularly grateful to Joseph Gibaldi, the general editor of the series, to Sonia Kane, and to Elizabeth Holland for their patience and guidance.

James F. Gaines, *Southeastern Louisiana University*
Michael S. Koppisch, *Michigan State University*

Part One

MATERIALS

Editions of the Plays in French

Complete and Collective Editions

The authoritative complete edition of Molière in French at the present time is Georges Couton's, prepared for Gallimard's Bibliothèque de la Pléiade collection in two volumes in 1971. The depth of annotation, the completeness of supporting texts located in appendices, and the reliability of the texts themselves make this edition stand out. The Classiques Garnier's edition by A. Jouanny, also in two volumes, ranks a close second and marks a distinct improvement over the same series' earlier Maurice Rat edition, which was thoroughly unreliable. Pierre-Aimé Touchard's edition in the Intégrale collection, jointly published by Editions du Seuil and Macmillan (but now out of print) is still available in many libraries, but its light annotation makes it less useful than either the Couton or the Jouanny editions. Researchers still find themselves consulting the venerable edition in thirteen volumes that Eugène Despois and Paul Mesnard turned out between 1873 and 1900, which was the definitive text before Couton. The first nine volumes contain the plays, the tenth a biography by Mesnard that took into account the discoveries of Moliéristes in the heyday of archival expeditions, the eleventh a bibliography that contains much relevant material on the eighteenth and nineteenth centuries even though it is now outdated, and the last two a lexicon that still serves readers well today. Although the 1682 *Œuvres de Monsieur de Molière*, edited by La Grange and Vivot, is not available in facsimile, the above editors account well for the accuracies and inaccuracies of that first collective edition, and the full set of engravings by Pierre Brissart and Jean Sauvé are now available in various handy sources, including Stephen Dock's *Costume and Fashion in the Plays of Jean-Baptiste Poquelin Molière*.

A paperback edition of the *Œuvres complètes* is available from Garnier-Flammarion, in four volumes edited by Georges Mongrédien; though its texts are reliable and its prices relatively modest compared with those of other complete editions, the brevity of its supporting material and its lack of annotation limit its value for those who are not already completely familiar with Molière and his world.

Individual Editions

The American teacher wishing to find a good French edition of one of Molière's plays is almost inevitably forced to choose between the Nouveaux classiques Larousse series and the Univers des lettres Bordas, both furnishing pocket-format texts that include a relatively rich collection of supporting documents and black-and-white illustrations. Of the two, Larousse offers books with slightly larger print and, in most cases, more abundant documentation. Bordas offers better illustrations, which generally show stage interaction rather than simply actors' publicity poses, and takes a more modern approach in its running commentary and questions. The Classiques Larousse edition of *Tartuffe* was prepared by Pierre Clarac. Other Larousse volumes are devoted to *L'Amour médecin*, *Amphitryon*, *L'avare*, *Le bourgeois gentilhomme*, *La critique de* L'école des femmes, *L'impromptu de Versailles*, *Dom Juan*, *L'école des femmes*, *Les femmes savantes*, *Les fourberies de Scapin*, *Le malade imaginaire*, *Le médecin malgré lui*, *Le médecin volant*, *Le misanthrope*, *Les précieuses ridicules*, and *Scènes choisies*. Bordas offers a largely similar selection, omitting *L'Amour médecin* but including *George Dandin* and *Monsieur de Pourceaugnac*.

In addition to these two imposing publishers, others in France offer less compendious series. Didier's Classiques de la civilisation française series contains individual volumes of *Tartuffe*, *L'avare*, *Le misanthrope*, *Le bourgeois gentilhomme*, *Les femmes savantes*, and *Le malade imaginaire*. They present a great deal of supportive glossing and illustration, so much that at times one has difficulty finding the text itself. The opposite is true of the Nouvelles classiques illustrées Hachette, which have rather light annotation; since they are published in collaboration with the Comédie Française, they tend to feature illustrations only of that troupe's productions, which is not always an advantage. This series includes *L'avare*, *Le bourgeois gentilhomme*, *Dom Juan*, *L'école des femmes*, *Les femmes savantes*, *Les fourberies de Scapin*, *Le malade imaginaire*, *Le médecin malgré lui*, *Le misanthrope*, *Les précieuses ridicules*, and *Tartuffe*, some of these volumes available with a separate teacher's manual (in French, of course).

In England, Blackwell's French Series contains distinguished editions of *L'école des femmes*, *Dom Juan* (both edited by W. D. Howarth), and *Le misanthrope* (edited by Gustave Rudler). Also in Britain, Nelson Publishing's French Classics series offers editions of *Tartuffe* (prepared by R. P. L. Ledesert), *L'avare*, *Le bourgeois gentilhomme*, *Le misanthrope* (all edited by R. A. Wilson), and *Le malade imaginaire* (edited by both Ledesert and Wilson).

An American volume of *Tartuffe*, edited by Hallam Walker for Prentice-Hall in 1969, is no longer in print but may be found in some libraries. A reprint of Haskell Block's edition for the Crofts Classics series may be obtained from Harlan Davidson.

In Britain, Peter Nurse's 1965 edition of *Le malade imaginaire* is available from Oxford University Press (Clarendon French Series); it has fine notes and introduction. The same series contains Gaston H. Hall's well-known edition of *Les femmes savantes*.

Finally, a most interesting edition of *La jalousie du Barbouillé* together with *George Dandin* has been prepared by J. A. Peacock for the Exeter University French Series.

Anthologies

Recent wholesale changes in the American publishing business have whittled down the range of French anthologies to a very few. Harcourt Brace still offers the 1965 edition of Morris Bishop's two-volume *Survey of French Literature*, the first volume of which features *Le bourgeois gentilhomme*, accompanied by a short introduction and moderate annotation. The first volume of Robert Leggewie's *Anthologie de la littérature française*, third edition (Oxford University Press), also contains *Le bourgeois gentilhomme*, with a short French introduction and light French glossing. (Previous editions of these anthologies had offered instead *Le malade imaginaire* and *Le misanthrope*, respectively.)

Editions of the Plays in English

Collective Editions

At the present time there is in print no English edition of the complete works of Molière that is suitable for classroom use. Several different collective translations, however, are available. Donald Frame translated two volumes of Molière for the paperback Signet Classics series, including in the first of them *The Misanthrope, The Mischievous Machinations of Scapin, The Doctor in Spite of Himself, The Miser, The Would-Be Gentleman, The Learned Women*, and *The Imaginary Invalid*; and in the second *Tartuffe, The Ridiculous Précieuses, The School for Husbands, The School for Wives, The Critique of the School for Wives, The Versailles Impromptu*, and *Don Juan*. Frame translated verse with verse and prose with prose. The original translation was prepared in 1968.

Another paperback series was edited by John Wood for the Penguin Classics. One volume contains *The Miser, That Scoundrel Scapin, The Would-Be Gentleman, Don Juan*, and *Love's the Best Doctor (L'Amour médecin)*; the other includes *The Misanthrope, Tartuffe, The Imaginary Invalid, The Doctor in Spite of Himself*, and *The Sicilian*. Wood's translations date from 1953.

Richard Wilbur's poetic translations, perhaps the most elegant ever done, are available from Harcourt Brace: *The School for Wives, The School for Husbands, The Learned Ladies*, and *Tartuffe* appear individually, and *Tartuffe* is combined with *The Misanthrope*. *The School for Wives* and *The Learned Ladies* were published together in 1978 and again in 1991, as were *The School for Husbands* and *Sganarelle; or, The Imaginary Cuckold* in 1993. Wilbur's versions date from 1965 to 1993. All these plays except *The School for Husbands* are combined in another Harcourt Brace volume entitled *Four Comedies*. The same translations (minus *The Learned Ladies*) appear in a volume published in Britain by Methuen under the title *Five Plays*, the fourth and fifth being Alan Drury's translations of *The Miser* and *The Hypochondriac*. Like the Wilbur translations that are mentioned below in the section "Anthologies," those in *Five Plays* lack the translator's short but excellent introductions, for which a piece by Donald Roy is substituted.

More recently, Albert Bermel prepared a series of translations for The Actor's Molière series, published by Applause Theater Book Publications. He paired *The Doctor in Spite of Himself* with *The Bourgeois Gentleman*, *The Miser* with *George Dandin*, and *Scapin* with *Don Juan*. Bermel took some liberties with Molière's text, cutting and blending parts, rhyming some prose and even adding a few rhymes of his own confection. Separately, he provided the translations for Ungar's *One-Act Comedies of Molière*; the book was originally published under the title *The Genius of the French Theater*. Applause has also published a collection entitled *The Misanthrope and Other French Classics*, containing the Richard Wilbur translation and edited by F. Bentley, but apparently it has been distributed only in the United Kingdom.

Another series of acting booklets—translated by Miles Malleson, published in Britain by Acting Editions, and only rarely available in America—includes volumes of *The Miser*, *The Prodigious Snob* (*Le bourgeois gentilhomme*), *The Imaginary Invalid*, *Tartuffe*, *The School for Wives*, and *Sganarelle*.

Absolute Classics, of Bath, England, has published a one-volume edition of Ranjit Bolt's rhymed-couplet versions of *Tartuffe* and *The Sisterhood* (*The Learned Ladies*), the texts having been originally prepared for productions at Peter Hall's Playhouse Theatre and at the New End Theatre, in Hampstead.

In 1969 Heinemann published, in a single volume, Allan Clayson's prose translations of *The School for Husbands*, *The Flying Doctor*, *The Uneasy Husband* (*Sganarelle, ou le cocu imaginaire*), and *Love Is the Best Doctor*. Augusta Gregory's quasi-Irish translation, called *The Kiltartan Molière*, originally published in 1910, is still available from Ayer Company Publishers in reprint form. Another collection, *Eight Plays by Molière*, is available from Amereon. In Britain, I. Maclean and G. Gravely's translation of Don Juan *and Other Plays* is available in the World's Classics series of Oxford University Press.

Individual Editions

Besides the Wilbur translation of *Tartuffe* already mentioned, the play has also been rendered into English by Renée Waldinger for Barron's Educational Series; this paperback edition is entirely in prose. The same series includes Wallace Fowlie's translation of *The Miser*, Eric M. Steele's verse rendition of *The School for Wives*, and Herma Briffault's *Middle-Class Gentleman*. These four volumes date, respectively, from 1959, 1965, 1977, and 1957.

For a production by the Royal Shakespeare Company in 1983 Christopher Hampton prepared a translation of *Tartuffe* that was later published by Faber and Faber of London; Hampton's translation is in unrhymed iambics, and his stage directions introduce the character of Laurent in several scenes. The same publisher has produced Hampton's translation of *Don Juan*.

Another version of *Tartuffe*, published and available mainly in England, was translated by Liz Lochhead for Polygon. Among older translations of the play that, though not in print, are sometimes available in libraries is the 1962 acting version by James Rosenberg for Chandler. Donald Sutherland's 1962 translation of *Scapin*, also for Chandler, is another such volume.

Oscar Mandel's 1977 translation of *Amphitryon* is published by Spectrum Productions. W. Hannon's 1963 version of *The Reluctant Doctor* is available from Theatre Arts. Tony Harrison's version of *The Misanthrope*, commissioned by the National Theatre of Great Britain in 1973, is available from Rex Collins (the American edition, printed by Third Press, is apparently out of print). Meanwhile, Jeremy Sams's *The Miser*, also prepared for the National, appeared in the Methuen New Theatrescripts series in 1991.

The Imaginary Invalid is available in Britain from Hansbury Plays in a translation by B. Briscoe. An Australian version of *Don Juan*, prepared by N. Enright, was published as part of by the Current Theatre Series.

Anthologies

American students who encounter Molière in world literature or drama classes will almost certainly read the Richard Wilbur translation of either *Le misanthrope* or *Tartuffe*. The former is featured in St. Martin's *Stages of Drama* (ed. Carl Klaus, Miriam Gilbert, and Bradford S. Field, Jr.); *The Norton Introduction to Literature: Drama* (ed. Carl E. Bain); *The Bedford Introduction to Literature* (ed. Michael Meyer); Little, Brown's *Types of Drama* (ed. Sylvan Barnet, Morton Berman, and William Burto); and the University Press's *Elements of Literature* (ed. Robert Scholes, Carl Klaus, and Michael Silverman). *Tartuffe* appears in volume 2 of *The Norton Anthology of World Masterpieces* (ed. Maynard Mack); *The Harcourt Brace Jovanovich Anthology of Drama* (ed. W. B. Worthen); and *Twenty-Three Plays* (ed. Otto Reinert and Peter Arnott). One alternative to Wilbur's *Tartuffe* is Christopher Hampton's, which appears in Methuen's 1991 *Landmarks of French Classical Drama* (ed. David Bradley). Of the books mentioned above, the Harcourt Brace anthology and *Stages of Drama* seem to offer the most extensive documentary support for students unfamiliar with the French literary tradition.

Macmillan's *Masterpieces of the Drama* (ed. A. W. Allison, A. J. Carr, and A. M. Eastman) uses a Lloyd C. Parks translation of *The Miser*, with minimal support and no annotation, largely because it forms a nice contrast with such other selections as *The Merchant of Venice* and *Volpone*. (Oddly, *The Miser* directly precedes William Wycherley's *The Country Wife*, which owes so much to another Molière play, *L'école des femmes*.)

Required and Recommended Readings

The sheer mass of scholarly and critical writing on Molière is daunting. For the thirty-year period spanning 1942 to 1971 alone, Paul Saintonge includes in his bibliography almost 1,400 entries; for the preceding fifty years, he and Robert Christ had compiled 3,316 items. Everything from bibliographies to collections of historical documents, from biographies of the author to detailed critical studies, is available to assist—or, if improperly handled, bewilder—the student of Molière. Since most of the teachers who participated in our survey must regularly introduce *Tartuffe* or other Molière plays to students for whom their reading will be a multifaceted initiation—to Molière, to the play, to studying a difficult work in French, to the seventeenth century in France—it is not surprising that many instructors do not require collateral readings. These teachers choose, rather, to have students devote all their attention, in the classroom and in homework assignments, to the text itself. Those who do require outside reading recommend many of the same works that they suggest as especially appropriate for the nonspecialist teacher. What most of us probably agree on is that our undergraduate students will derive the greatest benefit from recommended and required readings that are relatively straightforward and easily accessible in libraries.

Although first published in 1954, John Lough's *An Introduction to Seventeenth Century France* remains a useful book for its intended audience: "those who, in schools and universities or outside them, approach seventeenth century France through the great works of its literature" (v). Chapters 5, 6, and 9 in this book, read together, will give students a general notion of the period's history. A broad but fine introduction to comedy in France is Pierre Voltz's *La comédie*. The chapter on Molière treats the major plays, with special attention to *Tartuffe*, and several passages from Molière's opus are anthologized in parts 2 and 3 of the volume. As Voltz sees the play, *Tartuffe* is the first of Molière's comedies to focus on a group of characters, the bourgeois family, rather than on a single central figure (as is typical in farce). To give students a lively picture of the sweep of seventeenth-century French letters, teachers might assign Will G. Moore's book *French Classical Literature*. Moore resists criticism that portrays the period's great writers as restrained by a need to imitate ancient texts and strive for a limpid literary perfection. His clear, direct prose will communicate to students the surprise and excitement of the texts he discusses. The title of his chapter on Molière, "The Discovery of Comedy," indicates Moore's conviction that Molière is an innovator, not a dramatist looking back to ancient comedy.

Students in more advanced courses will read with great profit Paul Bénichou's classic study *Morales du grand siècle*, which has been translated into English as *Man and Ethics: Studies in French Classicism*. Distinguishing three dominant ethics in seventeenth-century French thought—the heroic, the austerely Christian, and the worldly—Bénichou develops his reading of classical humanism through insightful interpretive essays on Corneille, Pascal, Racine, and Molière. The essay on Molière could be assigned alone. In it, Bénichou argues against the view of critics for whom Molière's comedy propounds the virtue of bourgeois good sense and the ethic it implies. An extended study of Molière and his theater appropriate for advanced students is René Jasinski's *Molière*, which approaches its subject in the traditional style of setting out the author's life and works in some detail. A more speculative but very readable study in this genre is *La vie de Molière*, by Ramon Fernandez, translated into English in 1958 and later republished in French under the title *Molière ou l'essence du génie comique*. Fernandez has left his mark on much of Molière criticism. Recently, in 1991, Peter Nurse acknowledged this influence in his *Molière and the Comic Spirit*, a good contemporary introduction to the playwright. Andrew Calder's *Molière: The Theory and Practice of Comedy* is another general work appropriate for the nonspecialist.

Any number of works mentioned in the section "The Teacher's Library" might also serve students well. Responses to our questionnaire indicate that Molière specialists will recognize in both the student and teacher readings some of their own favorite books on Molière.

The Teacher's Library

Whether one is doing it for the first time or the fiftieth, to teach *Tartuffe* or other Molière plays is always a challenge, and nothing can substitute for the years of reading, studying, and attending performances that the best teachers will have behind them. Even the seasoned teacher of Molière, however, will undoubtedly want to consult some secondary materials before taking up in class a play as complicated as *Tartuffe*. Only a few specialists will be abreast of the latest in Molière scholarship each time they teach his plays, but, as our survey's results indicate, there is a substantial body of writing about Molière that will help instructors, specialists and nonspecialists alike, understand and teach Molière better.

A writer as widely read and performed as Molière is probably taught, in this country, as often in English as in French. There is no experience quite like reading Molière in French or seeing a good French production of one of his plays, but fortunately, fine English translations of his work do exist. There is, likewise, no shortage of excellent criticism of Molière in English. In fact, much of the best recent writing about Molière has been in the English language. In the suggestions that follow, we include works, without regard to the language in which they are written, that are potentially useful for a reader preparing to teach Molière. Those who teach in English will find good critical writing at their disposal, as will intellectually adventurous students in search of criticism in English. It goes without saying that the bibliographical information presented here is intended to assist teachers of Molière. Those who write about Molière will need to do far more exhaustive bibliographic work.

Reference Works

Teachers will find their best source of bibliographic information in the two volumes on the seventeenth century of the critical bibliography generally referred to as the "Cabeen," after the name of one of its original general editors. The first volume, edited by Nathan Edelman, covers works published up to March 1959. H. Gaston Hall's supplement appeared in 1983. Both volumes include a section on Molière. Works listed are judiciously chosen, and each title is followed by a brief descriptive statement about its contents. This information permits the reader to form in advance some judgment about how useful an entry is likely to be. These volumes are indispensable tools for teachers and scholars. Another critical biography, *French 17*, edited by J. D. Vedvik, is updated annually. Otto Klapp and the MLA also issue comprehensive bibliographies that, though not critical, are invaluable for the teacher who wants to track down a specific book or article.

Part 3 of Henry Carrington Lancaster's *A History of French Dramatic Literature in the Seventeenth Century* focuses on Molière and the period during which he produced his most important plays. This standard reference work gives much historical information about Molière's theater and the individual plays. Teachers who want to delve deeply into the historical documentation available on Molière, his family, and his troupe can refer to the archival work of Madeleine Jurgens and Elizabeth Maxfield-Miller. Sylvie Chevalley's *Molière en son temps* is a magnificently illustrated *album d'images*. It makes no claim to add to current knowledge of Molière but will give students a visual sense of Molière's theater and its historical moment. The full-color plates of Madeleine Béjart playing Magdelon in *Les précieuses ridicules* and of La Grange in the role of La Grange can make the play come to life for our students, most of whom will never have seen such costumes.

Background Studies

For extensive information about the literary background against which Molière must be read, it is hard to recommend a better work than Antoine Adam's *Histoire de la littérature française au XVIIe siècle*, whose third volume includes a long chapter on the great comic dramatist. Clearly written and superbly documented, Adam's work—though published between 1948 and 1956— remains authoritative. It is always sensitive to both the literary and historical dimensions of the period. Less comprehensive and certainly not as helpful on the work of Molière himself, Adam's *Grandeur and Illusion*, as he says in its preface, "seeks to exhibit as clearly as possible the fundamental relationships that existed between French society in the seventeenth century and the literature it created" (ix). Denis Hollier's *A New History of French Literature* is a very different kind of literary history from those of Adam and other traditional literary historians. Contributors to it write about the seventeenth century (and other periods) from a variety of critical perspectives. Especially relevant for teachers of Molière is Gérard Defaux's chapter, "The Comic at Its Limits" (334–40). Defaux suggests here what he sees as the "coherence and internal dynamism" (336) of an opus that evolved from a moral to a more aesthetic vision. Among contributions to Hollier's history that will help teachers enrich classes on Molière are those of Jean-Marie Apostolidès ("From *Roi Soleil* to *Louis le Grand*," 314–20) and Jacques Guicharnaud ("The Comédie-Française," 354–58).

Georges Bordonove's biography of Molière is an excellent introduction to the playwright and his work. The more recent biography of Francine Mallet is less straightforward and not as well written. For English-speaking readers, Hallam Walker's *Molière: Updated Edition* is a most serviceable volume. It is a good general presentation of Molière, with a concluding chapter that gives much concise bibliographical information. For both background reading and an outline of a number of the major critical perspectives on Molière up to the mid-1960s, Jacques Guicharnaud's *Molière: A Collection of Critical Essays* is still excellent. A handy source for Gustave Lanson's influential essay "Molière and Farce" (20–28), this volume also includes selections from works by some of the most important critics of Molière.

Critical and Scholarly Approaches

Although the number of book-length studies of Molière's theater is large, there are certain works that have, over the years, become essential reading for teachers and scholars. Extremely different in both tone and approach, Jacques Guicharnaud's *Molière: Une aventure théâtrale* and Lionel Gossman's *Men and Masks: A Study of Molière* are two such works. Taking Molière as a dramatist above all else, Guicharnaud analyzes in great detail *Tartuffe*, *Dom Juan*, and *Le misanthrope*. The critic becomes an extraordinarily alert spectator who tries to miss nothing in these three plays. Gossman's stance is far more philosophical and emphasizes the dynamics underlying relations between self and other in the plays he discusses. His book is one of the most richly suggestive readings of Molière available. In his *Molière, ou les métamorphoses du comique*, Gérard Defaux studies the evolution of Molière's theater toward a "perspective . . . maintenant plus esthétique qu'éthique" (292).

In 1949 W. G. Moore published a study, *Molière: A New Criticism*, founded on the simple, if telling, contention that Molière's plays are "comedies written and performed according to the theatrical conditions prevalent in Paris in the middle of the seventeenth century" (50). Shortly after the publication of Moore's book, René Bray, in *Molière: Homme de théâtre*, took the tack that Molière ought to be viewed not as a man of letters but rather—and almost exclusively—as an "homme de théâtre" (8). More recently, Jim Carmody's *Rereading Molière: Mise en Scène from Antoine to Vitez* has tellingly analyzed specific productions of *L'école des femmes* and *Tartuffe* by some of France's greatest twentieth-century directors. Since Moore and Bray, critics and teachers have remained aware of the centrality of theater and performance in studying and teaching Molière. His brilliant portrayal of characters has, of course, invited psychological studies of the plays. Charles Mauron's "L'évolution créatrice de Molière," a chapter in his *Des métaphores obsédantes au mythe personnel* (270–98), develops a Freudian approach to the plays. Reaching out to anthropology and philosophy as well as psychology, Harold Knutson's *Molière: An Archetypal Approach* is systematic but less reductive than purely Freudian studies tend to be. Ralph Albanese's *Le dynamisme de la peur chez Molière* and James Gaines's *Social Structures in Molière's Theater* are both book-length sociocritical readings of Molière that include extended discussions of *Tartuffe* and other plays. Each investigates in its own way how social and literary structures intersect in Molière's theater.

Marcel Gutwirth's thematic study of Molière, *Molière ou l'invention comique*, and Judd Hubert's *Molière and the Comedy of Intellect* are more eclectic in their approach to the plays. Both works provide thoughtful insights about Molière's masterpieces. More recently, Ronald Tobin, while emphasizing the gastronomical in his delightful book entitled Tarte à la Crème: *Comedy and Gastronomy in Molière's Theater*, discovered that "each of the plays that finally emerged as most interesting called for a different analytical method" (xii). Instructors can use many of the textual details that Tobin discusses to initiate fruitful discussions in the classroom. In *Molière ou l'esthétique du ridicule* Patrick Dandrey develops the hypothesis that the "peinture vraisemblable des moeurs et le souci de donner à rire" ("the believable portrayal of manners and the desire to provoke laughter") (389) merge in Molière's theater to create a comic vision of humankind. Max Vernet's *Molière: Côté jardin, côté cour* is a densely written philosophical analysis of Molière from which teachers of very advanced students will glean suggestive insights.

The critical works mentioned here are not meant to constitute a complete reading list for teachers of Molière. What one reads in order to prepare a class will depend on many factors, including the level of the class, the students' preparation, and the context in which Molière is being taught. What the critical studies suggested all share is a sense of the joy of seeing, reading, and teaching Molière. It is this sense that good teachers will also want to communicate to their students.

Aids to Teaching: Video and Media Resources

Only recently have teachers of *Tartuffe* been able to benefit from the release of two outstanding and reasonable video versions of the play. Gérard Depardieu's French version features the renowned Gallic screen presence (he plays the title role and directed as well), who will be familiar to some students from such previous roles as Martin Guerre and Cyrano. This 1984 video, based on Jacques Lassalle's production at the Théâtre National de Strasbourg, was originally produced by Margaret Ménégoz for Les Films du Losange, D. D. Productions, Gaumont, and TF1 productions; it was released in Europe by Gaumont. The version in North American VHS format (with English subtitles) was reissued in 1991 as part of the Connoisseur Video Collection and is available from Tamarelle's and Applause Learning Resources. With Depardieu's wife, Elisabeth, and François Périer also in the cast, it is most welcome as a classroom and laboratory resource that allows students to put the poetry of Molière's text into a fuller context, complete with gesture and timing. The costumes of this version are more nineteenth than seventeenth century for the most part, but this anachronism may actually help make the play accessible for some students.

An English version of the 1984 Royal Shakespeare Company production directed by Bill Alexander stars Antony Sher in the title role, supported by Allison Steadman and Nigel Hawthorne. Though it lacks the linguistic authenticity of the French version, it is an extremely successful performance that is useful as a theatrical contrast to Depardieu's, as a supplement in courses on French drama in translation, and as a teaching tool for those who might wish to use contrasting scenes in French and English for intermediate or advanced language studies or as an aid in textual translation. This video can be obtained from Filmic Archives, Facets, and Tamarelle's.

Another French-language video version of *Tartuffe*, available from Films for the Humanities, is the 1990 release (originally filmed in 1986), directed by Albert Schimel and produced by Pierre Badel and the Société des Comédiens Français. (A fourth version of the play is included in the Plaisir du théâtre series of the Society for French American Cultural Services and Educational Aid (FACSEA), mentioned below.) The same society has done a production of *Le misanthrope*, directed by Bernard Girod and produced by the venerable Pierre Dux. Based on a 1986 production, the video was released in 1990. Films for the Humanities likewise offers an English-language version of the play (Wilbur translation, also 1990), starring Edward Petherbridge. At only fifty-two minutes, however, this version must make some liberal cuts in a comedy that usually runs a solid two hours.

Films for the Humanities offers a variety of additional French-language Molière titles: a 1989 release of a 1985 performance of *L'école des femmes*, produced by Bernard Soble for TF1, without subtitles; a 1989 black-and-white release of a 1975 performance of *Dom Juan*, directed by Marcel Bluwal and produced by Claude Ventura and Claude Savet for INA, also without subtitles; a 1989 release (performed the same year) of *Les fourberies de Scapin*, directed by Pierre Boutron and produced by Paul-Robin Benhaouin for Technisonor; and, finally, versions of *Le médecin malgré lui* and *Le malade imaginaire*, both originally done in 1986 for the Société des Comédiens Français and released in 1989, the former directed by Jean-Louis Picavet and produced by Lazare Iglesias, the latter produced by Technisonor.

There are two French-language versions of *Le bourgeois gentilhomme* available, the first a well-known but now dated 1958 Comédie-Française version, directed by Jean Meyer and starring Louis Seigner, supported by Jean Piat and Michèle Grelier. With accurate period costumes and original music by Lully, this is one of the most "archaeological" of Molière performances, but its opulent re-creation of classicism is almost too self-conscious, and Seigner's interpretation of the protagonist is buffoonish to the point of utter obnoxiousness. Originally released in America by Video Images in the Video Yesteryear collection, this title is available from Applause Learning Resources. The second, offering a newer approach, is a 1989 release of a 1982 performance directed by Christian Guy-Bleir and produced by Dirk Sanders for Le Grand Circus. It is distributed by Films for the Humanities. The first of these videos has subtitles.

FACSEA presents Molière plays in two video collections. The series Collection Molière: Plaisir du théâtre contains 1989 versions of *L'avare*, *Les fourberies de Scapin*, *Le médecin malgré lui*, *Le misanthrope*, *Les précieuses ridicules*, and *Tartuffe*, the first directed by Jacques Mauclair and all the others by Jacqueline Duc. The second series, Collection Comédie-Française, includes a 1976 version of *Le malade imaginaire* and a 1977 version of *Les femmes savantes*. All these are modestly priced.

Not to be overlooked is a video, especially appropriate for use in survey courses or those introducing students to Molière, entitled simply *Molière*, which features Antony Sher as the playwright. The drama is based on Mikhail Bulgakov's biographical novel, which places Molière in a social and historical context teeming with political and religious confrontation. Like Sher's *Tartuffe*, this production stems from a 1984 Royal Shakespeare Company stage version directed by Bill Alexander. It is available from Facets.

The increasing dominance of video has reduced the role of audio versions of Molière, and the demise of the turntable in favor of compact discs has made the former range of LP recordings of Molière plays extinct. The numerous plays formerly carried by the Encyclopédie Sonore, Pathé/EMI, and Playette/ Comédie-Française labels and distributed by the Wible Language Institute have not, at the time of this writing, been rereleased in convenient cassette editions. Nevertheless, audio can still play a vital role in an integrated language-learning and literature program. As long as the language laboratories and the portable cassette players exist, there will be a place for cassette recordings (listed below), and we can hope that some of the older LP material will be rereleased in compact-disc format and made available in North America.

The widest selection of cassette recordings of Molière plays seems to be offered by the Olivia and Hill Press of Ann Arbor. Their two-cassette packages, moderately priced, include Comédie-Française productions of *Tartuffe* (featuring Michel Etcheverry, Jean Le Poulain, and Denise Gence), *L'avare* (starring Michel Aumont and Françoise Seigner), *Dom Juan* (with Francis Huster and Jacques Toja), *Les femmes savantes* (François Chaumette, Françoise Seigner, and Denise Gence), and *Le misanthrope* (Michel Duchaussoy, Bernard Dhéran, and Dominique Constanza). All these recordings were originally broadcast over the France-Culture radio network. Olivia and Hill also offers an award-winning recording of *Le bourgeois gentilhomme* (featuring Jacques Fabbri and Arletty, with sumptuous musical support), as well as recordings of *Les fourberies de Scapin* (with André Roussin, Roger Mollien, and Jean Parédès), *Le malade imaginaire* (a musical companion to *Le bourgeois gentilhomme*, with Michel Galabru and Guy Bedos), and *Le médecin malgré lui* (André and Georges Bellec, Françoise Soubeyran, and Paul Tourenne)—all in two-cassette sets. A single-cassette release contains *Les précieuses ridicules*, starring Jean Parédès.

Applause Learning Resources offers two audiocassettes with selections from *Tartuffe*, *Les femmes savantes*, *Le bourgeois gentilhomme*, and *Le malade imaginaire*.

Part Two

APPROACHES

Tartuffe Goes to School: The Formation of Academic Discourse in Nineteenth-Century France

Ralph Albanese, Jr.

> What, then, is this *Tartuffe*, the very name of which
> appears to be an evil force, which elicits so much applause
> on the one hand, and so much recrimination on the other?
> —Abbé Figuière

In the wake of more than a century of partisan academic writing about Molière's controversial comedy, during which time the play has been claimed as a powerful symbol by many different camps involved in pitched ideological battles, one cannot approach the problem of teaching it without some preliminary grounding in the role it played in nineteenth-century French schools. These institutions of secondary education and the instructors who dominated them exercised a preponderant role in the formation of a cultural elite that persists well into the twentieth century, as Jacques and Mona Ozouf have demonstrated in their landmark study *La république des instituteurs*. Whenever evoked in a modern or postmodern cultural context, even outside France, *Tartuffe* still carries with it a considerable amount of polemical baggage. It may be argued that it delves far closer to the level of persistent cultural preoccupations than any of Shakespeare's plays, for instance, and that one must look to *Don Quixote* or *War and Peace* to find a literary text so thoroughly joined to a particular concept of nationhood.

The above-quoted rhetorical question, placed near the beginning of Abbé Figuière's introduction to his critical edition of *Tartuffe*, summarizes succinctly the fortune of this highly polemical play in nineteenth-century France (10). The creation of this particular academic edition represents, in fact, a direct reaction to the inscription of the play on the official program of the *Classe de rhétorique* (later to become the *Classe de première*) in 1880. Students enrolled in religious schools were considered a captive audience—"Since our youth in Christian educational establishments is now condemned to study [*Tartuffe*]"— and the Abbé Figuière proposes, through his reading of the play, a detailed answer to his question.

Deeply rooted in nineteenth-century French politics, anticlericalism represented a particularly sensitive issue for the Republicans. The ideological battleground between church and state was, in fact, the school; the intense competition between public and private education reflected a conviction on the part of proponents of both the secular and the clerical ideal that each institution was the only legitimate purveyor of solid moral values. Education constituted a key social and political issue for supporters of *laïcité* ("lay politics") in that it provided the Republican nation-state with a clear justification for its coming into being, an excellent means of demonstrating the legitimacy of the principles of 1789. Playing on the fear that France could well become a clerical state, Republican ideology viewed clericalism as an unfortunate vestige of the Old Regime. According to this ideology, the church was public enemy number one, a force of obscurantism, both retrograde and pernicious, since its role would be to dictate morality. It was, quite simply, to have no role in the Republican blueprint for a new society. Reaching its militant phase between 1881 and 1887, the battle for secular education in France was characterized by the creation of a new cultural consensus that rejected the dogmas of the church.

"Culture" represented the principal manifestation of a national tradition and thus became a legitimate substitute for religion. Functioning within the framework of the school as a public service unit, teachers constituted a kind of "lay priesthood," serving as, in the words of Charles Péguy, "ministers and masters of the distribution of culture" whose aim was to promote the principles of civic education (530). It is hardly surprising, then, that *Tartuffe*, by becoming "required reading" in the *Classe de rhétorique* in 1880, was thrust into the public arena of culture and society, symbolizing the new catechism of militant Republican ideology. (Indeed, the official exclusion of *Tartuffe* from literary programs before 1880 recalls the original five-year ban on its performance from 1664 to 1669, when Molière's struggle to gain acceptance for the play became a virtual state affair). Its status as a *succès de scandale* has always stemmed, in part, from its prohibition in both the academic and theatrical arenas. Whereas before 1879 the official literary programs at the secondary level betrayed a general mistrust of comedy—within this ahistorical pedagogy, the selection of a particular author was irrelevant since this author merely served as a pretext for rhetorical development—from that year on, secondary education developed a systematic curriculum geared to classical authors, including Molière.

Rabelais was placed on the literary program of the Agrégation in 1879, no doubt because of the carnivalesque, subversive nature of the laughter he invoked (symbolically linked to revolutionary values dear to Republicans), and *Dom Juan* was added to this same program during the academic year 1879–80.

A celebratory discourse was thus created whereby the works of these authors served to confirm sociocultural values of the late nineteenth century. *Tartuffe*, as we shall see, represented a civic profession of faith within a state-controlled educational system bent on bolstering the Third Republic against its many enemies (e.g., monarchists, Freemasons, the army, and the church).

To grasp how thoroughly Molière's work—in particular, *Tartuffe*—served as a *machine de guerre* ("an engine of war") against the forces of clericalism, one needs at this point to examine the interrelation between two forms of discursive activity in nineteenth-century France: exegetical criticism and academic discourse. The transformation of critical discourse on Molière into a more codified school discourse constitutes a key institutional practice of the Republican school system (Albanese, *Molière*). Whereas *Le misanthrope* was glorified in the literary manuals as the perfect incarnation of worldly values, and *Les femmes savantes* was exalted inasmuch as it proposed an exemplary model of feminine virtue and propriety in the character of Henriette, *Tartuffe* retained its essentially polemical status throughout the century and came to dramatize the cultural politics of *laïcité*. Occupying a privileged place on an official list of nineteenth-century "Moliérophobes illustres," Louis Veuillot is no doubt the best-known representative of the Catholic exegesis directed against the comic poet (Le Hardy). After noting the immense popularity of *Tartuffe* among diverse segments of the *bonne bourgeoisie,* the author of "Molière et Bourdaloue" mocks public adulation of the dramatist, characterizing his work as "indestructible," since it has undergone various forms of analysis or, in the polemicist's opinion, deformation at the hands of numerous critics of socialist persuasion (Veuillot 5: 643). Veuillot considers his own critical stance audacious, since it runs counter to the vast majority of critics, who espouse, to varying degrees, Molière's ethics. Thus he ridicules the place of honor enjoyed by such critics in the "Church of Free Thought" and, more specifically, the status of secular sainthood bestowed on him by the general public. This unenlightened public has seen fit to canonize an essentially farcical writer ("un Scapin"). As far as *Tartuffe* is concerned, the Catholic critic denounces Molière's tendency to caricature the decent individuals—"les honnêtes gens"—of the play. Orgon is depicted as a perfect imbecile, and Cléante is reduced to the level of ineffective rhetorician; Damis is a mere fool, Mariane a timid *demoiselle de pensionnat* ("boarding-school girl"), and Elmire an indolent *bourgeoise*. Whereas all these characters are mired in passivity, Veuillot is scandalized that only Tartuffe takes the initiative to act: he alone "plots, acts, attacks, defends himself" (7: 95). In short, the average spectator risks being corrupted by the evil yet apparently successful ways of the hypocrite and so is simply unable to discern between true and false devotion. Finally, the immorality of Molière's life belies the moralizing pronouncements of Cléante and Alceste with which the dramatist publicly identified and the highly dubious lifestyle of Tartuffe and Sganarelle. Molière's vileness is such that one is tempted to evoke here the ironic maxim "Tartuffe, c'est moi."

Drawing on the major conclusions of exegetical criticism, academic discourse attempted to promote an exclusively sectarian reading of *Tartuffe*. A good example is the popular manual of Père Longhaye, which derides Sainte-Beuve for having praised the morality of the play. The Jesuit author seeks to discredit the notion that *Tartuffe* should serve as a standard-bearer for the anticlerical cause in nineteenth-century French politics. He does so by demonstrating the lack of verisimilitude in various characters of the play. Elmire's ambiguous reaction to Tartuffe's declaration of love (3.3) and her questionable strategy in playing the seductress (4.5)—a ruse that Father Longhaye calls not only a betrayal of the sense of personal dignity befitting a wife but also an "infamy" (171)—and the portrait of Orgon as a Christian turned fanatic by his spiritual director are, to be sure, morally inconsistent. Finally, Father Longhaye underscores the very impossibility of *Tartuffe* as an artistic enterprise, since the subject of religious hypocrisy is, by definition, offensive.

Returning now to Abbé Figuière's edition, it is clear that students enrolled in religious *lycées* and *collèges* were limited by a truncated reading of the play, one based on the repression of reprehensible, indeed "morally incorrect," passages such as the evocation of Dorine's *décolleté*: "Couvrez ce sein que je ne saurais voir" (3.2.860) ("Cover that bosom, girl"). Not only does the author justify the antiquated practice of self-flagellation, but he also imagines a more Christian dénouement, one in which a repentant Tartuffe confesses his abominable sins. Grounding his criticism of *Tartuffe* in the observations of L. Veuillot, Abbé Figuière first recalls the circumstances surrounding its performance in the 1660s: he denounces "l'intrépidité poqueline" (15) ("Molière's audacity") as well as "the husband of the Béjart women . . . transformed into a preacher of moral purity!" (17). Thanks to his strategy of vile flattery, Molière succeeded in having the king lift the prohibition against the play. Abbé Figuière then attributes the unctuous language of the *faux dévot* to the playwright himself: "Je puis vous dissiper ces craintes ridicules, / O Prince! et je sais l'art de lever les scrupules" (18) ("I can dispel those ridiculous fears, O Prince, and I know the art of suspending scruples").

For the majority of "lower-middle-class types, small-scale investors and minor merchants," the protagonist assumed a profoundly symbolic value and came to incarnate all practicing Christians (19). Although Molière claims to unmask the hypocrite, he is, in effect, creating an even more clever and impregnable cover for unscrupulous libertines. Decrying the absence of true believers in the play, Abbé Figuière extensively cites Veuillot, who contends that Orgon's extreme gullibility makes him appear more monstrous than Tartuffe, particularly during the scene in which Orgon disinherits his son (3.6).

Representatives of church-oriented academic discourse thus accused Molière of demeaning Christians and Christianity by promoting a kind of new-age humanist religion. Numerous critics portrayed Cléante as a proponent of secular humanism, an Enlightenment intellectual who addresses the issue of religious belief and practice in deistic terms. This apostle of human and humane devotion, who remains even-tempered throughout the play, exalts the virtues of moderation and reason and, in the process, opposes the truly devout to the *fanfarons de vertu* ("braggarts of virtue") who, in their overly rigorous practice of Christian virtues, display a spectacular sense of piety. Cléante's discourse in praise of genuine piety serves as a powerful lesson not only to loyal subjects of the monarchy but, more important in the eyes of the nineteenth-century teaching corps, to model citizens of the Third Republic. According to this Republican perspective on *Tartuffe*, the progress of *laïcité* is perhaps best measured by the triumph of the king at the end of the play: ultimate guarantor of truth, justice, and the French way, to say nothing of national unity, Louis XIV ensures the victory of the state over the dangers of religious fanaticism. The panegyric of the king figure implies the legitimate assertion of power over the *faux dévot's* blatant usurpation of power. As an enterprise in demystification, then, *Tartuffe* dramatizes both the unmasking of the impostor and the denunciation of Orgon's obsessive credulity. The king's exemplary discernment underscores the powerlessness of the family to deal with the deleterious effects of Orgon's infatuation with Tartuffe. The *père de famille's* reintegration within the monarchical order highlights the political function of the bourgeoisie, whose principal traits under Louis XIV are loyalty, hard work, and productivity.

The exegesis of Sainte-Beuve and Nisard, for example, contributed significantly to this secular reading of *Tartuffe*. For Sainte-Beuve, the play incarnates the tenets of free thought and offers lasting therapy against the evil wrought by political or religious fanaticism; such moral extremism is, in fact, a manifestation of *démesure* (imbalanced values) or, more specifically, of *impudeur* (lack of self-control):

> To love Molière is to be forever cured, not (I would say) of base and scurrilous hypocrisy, but rather of fanaticism, intolerance, and harshness, of all that may cause one to be cursed or condemned.   (277)

For Nisard, the main pleasure derived from a performance of Molière is of an ethical rather than an aesthetic nature. Hence the significance attributed to the dramatist's precepts:

> . . . hatred of viciousness, scorn for persons both uncivil and ridiculous, love of that which is good, natural, and true; all that emanates either from the maxims of duty or the counsel of benevolence; all this comes from the heart of Molière.   (140)

Nisard's notion of "distributive justice," moreover, stems from the corrective function of comedy: the virtue of one's character or the lack thereof determines the degree to which one is rewarded or punished in this theater. This notion is in keeping with the debate on the issue of "moralism" that characterizes the discourse of Tartuffe, Orgon, and Mme Pernelle, as well as that of Cléante and other members of the family, as they relate to the character of the *faux dévot*; the numerous portraits of the hypocrite are designed to create a sense of moral opprobrium, as were the character analyses that French *lycéens* of the period were typically required to draft. In Nisard's view, then, *Tartuffe* offers a valuable warning against the dangers of religious hypocrisy; Moliéresque laughter constitutes an instrument of human solidarity in the light of its tendency to promote a feeling of consensus and social harmony.

A brief review of a few subjects drawn from *Tartuffe* for French composition will help elucidate the workings of nineteenth-century pedagogical practices. On the basis of their study of Molière's preface to the play, students are asked to analyze the role and function of comedy: "Is it true, as Molière says in the préface to *Tartuffe*, that the purpose of comedy is to correct human vices?" (Paris, Devoir de licence, Jan. 1882; Hémon 46). For another assignment, students are to imagine the letter in which the playwright expresses gratitude to Boileau for his support in the battle to have *Tartuffe* approved for public performance: "Suppose that Molière is writing to Boileau to thank him for this proof of his courageous friendship" (Hémon 441). Another topic of French composition engages students in a debate between two antithetical forms of devotion, the rigorous stance of the preacher, Bourdaloue, and the more enlightened pose of the worldly moralist, Saint-Evremond (Agrégation de grammaire, 1905; *Revue universitaire* 14 [1905]: 267). Evoking Ferdinand Brunetière's view that Molière openly attacked organized religion in *Tartuffe*, the following question invites students to reflect on the disruptive effect of the church on society:

> Is it true, as one recent critic (Mr. Brunetière) maintains, that Molière attacks religion in *Tartuffe* and represents it as lethal to domestic peace and destructive of common sense and instinctive goodness?
> (Caen, Devoir de licence, May 1890; Hémon 46–47)

Students could also bear in mind the perverted friendship between Tartuffe and Orgon in answering this examination question: "How can friendship assist the development of our moral being?" (Agrégation des lettres, 1897; *Revue universitaire*, 6 [1892]: 79).

The transformation of Moliéresque dramaturgy into Republican pedagogy is an important sociocultural reality of late nineteenth-century France. In one of the most reedited literary manuals of the period, E. Géruzez envisages Molière's theater as a public service enterprise offering French students and nonstudents alike "a course of ethics in dramatic form" (164). Given its therapeutic and reformist value in the face of hypocrisy, a notorious *vice du siècle,* Moliéresque satire dramatizes the humanist ideal of truth and good and, by extension, underlines moderation and reason as the cornerstones of Republican pedagogy.

To the extent that the formation of school discourse draws on the history of French pedagogy, this discourse sheds light on the constitution of an archaeology of knowledge that, although primarily relevant to French schooling of the period, necessarily informs current practices as well. Molière's modernity can perhaps best be measured by his direct contribution to the secular vision underlying Republican institutions. If, from 1880 on, *Tartuffe* acquired canonical status in French literature, it is largely because the comic author had become a cultural icon of sorts, a living symbol of national patrimony. His work served as a rallying point for civic consciousness, a fundamental point of articulation in the formation of a national ethos. *Tartuffe* is particularly problematic in that it invariably either fascinated spectators or deeply troubled them. As we have seen, the play crystallized the politics of division in nineteenth-century France, the sociopolitical and ideological dimensions inherent in *laïcité,* and the intense struggle between public and congregationist schools. Desirous of a stronger sense of group cohesion, the Republican School charged secondary education with the task of dispensing moral value predicated on a secular ethic. Literary history, in short, constituted a means of developing cultural identity and, in the process, served as a compensation for the long-standing political disunity of the French. It should come as no surprise, then, that the basic paradigm presented by *Tartuffe* of the *fauteur de trouble* who upsets the family order ultimately gives rise to the need for a reassurance of cultural unity in the spectacular triumph of the king figure. The issue of religious-political fanaticism, which took on particular importance during the period of Republican militantism, is, of course, central to the play. Indeed, from the Restoration to the Third Republic, the antagonism between liberalism and conservativism, between secular humanism and religious orthodoxy, manifested itself most acutely in the battle for lay education. The polemical nature of *Tartuffe* showed that a unified French cultural tradition took precedence over the divisions wrought by the forces of clericalism.

NOTE

I would like to thank Richard Marcus and Will Thompson for their editorial assistance in the preparation of this article.

Authority, Language, and Censorship

Ronald W. Tobin

If one were to develop a pedagogical strategy for introducing students to the major features of Molière's *Tartuffe*, one would have to draw attention to the roles played by language and religion. The latter topic—Molière and Religion—has been treated in thousands of student papers and by a host of critics, from the conservative writers of the early twentieth century, like Ferdinand Brunetière and Emile Faguet, through biographically oriented scholars like Ramon Fernandez and François Mauriac, to such modern thinkers as Philip Butler, John Cairncross, Thérèse Goyet, and Raymond Picard. Some see Molière as opposed to institutional Christianity; others perceive an attempt by the dramatist to reconcile the "two religions"—one worldly, the other strictly orthodox—portrayed in *Tartuffe*.

To be sure, *Tartuffe* was not the first opportunity for conflict between Molière and the "dévots" ("devout persons"), yet it forms a special case, not only because of the protracted struggle between the playwright and his detractors but also because of the particular nature of the play's language. If one typically finds in Molière's comedies a lexicon dominated by education (as in the two *School* plays and *The Learned Ladies*), violence, gastronomy, and pleasure; and if religion is a code that naturally informs *The School for Wives*, *Dom Juan*, and *Tartuffe*, it is surprising to discover, particularly in *Tartuffe*, a profusion of expressions having to do with the speech act. In fact, the frequency of verbs used in *Tartuffe* to describe human discourse is striking: *causer* ("to chat"), *conter* ("to recount"), *jaser* ("to chatter"), *parler* ("to speak"), *quereller* ("to quarrel"), *reporter* ("to carry back a message"), *sermonner* ("to preachify"), *médire* ("to slander"), and, above all, *dire* ("to say, speak"). Since the theater is an audiovisual experience, verbs of hearing (*entendre*, "to hear"; *écouter*, "to listen") and of seeing (especially *voir*, "to see") occur often. But in *Tartuffe* they are clearly less abundant than verbs about speaking. Indeed, the code of the speech act—*la parole*—predominates in the comedy, and in its very logocentricity *Tartuffe* may be represented to students as the epitome of French classical theater.

Moreover, the two main themes we are tracing are interdependent because the "sayings" of the religious hypocrite—the *faux dévot*—assume godlike proportions so that Tartuffe's discourse has become, for Mme Pernelle and her son Orgon, a transposition of the Logos. Since in their eyes Tartuffe is the embodiment of religious sentiment, the impostor succeeds in imposing himself as if he were a sacred text that one must treat with appropriate respect, even reverence: in a word, one must *listen* to this text because it speaks from and with authority.

To give this phenomenon its due, let us look at the evidence contained in the text itself, and let us begin with scene 1, in which Mme Pernelle turns her verbal shotgun on the family and fires at one member after another. In the first place, Pernelle complains that she is leaving Orgon's house "much vexed in spirit" (1.1.9) ("fort mal édifiée"), that nothing therein commands respect since everyone speaks up in an interminable cacophony. Their gratuitous expression of opinions, in effect valorizing all doctrines equally, shocks her to the point that she is driven to attack the servant Dorine, accusing her of talking too much and wanting her say in everything (13–15). The son Damis has only to open his mouth and he becomes the next object of her wrath. Pernelle would impose her speech on all: "You're a dunce, grandson, / And your grandmother tells you so" (16–17; my trans.). For Mariane she has reserved a dictum that she evidently holds dear: "But you know what they say about still waters. / I pity parents with secretive daughters" (23–24). Finally, she launches her ultimate salvo against Cléante, the intellectual leader of the opposition: "You're full of worldly counsels, which, I fear, / Aren't suitable for decent folk to hear" (37–38).

One cannot miss the point: the family's sin consists in having yielded to the impulse to speak rather than simply having listened. When Tartuffe's name is first mentioned (41), Pernelle leaps at the opportunity to specify the evil that has been allowed to fester:

> And [Tartuffe] practises precisely what he preaches.
> He's a fine man, and should be listened to.
> I will not hear him mocked by fools like you.
>   (42–44)

(The French word used by Pernelle for "mocked"—*quereller*—makes her meaning obvious, for it signifies "to attack with hostile *words*.")

Pernelle repeats the key to her personal interpretation of Tartuffe when she responds to Dorine's remark ("You see him as a saint" [69]) with "You all regard him with distaste and fear / Because he *tells* you what you're loath to hear" (75–76; emphasis added). Since, for Pernelle, Tartuffe's words are divinely inspired, the character himself must be the vehicle of a celestial plan. If Tartuffe does not carry all the moral weight of the king, the chosen representative of God on earth, he does resemble Louis XIV in that he is God's "spokesperson" in one corner of His realm—and at the end of the play Molière implicitly contrasts the ways in which Louis XIV and Tartuffe use words.

And so for Pernelle—and Orgon, too—the ideal system would be the following:

God = author/sender
Tartuffe = text/message
Pernelle and Orgon = mediators
Members of the family = (properly reverent) receivers

Mother and son see themselves, therefore, as the authorized—and author-itarian—exegetes of Tartuffe's discourse, responsible for the official commentary on the sacred message. Those who refuse to follow this line are designated as "libertines," and if such a thing were practicable, they would be condemned to silence until the day on which they opened their ears, then their eyes. Let us not mistake what is happening here: *within the play there is a debate raging about the very practice that had prevented the play from appearing for five years in public: censorship*. Larry Riggs even wonders whether Molière is not trying to engage the king in a dialogue about the right to plurality of voice in France (155–90).

Perceiving the danger inherent in Pernelle's repressive instincts, Cléante does not hesitate to point it out:

> Would you prevent people from talking?
> Life would be difficult indeed,
> If, fearing implication in silly stories,
> We stopped speaking to our good friends.
> And even if one decided to do so,
> Would you be able to stop everyone from chattering?
> (1.1.93–98)

To "stop [some]one from chattering" (*se taire*) becomes an irresistible phrase from this point on, as—well before Orgon's repeated use and abuse of "Be quiet" ("Taisez-vous" [2.2])—everyone discusses the right of free expression. Pernelle takes center stage once again to defend herself in a passage that is utterly logorrheic:

> Therefore you'd have us all keep still, my dear,
> While Madam rattles on the livelong day.
> Nevertheless, I mean to have my say.
> I tell you that you're blest to have Tartuffe
> Dwelling, as my son's guest, beneath this roof.
> . . . .
> And . . . you'd better heed him, and be sensible.
> . . . .
> One never hears a word that's edifying:
> Nothing but chaff and foolishness and lying,
> As well as vicious gossip in which one's neighbor
> Is cut to bits with épée, foil, and saber.
> . . . .
> And reputations perish thick and fast.
> As a wise preacher said on Sunday last,
> Parties are Towers of Babylon, because

The guests all babble on with never a pause;

. . . .

Enough, I'm going; don't show me to the door.

(1.1.141–66)

In the would-be logocracy that is *Tartuffe*, three verbs in particular are fundamental: to say (*dire*), to speak ill (*médire*), and to lie (*mentir*). As it happens, *dire* and *mentir* are usually reserved for use by the eponymous character, whereas the family members, desperately seeking to reveal the truth, are paradoxically constrained to speak ill (*médire*) of Tartuffe, especially in front of Pernelle and Orgon. This situation demonstrates that, even before *Dom Juan*, Molière had suggested that the world is turned upside down when a hypocrite—a sort of ill-intentioned wordsmith, a diabolical poet—creates havoc with social discourse.

The verbal inquisition of Pernelle in the first scene of the drama constitutes, as I have noted, a microcosm of the entire play because the debate turns around "to speak or not to speak"; that is, in terms of what transpires in classical tragedy, "to live or to die." If, as critics from the Abbé d'Aubignac in 1657 to Roland Barthes in 1963 have asserted, to speak is the basic form of action in classical theater, what can one say of a character who does not utter a syllable in the course of the first two acts but succeeds nonetheless in dominating attention? Tartuffe's tactic consists, of course, in not saying a word but having others talk constantly about him. Pernelle and Orgon serve as apostles: they listen to him, the better to repeat his oracular pronouncements.

In principle, every member of the family is supposed to receive the word as it comes down from Tartuffe, *deus absconditus* of the first two acts. But it is the role of Pernelle and Orgon to decipher its sense. If Christianity is defined as adherence to the doctrine of the divine Logos and by the central place accorded to the Scriptures, one has to conclude that in this so-called impious production ("production impie," as it was described), the believers regard Tartuffe as the incarnation either of the Word or of a sacred oral tradition, possessing all the prestige of a source wrapped in the approval of the highest authority. Consequently, his "text," which is at first identical with himself, has to be read by the others because Tartuffe is a verbal creation, a "self-made man" in the sense that the little Orgon knows of him Orgon learned from Tartuffe himself.

It goes without saying that the reception of this text is mixed. While the zealots Pernelle and Orgon accept it literally, Elmire seems to manifest an agnostic's indifference toward it. If Mariane in act 2, scene 2 appears ready to place her trust in the high priest Orgon, she soon adopts the attitude of the anti-Tartuffe cabal and joins Dorine, Damis, and Cléante in their atheism. Since classical comedy tends to promote social conformity at the expense of the disruptive initiatives of the individual, it is ironic to find the "individual" Orgon assuming, at least over the first four acts, the role of the comic principle seeking to enforce its collective orthodoxy. His tyranny, as one can guess, seeks to silence (*faire taire*) the others: he says so explicitly to Dorine several times in the course of act 2, scene 2; he shuts off debate with his brother, whose "language savors of impiety" (1.5.314); and after having repeatedly demanded that Damis be quiet, he asks his son to "retract" (3.6.1131; my trans.) his statement, to change his interpretation, to speak ill no more. When his son refuses, Orgon gives him his "malediction," thereby excommunicating him from the circle of the true believers in and readers of the Tartuffian text.

From all the evidence, one may judge that Tartuffe has chosen his victim wisely, for there is something in the genetic makeup of Orgon's psyche (and his mother's and his son's) that creates an irresistible desire to force one's will on others by cutting off debate. We might be tempted to call such a condition a dictatorship, in the etymological sense of a unit governed by a person whose oral pronouncements are to be treated as laws.

The problem Tartuffe faces, once he makes his first appearance onstage, is that the word has become flesh: the orality typical of this character betrays his two deepest impulses—to discourse and also to devour. In the course of the first two acts, Tartuffe anticipated the wise saying of Diderot's Neveu de Rameau: "Be a hypocrite, if you wish; just don't speak like one." In fact, he had not spoken at all: he remained the subject of interpretation. Molière himself gives us the key:

> One knows him straightaway by the identification marks ["marques"] that I give him; and from one end of the play to the other he does not say a word nor do a single thing which does not paint his character ["caractère"], for the spectators, as that of a wicked man.   (*Œuvres* 1: 884)

By choosing the terms *marques* and *caractère*, Molière brings into play the vocabulary of printing so that we may understand that we should really have no trouble reading this "typo-graphical" character.

We know that to defeat Tartuffe the family finally decides to abandon all attempts at "contra-dicting" Orgon, at least literally. They adopt a different strategy, one better suited to exposing an intrinsically performative being (a *hypocrites*, an "actor" in Greek): they will stage a play—or two—in an endeavor not to present yet another reading of Tartuffe but, rather, to make the character himself seen and heard.

To be sure, the speech patterns of the title character, which have been the object of innumerable commentaries, are part and parcel of performative speech acts, those designed to persuade and to seduce. Hypocrisy, whether it be Tartuffe's or Dom Juan's, implies the same techniques: to speak in order to act on the other's beliefs. By using his rhetoric for illegitimate purpose, Tartuffe commits what J. L Austin calls an "abuse" of the performance act, a true linguistic perversion (*How to Do Things* 16).

Whereas in their first meeting onstage Tartuffe tried to control Elmire through physical efforts, in the second rendezvous he turns to a plan of attack conceived along linguistic lines. It is, therefore, only when Tartuffe changes from the assertive to the performative, in the scenes with Elmire, that he destroys the authority of his text, that he begins, in truth, to destroy himself. The culmination of this development takes place precisely when Tartuffe explains to Elmire, apropos of her husband: "Our conversations are a source of joy for him, / And, thanks to me, he sees everything and believes nothing" (4.5.1525–26; my trans.). Critics usually read this declaration as simply an accurate statement of fact. It seems to me, however, that if Tartuffe used the truth to deceive in the scene of his "confession" to Orgon (3.6)—committing a form of "abuse" as far as his own real intentions were concerned—in the second encounter with Elmire (4.5) he is confident of telling the truth. Yet Molière, undoubtedly wishing to keep Tartuffe's character coherent, does not accord him the grace of truth-telling at this point. The other members of the family, we should recall, saw—or read—Tartuffe without believing him; it was only Pernelle and Orgon for whom seeing was believing. The fervent disciple Orgon abjures his faith only when he *hears* the profanation of the holy word. Because of his unshakable confidence in his performative powers, Tartuffe never believed Orgon capable of distinguishing the abstract text from its literary representation. It is precisely the mise-en-scène of this formerly sacrosanct writing, in the framework of a play within a play, that finally undermines the authority of the text and dispatches Orgon into the camp of the atheists, those who see and do not believe.

At the end of act 4, one is tempted to conclude that when a text is dramatized, it automatically loses its purity and is transformed into that artistic compromise we call theater. Once Tartuffe takes the initiative and becomes an active player, he runs some risks. Until this point Tartuffe had successfully enveloped himself in silence and discretion. The details of his true identity were never given: he consistently remained a creation of *dire* rather than *mentir*.

Nonetheless, Tartuffe is caught, after calumniating Orgon. Tartuffe changed roles and, in so doing, betrayed his essence by lying (*médire*), a function that previously belonged exclusively to the family in a play in which, before the king restores sanity, society's values are turned upside down. Moreover, this restoration apparently occurred after a confrontation, offstage, between those two "contra-dictory" beings, the king and Tartuffe. Instead of maintaining a prudent silence and keeping a secret—as he had assured Elmire he could in act 4, scene 5—Tartuffe insisted on taking advantage of the free access that the king offered to his subjects, and by his very speech act, the hypocrite revealed himself.

Without realizing it, Tartuffe confronts the greatest danger by exposing himself to the ear and the eye of the king. Leaving behind his familiar terrain —the field of religion—Tartuffe ventures into that of politics, which he now calls his "sacred duty" (5.7.1881). Tartuffe is at long last contradicted by the ideal spectator/reader, one who is able to distinguish the truth from falsehood, the factual from the "abusive." In fact, Louis XIV conducts himself as a wiser Tartuffe should have: he says nothing.

If Louis XIV does not participate in the word games that distinguish *Tartuffe*, he does guarantee their authenticity. Father of his country, he silences all debates (as the paterfamilias Orgon wanted to do) without pronouncing a single word. At the end, it is the king's body that incarnates the Logos; the example of effective and venerable silence stands in marked contrast to the self-destructive statements of the figure who earned Molière the reproach of "having put terms of piety in the mouth of the impostor" (*Œuvres* 1: 885). Henceforth, the family members, freed from Tartuffe's oppression, can express themselves openly, and they begin to do so, appropriately, by raising their voices in praise of the king and "the mercies he has shown" (5.7.1958; my trans.). Molière will ultimately enjoy this same privilege: his voice will survive all the attacks of his enemies who were unable to silence the truth of his plays.

"I? Leave This House?"
Space and Language in *Tartuffe*

Sylvie Romanowski

The study of literature in its historical and cultural context has developed as a result of two convergent trends: one is the reaction to, or the desire to move away from, a purely textual analysis emphasized by such critical methods as structuralism and deconstruction; the other trend is the shift in historical studies, from the *Annales* school of the 1920s on, to an examination of long-term social and economic developments and of everyday life of all social classes, not just of political events involving monarchs and the high nobility. These recent trends might seem to distance the text from both teachers and students, as we are no longer able to study the text alone and no longer able to derive from it universal truths that transcend all periods. But the gains far outweigh the apparent loss of immediacy.

The first trend, away from a purely immanent study of the text's inner meanings, does not negate the need for such a study but builds on it, for the text is the bedrock of ensuing interpretations. The second trend, toward contextualizing literature in its social and historical background, does not mean trying to acquire, say, an exclusively seventeenth-century perspective or getting into an author's mind or intentions. Rather, it means developing our own understanding of the text as enriched by our understanding of that era. The task of interpreting literature through the mediation of social and cultural history will be carried out by first determining what specific aspects the work focuses on, highlighting aspects that might otherwise be left unseen. Then these observations must be situated in the proper context so that we may understand what is at stake in a given work. This essay is an attempt to help teachers do so. It draws on the study of living spaces in the second half of seventeenth-century France. Observations about housing, which James Gaines usefully calls a "social indicator" (19), are then set in the larger social context of seventeenth-century France, a hierarchical society organized by "estates," which were a combination of economic class and rank determined by birth and which dictated certain norms of thought and behavior. More precisely, during this moment of history there occurs the struggle of a certain part of society, the upper strata of the middle class, to gain recognition from and access to the ranks of the nobility. This desire for social mobility and advancement can be set in the larger philosophical context of the early modern period, which, from the Renaissance on, emphasized the autonomy and strength of the individual self. The mediated understanding through philosophical and social history allows students to see both continuity and difference between that period and our own and stimulates a more imaginative understanding of a work written in a past era.

In *Tartuffe*, the role of space in the sense of dwelling, of the house in which the action takes place, is emphasized by the frequency of the word *céans* ("here," "in this place"), which appears fourteen times—more than in any other play by Molière, as Quentin Hope (43), Marcel Gutwirth (*"Tartuffe"* 35) and Gérard Ferreyrolles (46–47) point out. In *Tartuffe*, as in most other plays by Molière, the characters are very aware of their own language. In Molière's world, speaking is a form of doing, and doing means speaking and having power, having the upper hand. This essay explores the special role of space and house in the play and the general awareness of language in Molière's plays as a means of understanding the role of language and space in the social context of Molière's time.

Space is emphasized from the beginning of the play by the movement of the characters and by their words. The noisy and prolonged exit of Mme Pernelle takes up the entire first scene, in which six of the fourteen occurrences of the word *céans* are found. The movement of the characters on the stage is emphasized by their words: Mme Pernelle says, as she is trying to leave, "[Q]ue d'eux je me délivre" ("[I]t's time I left this place"), and Elmire replies, "Vous marchez d'un tel pas qu'on a peine à vous suivre" (1.1.1–2) ("I can't keep up, you walk at such a pace"). Mme Pernelle replies, "[N]e venez pas plus loin" (3) ("No need to show me out"), and Elmire asks, "[D]'où vient que vous sortez si vite?" (6) ("But, Mother, why this hurry? Must you go?"). Mme Pernelle has observed in her son's lifestyle a recent change tending toward luxury that offends her: her daughter-in-law is "dépensière" (29) ("much too free with money") and "vêtue ainsi qu'une princesse" (30) ("so elaborately dressed"). There are carriages and servants constantly at the door and entirely too much social activity. Dorine and Damis also complain that the space of the house has been invaded: Tartuffe not only lives there but wants to dominate both the master and the servants: "un inconnu céans s'impatronise" (62) ("see this man usurp the master's place"). Space is emphasized both by the movement of Mme Pernelle's exit and by the indications that recent changes have taken place in the house.

What Mme Pernelle castigates here is a new lifestyle belonging to a specific class, the nobility. In the seventeenth century and in general in the ancien régime, one's social class and profession were much more visible to an observer. Middle-class people did not dress like the aristocracy, and members of various professions wore specific garments. The words used by Mme Pernelle show clearly that Orgon is moving upward from a middle-class lifestyle to an aristocratic one. In short, Orgon is a "bourgeois gentilhomme" but not a ridiculous one—or at least not in the same way as M. Jourdain.

In this new lifestyle, Mme Pernelle reproaches an excess of spending, suggesting that the mother and the son are not living in the same manner. She belongs in the middle-class world, where one lives discreetly without calling attention to oneself, while her son's aristocratic world is open, public, permeable. Not for nothing does Dorine say that their family is open to a "blâme public" (1.1.116) ("public censure"; my trans.). As Jürgen Habermas shows, in the seventeenth century public space belonged to the aristocracy, while the bourgeois were generally "private persons" (*Structural Transformation* 28). Orgon has moved up to the public world, probably to what Habermas calls the "thin . . . upper stratum" of the bourgeoisie (31), as his reward for having served his prince well during the civil war of the Fronde (1.2.181–82). One aspect of the public life of the aristocracy and of the upper middle class was the ownership of a house that showed one's rank and wealth. At the time Molière was writing—that is, at the beginning of the reign of Louis XIV—numerous aristocratic dwellings, called *hôtels*, were being constructed in Paris. These *hôtels* had a series of differentiated rooms in which to receive visitors in the *assemblées* condemned by Mme Pernelle (1.1.158): after the courtyard came the vestibule, the *anti-chambre* (antechamber), and the *chambre de parade* (ceremonial hall), the principal reception room for people who had not been limited to the *anti-chambre*. In the actual living quarters were a bedroom, often called the *chambre à alcôve* (a room with an alcove, or a room that is like an alcove); a *garde-robe* (clothes closet); an *arrière-garde-robe* (back closet) for the toilet; and often other little rooms or closets with various uses. According to the wealth and the space available, grander dwellings could also have galleries and libraries, as well as a chapel, usually situated on the upper floor. The living quarters were generally on the upper floor and frequently double, one set of rooms for the husband and one for the wife (Dennis; Elias; Rybczynski).

Traces of this kind of highly differentiated aristocratic dwelling are found in the text of *Tartuffe*. Elmire says that she is going upstairs to await her husband (1.3.214). Cléante, her brother-in-law, will wait for Orgon in a more public space: "[J]e l'attends ici pour moins d'amusement" (215) ("I'll wait and greet him here"). Orgon thus finds himself cornered on his way upstairs to see his dear Tartuffe; I suggest that his famous exclamation "Le pauvre homme!" (1.4) ("Poor fellow!") is a perfunctory phrase he utters without too much thought, since all he wants to do is dash off. In act 2, scene 1, before talking with his daughter, Orgon verifies that there is no one in a "petit cabinet," a little closet from which Dorine will emerge in the next scene. In act 3, Tartuffe comes down, probably from the chapel— "son valet dit qu'il prie" (3.1.844) ("his man / Says he's almost finished with his prayers")—to the "salle basse" ("room on the lower floor"), a more ceremonious and impersonal space where he and Elmire will talk. Elmire thus puts a certain distance between herself and her guest. Nearby there is a *petit cabinet*, as existed in many *hôtels* of this period, which were built in irregular spaces accommodating small closets to be built in leftover corners. In act 4, Cléante and Tartuffe are no doubt meeting on the ground floor, for Tartuffe interrupts the conversation to go "là-haut" ("upstairs") to fulfill a pious duty in the chapel on the upper floor (4.2.1267). And in this more public room on the ground floor, Elmire will have Tartuffe come again to play the seduction scene with Orgon hidden under the table:

"Faites-le-moi descendre" (4.4.1359) ("Have him come down"), she says. Elmire also asks Tartuffe to go and see if her husband is "dans cette galerie" (4.5.1522) ("in this gallery"; my trans.). Such galleries were large rooms for elaborate receptions, like the Galerie des Glaces at Versailles, usually (but not always) on the ground floor.

Orgon's dwelling follows the aristocratic model: differentiated, large, with two floors, a gallery, and a chapel. Many such *hôtels* were built in Paris between 1650 and 1660, a moment of expansion under the regime of the young king, a time when the older elites were passing from the scene (Millon; Romero, "Tropes"). The word *hôtel*, however, never appears in the play: *maison* is used instead. This is highly significant, for the latter word referred strictly to middle-class houses. The word *hôtel* was reserved for the nobility, *palais* for the king and princes of royal blood. Norbert Elias quotes the pithy summary in the article "Hôtel" of the *Encyclopédie*: "Dwellings take different names according to the different estates of those occupying them. We speak of *la maison* of a bourgeois, *l'hôtel* of a noble, *le palais* of a prince or a king" (54). A middle-class owner of a fairly large aristocratic *hôtel*: such is the contradiction of Orgon's ambivalent position in society. This ambivalence was indicated in the 1962 and 1973 stagings by Roger Planchon, who showed a space in the process of being torn up and rebuilt (Corvin; Merle; Millon; Romero, "Tropes").

A more fundamental process is at work here. The construction of private, freestanding residences took place at the same time that the concept of an independent, autonomous self became dominant (Reiss; Greenblatt). To use Stephen Greenblatt's words, the self "fashions itself" an identity through language (9) and, I would add, not only through language but also by the construction of a separate residence. This construction is a spatial equivalent of what was understood then in psychology: that individuals were masters of their own destinies and through their willpower exerted control over their lives. In seventeenth-century France, the king, who was at the top of the social hierarchy, gave the example by leaving the Louvre, the medieval residence of his forebears, and building a new palace at Versailles. Nobles were building their *hôtels* in the Marais, and middle-class people on their way to nobility were building their *maisons*, imitating aristocratic house plans.

Orgon is not entitled to use the word *hôtel*. In his lifestyle, however, he is nevertheless overstepping the boundaries of his social class by behaving like a nobleman: the charge of usurpation can thus be leveled not only at Tartuffe, who "céans s'impatronise" (1.1.62) ("usurp[s] the master's place"), but also at his master. They mirror each other in being social climbers, which may explain in part their mutual fascination. Tartuffe, we are told, was from a poor background (1.1.63–64). If he were to marry Mariane, he and she would be relegated to the most humble of small towns in the provinces and would have to attend the local carnival and to sit on a "siège pliant" (2.3.663) (a folding chair, or, in Wilbur's version, "a kitchen chair"). At a time when the nature of the seat prescribed was a crucial indicator of social status, this detail shows the humble status likely to be Tartuffe and Mariane's lot. In a parallel move, Orgon, from a middle-class background, wants to climb into the class above him; indeed, Orgon and Tartuffe are more alike than different from each other, as Jacques Guicharnaud notes (*Molière: Une aventure* 168). Orgon does not go so far as to say the forbidden word *hôtel* but uses the term that properly belongs to him as a middle-class person, *maison*. There is also, however, the convenient word *céans*, which is vague and neutral, designating only an interior space without connotation of rank, an expression that therefore suits Orgon's ambivalent status particularly well.

Orgon's ambivalence is further reinforced by the two meanings of the word *maison*. In reference to dwellings, it was opposed to the aristocratic *hôtel*, but in reference to the social unit, *maison* meant the aristocratic family and lineage as opposed to the middle-class *famille*. Elias sums up the difference between the two words used to refer to the family unit of husband and wife: "In the usage of the ancien régime, the term 'family' is more or less restricted to the upper bourgeoisie, that of the 'house' to the king and high aristocracy" (50). The aristocratic sense of family or lineage appears in M. Loyal's speech: "Toute votre maison m'a toujours été chère" (5.4.1737) ("I've always held your family most dear"). The irony is extreme here, because at the very moment that Monsieur Loyal is praising the noble *maison* of Orgon, he is seizing the latter's *maison* in the literal sense. No wonder that Dorine says a bit later, "Ce Monsieur Loyal porte un air bien déloyal!" (1772) ("This man Loyal's a most disloyal sort!").

Orgon's house is thus not a simple passive space containing people moving about. It is complex and visible as one of the crucial elements of the play's structure and value system, and as such it participates in the action of the play: it is as much at stake as a character—say, Mariane, who, as the daughter wishing to marry against her father's wishes, furnishes the traditional comic plot. It is a space with multiple meanings given to it by the characters who invest it, lose it, and regain it at the end. It is also a space filled with language, and that makes sense, since language, along with dwelling, is one of the prime instruments by which the self "fashions" itself: "Self-fashioning is always, though not exclusively, in language," says Greenblatt (9). I will now analyze the parallel progression of space and language throughout the play until the dramatic expulsion of the entire family by Tartuffe.

Orgon's house is filled with language: as Mme Pernelle points out, everyone speaks too much and too loudly. To Dorine, who is "un peu trop forte en gueule" (1.1.14) ("far too saucy"), she says, "Vous vous mêlez sur tout de dire votre avis" (15) ("You push in everywhere and have your say"); to Cléante she says, "Sans cesse vous prêchez" (37) ("You're full of worldly counsels"). From the rest of the family come similar complaints against Tartuffe, who is accused of making "un vacarme à nous rompre la tête" (82) ("[P]rophesy[ing] against us all"). The remainder of the opening scene revolves around the question of language; witness the accumulation of terms meaning to speak or to say:

"querellé" (44) ("mocked"), "cause" (93) ("talk"), "médire" (106) ("besmirch"), "sots discours" (95) ("stupid speeches"; my trans.), "sots caquets" (100) ("tittle-tattle"), "semer la nouvelle" (109) ("spread the joyous news"), "jaser" (143) ("rattle on"), "discourir" (144) ("have my say"), "conversations" (151) ("conversations"; my trans.), "propos oisifs, chansons et fariboles" (154) ("[n]othing but chaff and foolishness and lying"), "mille caquets divers" (159) ("a thousand different cacklings"; my trans.), "babille" (162) ("babble"), and "conter" (163) ("told a story"). Language proliferates: the language of others—neighbors' rumors that multiply about this family—as well as the family's own language. Mme Pernelle's tirade is finally interrupted at the moment when one senses that she is about to embark on the telling of a story. She is stopped in her tracks by an alert Cléante, who snickers as if he already knew what was coming (164–65). She ends the scene with a vulgar command to Flipote and slaps the mute servant, who, being speechless, seems barely human.

Tartuffe's and Orgon's excessive language is described in act 1, scene 2: although Mme Pernelle speaks too much and admires Tartuffe too much, there is worse, for, according to Dorine, Orgon "l'appelle son frère, et l'aime dans son âme / Cent fois plus qu'il ne fait mère, fils, fille, et femme" (1.2.185–86) ("calls him brother, and loves him as his life, / Preferring him to mother, child, or wife"). Orgon quotes Tartuffe constantly (1.2.196), and "tous les mots qu'il dit sont pour lui des oracles" (198) ("each word / Oracular as those that Moses heard"). Even Tartuffe's servant, Laurent, is guilty of similar excesses: he comes to lecture the servants with wild eyes (205).

Language continues to flow abundantly in the early part of the play. In act 1, scene 5, Orgon and Cléante wage a duel of long, wordy, and repetitious tirades; the champion is Cléante, who delivers a speech of fifty-seven verses. Then it is Dorine's turn to wield domination through her use of language, even over her master, with her interruptions and later through her deliberate silences (2.2). She also shows her linguistic power in the tirades describing the provincial life that awaits Mariane if she marries Tartuffe (2.3), and she evokes briefly the power of Elmire's speech over Tartuffe: "Il se rend complaisant à tout ce qu'elle dit" (3.1.836) ("He hangs upon her words, seems most devoted"); Dorine's last moment of power onstage is her daring outburst to Tartuffe, when she bravely confronts Tartuffe, accusing him of lechery and assuring him that she is not in the least attracted to him (3.2.863–68).

In the middle of the play, however, the characters' ability to speak and make themselves heard diminishes. Mariane is the first to be reduced to silence by her father, as she is the weakest person in this universe. Dorine reproaches her: "Avez-vous donc perdu, dites-moi, la parole?" (2.3.585) ("Well, have you lost your tongue, girl?"). The equivalence of speech with action is indicated in Mariane's question "[Q]ue veux-tu que je fasse?" (589) ("What do you want me to do?"; my trans.) and in Dorine's answer: "Lui dire . . ." (591) ("Tell him . . ."). Mariane admits that she is weak because she cannot talk back to her father (597–98). In act 3, scene 3, Dorine loses her linguistic force, and all the other characters are, one by one, also reduced to powerlessness. Elmire complains that Tartuffe is squeezing her fingertips too hard (according to the stage direction before line 912), a squeezing that feels more like a suffocation, judging from her reply: "Ouf! vous me serrez trop" (3.3.914) ("Ooh! Please! You're pinching!"). He dominates her body and pursues her by pushing his chair against hers, and he monopolizes the conversation with his long speeches (3.3).

From the time he comes onstage in act 3, Tartuffe occupies a space with his abundant language, reducing the others to silence. Concurrently, there is a reduction in the spaces represented onstage. Damis comes out of a *petit cabinet* (3.4) and will soon be chased out of the house in words that emphasize the space he is to leave: "[Q]ue de ma maison on sorte de ce pas" (3.6.1136) ("Out of my house this minute!"). The stage directions just before line 1149 further emphasize this expulsion: "[Orgon] court tout en larmes à la porte par où il a chassé son fils" ("He runs, in tears, to the door through which he has just driven his son"). Tartuffe also stresses the confines of a space that cannot contain both Damis and himself: "Et s'il rentre céans, c'est à moi d'en sortir" (4.1.1208) ("If he comes back, then I shall have to go"). Tartuffe cuts off Cléante rudely and reduces him to the inarticulate protest "Ah!" (1269). Orgon will soon disappear under the famous table, and Elmire's speech will dissolve in coughing (4.4; 4.5). Worse yet, Orgon and his entire family are chased out of the house in act 4, scene 7. Orgon—who just said to Tartuffe, "Dénichons de céans" (1554) ("Just leave this household, without more ado")—hears him reply, "La maison m'appartient" (1558) ("This house belongs to me") and "[J]'ai de quoi . . . faire repentir / Ceux qui parlent ici de me faire sortir" (1562–64) ("I've means to . . . make you grieve / That ever you dared order me to leave"). Orgon, who would not believe others' accusations against Tartuffe, is now powerless to convince his own mother about Tartuffe's misdeeds (5.3). Dorine comments ironically, "Juste retour . . . des choses . . . / Vous ne vouliez point croire, et l'on ne vous croit pas" (1695–96) ("It's your turn now, Sir, not to be listened to; / You'd not trust us, and now she won't trust you"). His complete defeat in both linguistic and spatial domains is marked by the exclamation "Moi, sortir de céans?" (5.4.1752) ("I? Leave this house?").

It may be hard to believe that the situation can get worse, but it does. Concrete details of Orgon's move out of the house are given by M. Loyal: Orgon must hand over the keys to his front door (1786), presumably the same door through which he had chased his own son a few scenes ago, and "vuider de céans jusqu'au moindre ustensile" (1790) ("move out all . . . furniture, every stick"). Planchon emphasized the reduction in space and the general darkening of the mood by using a somber and hostile set, with high bare walls, little light, and only a small sky-blue door at the back (Corvin 121–23, 135–37). The constriction of space is indicated by the words "gîte" (5.7.1862) ("lodging") and "prisonnier" (1863). Orgon calls Tartuffe's insulting language "injures" (1867) ("insults"; my trans.), and Tartuffe uses the very contemptuous word "criaillerie" (1897) ("clamor") in his last moment of power, before the dramatic reversal that will close down on Tartuffe and in turn reduce his space to that of the prison cell (1902).

After the fall of Tartuffe, Orgon does not really recover his power of speech, for speech now belongs to the king's envoy, charged with Tartuffe's arrest. What Orgon would like to say, no doubt a string of insults against Tartuffe, is cut short by Cléante, who reminds Orgon that the most important act he must perform is to thank the king. In the perspective of this analysis, the officer's speech must also be considered. A clear contrast has been made between a family reduced to powerlessness and homelessness and the prince who knows and sees everything, whose vision is not blocked by any opacity. Not only is Tartuffe transparent (1919–20) to the king, but so are all the citizens of his kingdom, for he is "[u]n Prince dont les yeux se font jour dans les coeurs" (1907) ("[a] Prince who sees into our inmost hearts"). This power to see through space is augmented by his power of speech:

> D'un souverain pouvoir, il brise les liens
> Du contrat qui lui fait un don de tous vos biens,
> Et vous pardonne enfin cette offense secrète
> Où vous a d'un ami fait tomber la retraite.
> (1935–38)

> The King, by royal order, invalidates
> The deed which gave this rascal your estates
> And pardons, furthermore, your grave offense
> In harboring an exile's documents.

It is interesting to compare the king's power to speak and forgive with the power expressed in a similarly forgiving speech, that of the priest or of Christ: "I will give you the keys of the kingdom of heaven: whatever you bind on earth shall be considered bound in heaven; whatever you loose on earth shall be considered loosed in heaven" (Matt. 16.19 [*Jerusalem Bible*]). Planchon emphasized the keys to Orgon's little kingdom, which had already appeared in M. Loyal's speech, by directing that they be held by Elmire in act 4, scene 5 (Merle 40), and he further underlined the religious connotations by staging the last image of Orgon's family before the expulsion as a Last Supper (Corvin 136). The religious meaning of the king's envoy is not lost on Dorine, who, ever perceptive, exclaims "Que le Ciel soit loué!" (1945) ("Heaven be praised!").

The unusual frequency of a particular word, *céans*, points to a significant aspect of the play's conflict, in which a well-defined space is at stake. For modern-day spectators, the conflict in this play centers not on the problem of a young girl who is forced by her father to marry someone she hates, a conventional plot of seventeenth-century comedies, or on the matter of defining the difference between a true believer and a *faux dévot* (religious hypocrite), a crucial problem in Molière's time. Our meaning is elsewhere.

However, our meaning is also profoundly anchored in Molière's text and period, for it is the period during which a certain concept of the self took hold and, with it, a particular concept of dwelling space. There is spatialization of the self, which occupies a certain place, and personification of the space, which plays a role like a character: such are the meanings that are found here, "céans," in Molière's text and world. These are processes that we can recognize, for whether we call ourselves modern or postmodern, we are heirs to the concepts of space and person elaborated in the seventeenth century.

Love in *Tartuffe*, Tartuffe in Love

Jules Brody

As the curtain goes up on *Tartuffe,* we are offered a first view of "love," in the guise of familial affection and worldly courtesy. These are the feelings communicated in a wordless scenic language by Elmire as she accompanies her mother-in-law to the door. The old lady's reaction, brusque and uncalled for, serves both to lay out the drama's background and to anticipate things to come: "Laissez, ma bru, laissez, ne venez pas plus loin: / Ce sont toutes façons dont je n'ai pas besoin" (1.1.3–4) ("Don't trouble, child; no need to show me out. / It's not your manners I'm concerned about"). The word *façons* subsumes in advance the long indictment by Mme Pernelle of modern-day Parisian manners and social life that monopolizes the opening scene of *Tartuffe.* Her rejection of Elmire's solicitous, affable "manners" targets a conception of human relations in which the pleasures and entertainments of polite society play a central role. Despite her edifying "leçons" ("advice"), her son's home has become the scene of one riotous, endless party (10–12). This observation launches a detailed denunciation of the entire household, by order of ascending social rank, from the "saucy" servant girl (14) to the "dunce" of a son (16–17) and the hypocritical daughter who hides her scandalous lifestyle behind a façade of respectability. Mme Pernelle blames the waywardness of her grandchildren on the poor example of their elders:

> Ma bru, qu'il ne vous en déplaise,
> Votre conduite en tout est tout à fait mauvaise;
> Vous devriez leur mettre un bon exemple aux yeux,
> Et leur défunte mère en usait beaucoup mieux.
> Vous êtes dépensière; et cet état me blesse,
> Que vous alliez vêtue ainsi qu'une princesse.
> Quiconque à son mari veut plaire seulement,
> Ma bru, n'a pas besoin de tant d'ajustement.
>
> (1.1.25–32)

> And as for you, child, let me add
> That your behavior is extremely bad,
> And a poor example for these children, too.
> Their dear, dead mother did far better than you.
> You're much too free with money, and I'm distressed
> To see you so elaborately dressed.
> When it's one's husband that one aims to please,
> One has no need of costly fripperies.

This speech defines at the outset the relative positions and values of those who are assembled under Orgon's roof. We learn, for example, that he is a widower and that Elmire, as his second wife, is closer in age to his late-teenage children than to Orgon himself. (In the original production, her role was played by Molière's daughter [Mongrédien 1: 337].) So the conflict is not merely between two different sets of social and moral values but between two generations and between two distinct lifestyles. The stodgy, old-fashioned mind-set of the age of Louis XIII is pitted against the worldview of the "young court" at Versailles, where *Tartuffe* was first performed in 1664 for the pleasure of the twenty-six-year-old Louis XIV and his mistress (Molière, *Œuvres* 1: 859–61; Apostolidès, *Roi-machine* 93–113).

Mme Pernelle's criticism of Elmire's wardrobe is an example: not only is Elmire "dressed like a princess," but her perceived values—her apparent desire to attract other men—smack of the freewheeling, self-indulgent behavior of the aristocratic upper crust. Nor is costume the only measure of Elmire's social orientation. What with the line of carriages at her front door, the crowds of noisy lackeys always hanging around (1.1.88–89), and the endless socializing (151), we have all the trappings of the Parisian yuppie lifestyle of the roaring 1660s. Further, we learn that during the wars of the Fronde, during Louis XIV's minority, Orgon had "served his King" (1.2.182), the mark of a politically connected family living close to the highest public function.

In brief, this opening expository scene, which teachers will need to explain in detail to their students, introduces us to one of those great, prosperous, upwardly mobile bourgeois families on which Louis's régime became more and more financially dependent with each passing year. In her dress, her pastimes, her manners, and her social attitudes, Elmire emerges as the very emblem of the elegant, newly established leisure classes of the age of Louis XIV. Mme Pernelle is pictured, in stark contrast, as the champion and the mainstay of the conservative religious right, nostalgic for the frugality, the discipline, and the family values of the "old court" and the good old days of the reign of Louis XIII.

The play's opening scene is also noteworthy in this respect: it contains the first in a series of verbal sketches of the title character. The purpose of these portraits of Tartuffe is to prepare for his late entrance at the beginning of act 3 and, in particular, to situate him socially with respect to the elegant milieu where he is viewed almost universally as an intruder. This distancing is clear from the very first mention of his name by Orgon's son, Damis: "Votre Monsieur Tartuffe est bienheureux sans doute . . ." (1.1.41) ("Your man Tartuffe is full of holy speeches"). The title "Monsieur" is a giveaway in a social context where everyone but "Madame Pernelle" goes only by a fine-sounding Grecian first name (Elmire, Damis, Cléante, Orgon), reminiscent of the courtly literary genres of pastoral and tragedy. The first thing we learn about "Monsieur Tartuffe" is that his physical demeanor is the outward expression of his more than questionable origins. Again according to Damis, "ce beau monsieur-là" (48) ("that handsome gentleman") is a "pied plat" (59) ("hay-seed"), literally a flat-footed, "pedestrian" clod who shuffles around in low-heeled shoes. A peasant in fact and at heart, Tartuffe, strictly speaking, does not even rate being called Monsieur. At best, he is "Monsieur Tartuffe" in the same way that Dom Juan's money-grubbing tailor is "Monsieur Dimanche."

As this verbal portrait develops, Dorine refers to Tartuffe as a barefooted "inconnu" ("nobody"): ". . . un gueux qui, quand il vint, n'avait pas de souliers / Et dont l'habit entier valait bien six deniers" (62–64) (". . . this beggar, who, when he first came, / Had not a shoe or shoestring to his name"). That a "Monsieur" Tartuffe of this description should have the run of a household like Orgon's raised the specter of an infiltration and a subversion, from below, of the fabric of upper-class life. The physical and social unseemliness of Tartuffe's presence here had a moral dimension as well. Why, asks Dorine, hasn't he allowed them any visitors of late? "Je crois que de Madame il est, ma foi, jaloux" (84) ("[I]f you ask me, / He's jealous of my mistress' company"). This assessment of Tartuffe's motives, setting the stage for his sexual advances to Elmire in act 3, scene 3, evokes an upside-down world in which rustic beggars can take over upscale bourgeois families and, worse, in which moral austerity and religious piety become tools of sexual conquest.

The subsequent installments in this verbal portrait further illustrate Tartuffe's vulgarity through a series of glimpses of his eating habits: he sits at the head of the table, where he packs in enough for six, grabs all the choice morsels, and belches right out loud (2.2.190–94). These fleeting references to the crudeness of Tartuffe's appetites will be developed in Dorine's first scene with Orgon:

ORGON.   Et Tartuffe?
DORINE.   Tartuffe? Il se porte à merveille.
                  Gros et gras, le teint frais et la bouche vermeille.
                                                        (1.4.233–34)
ORGON.   Ah. And Tartuffe?
DORINE.   Tartuffe? Why he's round and red
                  Bursting with health, and excellently fed.

And why shouldn't he be the picture of health, with what he consumes? The other night, Elmire was too ill to look at food, but that didn't bother Tartuffe:

Il soupa, lui tout seul, devant elle,
Et fort dévotement il mangea deux perdrix,
Avec une moitié de gigot en hachis.
                                (237–39)

He ate his meal with relish,
And zealously devoured in her presence
A leg of mutton and a brace of pheasants.

After supper, he got into his warm bed, and after a good night's sleep he started off the next day with four big glasses of wine (245–55).

Tartuffe's existence is depicted as a masterpiece of comfort, well-being, and sensuality. This man, purportedly of God, is reported to us as a monster of corporality. Whereas Orgon sees in him a disembodied soul, what Molière shows us at work in Tartuffe's behavior is a mouth, a belly, an appetite, and, in a manner of speaking, a penis. In symbolic terms, the triumph of this grasping low-class bumpkin over his elegant antagonists forebodes a metaphysical victory of body over spirit, ugliness over beauty.

In act 2, scene 1, Orgon informs his daughter, Mariane, that she must marry Tartuffe. Dorine, as the mouthpiece of good sense and reality, denounces this choice by a man of property of a "gendre gueux" (2.2.484–85) ("beggar son-in-law") as what was called in that day a "mésalliance." Her refrain throughout is, How can a man like you marry a girl like her to a creep like him? In the French text her disbelief is marked by the recurrent word *tel* (such): "une telle alliance" (482, 638) ("such a marriage"), "un tel époux" (579) ("such a spouse"), "un tel mari" (648) ("such a husband"; my trans.). In defense of his decision, Orgon maintains that Tartuffe has a noble lineage: "Et tel que l'on le voit, il est bien gentilhomme" (494) ("Poor though he is, he's a gentleman just the same"). Such as he is, that is, contrary to appearances, he belongs to the landed gentry. But appearances count, Dorine insists:

> Parlons de sa personne, et laissons sa noblesse.
> Ferez-vous possesseur, sans quelque peu d'ennui,
> D'une fille comme elle, un homme comme lui?
> (2.2.502–04)

> Let's speak, then, of his person, not his rank
> Doesn't it seem to you a trifle grim
> To give a girl like her to a man like him?

In Dorine's view, Mariane is to Tartuffe as Beauty is to the Beast. And Molière makes Orgon admit as much: "Sans être demoiseau, / Tartuffe est fait de sorte . . ." ("Tartuffe is no young dandy, / But, still, his person . . ."). And Dorine replies ironically: "Oui, c'est un beau museau" (559–60) ("[Tartuffe] is as sweet as candy"). Tartuffe's reported physique is, at this point, a verbal emblem. Later, once we lay eyes on him, it becomes the scenic vehicle of a number of implicit value judgments—"disgusting," "repugnant," "hateful"—that were earlier conveyed by the description of his gluttony and his table manners.

In the next scene, Dorine puts the finishing touches to her physical and moral sketch of Tartuffe:

> Il est noble chez lui, bien fait de sa personne;
> Il a l'oreille rouge et le teint bien fleuri:

> Vous vivrez trop contente avec un tel mari.
> (2.3.646–48)

> He's a great noble—in his native town;
> His ears are red, he has a pink complexion,
> And all in all, he'll suit you to perfection.

Here again, the physical and moral aspects of Tartuffe coincide. Echoing her earlier comment on his "rosy skin and red lips" (1.4.233–34; my trans.), Dorine graces Tartuffe with a "sanguine" constitution, which, according to that era's theory of the humors, denoted a full-blooded temperament, powerfully inclined to the pleasures of the flesh (Molière, *Œuvres* 1: 1350). At this point, we are left with a full, vivid mental picture of the still unseen Tartuffe as a grubby, ruddy, horny social climber who has managed, incredibly, to penetrate the highest reaches of the beau monde.

As final object of this feat of social "penetration," Mariane, Dorine warns her, will end up being "tartuffiée":

> DORINE.   . . . Tartuffe est votre homme, et vous en tâterez.
> MARIANE.   Tu sais qu'à toi toujours je me suis confiée: Fais-moi . . .
> DORINE.   Non, vous serez, ma foi! tartuffiée.
> (2.3.672–74)

> DORINE.   Tartuffe's your cup of tea and you shall drink him.
> MARIANE.   I've always told you everything and relied . . .
> DORINE.   No. You deserve to be tartuffified.

In its most obvious sense, the word *tartuffiée* means "married to Tartuffe." But this bizarre proper name overlies a curious etymological and semantic substratum that deserves to be uncovered. In Italian *tartufo* means "truffle"; in French the word is *truffe*. From the Middle Ages to Molière's day, this exotic tuber carried suggestions of trickery and deception, perhaps also of lechery, since the truffle was legendary as an aphrodisiac (Brody 238–40). Tartuffe's name is the phonic equivalent of his physical and moral ugliness, evoking as it does the bulbous meat of that luxurious black mushroom—the same color as his somber religious garb—that grows underground and is hunted out with the help of pigs. By its immediate associations and its place in the scale of the unaesthetic, *Tartuffe* as mere word rivals the visually and psychologically displeasing associations of other Molière character names like M. de Pourceaugnac (*pourceau* means "hog"), Dr. Purgon (*purge*, "enema"), and George Dandin (*se dandiner*, "waddle like a duck").

The ultimate impact of the statement "vous serez tartuffiée," however, must be sought in its context, where the words echo and relay the sexually charged sentence "Tartuffe est votre homme, et vous en tâterez." This tactile and gustatory metaphor admits of a number of complementary paraphrases—"You will touch him, feel him, taste him, ingest him"—all of which are semantically equivalent variants of the implicit constant "You will know Tartuffe physically"— "in the flesh," as we say. Mariane will be "tartuffified," first and superficially, by becoming Mme Tartuffe but also, far more grievously, by being filled up with Tartuffe, in the sense of the modern French verb *truffer* ("to stuff," as with truffles): she will be crammed full of Tartuffe in the same way as we fill a turkey or a goose with stuffing. At this high point in Dorine's depiction of the fate to be endured by the future Mme Tartuffe, she is saying, in effect, "If you don't shape up, my dear, you're gonna have a bellyful of this fucker." The equivalent in today's French vernacular would be: "Tu ne vas pas tarder à te le farcir."

The participle *tartuffiée*, with its powerful associations of sexual invasion and possession, is literally the last word in the long and elaborate verbal portrait of Tartuffe that spans the play's first two acts. And it is highly significant that when Molière finally puts Tartuffe onstage in act 3, scene 2, it is in his capacity as "lover" or "amateur," in the neutral, crude senses of these terms: someone who loves to feast his eyes on women's bodies, who yearns to fondle and sample female flesh in any shape or form. As Molière observes in his preface to the play, "On le connaît d'abord aux traits que je lui donne" ("The audience recognizes Tartuffe immediately from my description of him"). It is a simple dramaturgical fact that the two successive actions that initiate Tartuffe's effective presence on the stage are driven by the sexual energy that propels his course through life. Each of these scenic moments is subsumed in a single gesture and a single line. In our first glimpse of Tartuffe, he is ogling Dorine's breasts: "Couvrez ce sein que je ne saurais voir" (3.2.860) ("Cover that bosom, girl. The flesh is weak"). In the following scene, he has his hand on Elmire's knee: "Je tâte votre habit: l'étoffe en est moelleuse" (3.3.917) (["I am] feeling your gown; what soft, fine-woven stuff!").

Tartuffe's physical presence incarnates the full semantic content of his name and actualizes all the distaste that is inspired by the cumulative revelations of his manners, his ambitions, his sexual aggressiveness, his religious hypocrisy, his usurpations both of noble birth and of Orgon's house and hold. What Molière denounces in Tartuffe's demeanor and behavior is an all-encompassing acquisitive appetite that makes of him the exemplary, hyperbolic enemy of the reigning social order. The royal intervention at the play's denouement is not a dramatic convenience but a moral necessity.

Considering the number of Tartuffe's transgressions, the magnitude of his greed, and the scale of his depredations, it is tempting to see in him the embodiment of a force of nature given over to the extinction of culture, a veritable telluric power devoted to the destruction of the good and the beautiful. Tartuffe is a character conjured up out of a nightmare (Knutson 77–78), a maniacal, demonic presence that threatens the very foundations of civilization. Tartuffe, in a word, is the evil spirit that must be exorcised if justice is ever again to prevail over fraud, equity over brute force, spirit over flesh, love over animality, if a "doux hymen"("sweet union") is, as Orgon hopes, ever to "couronner en Valère / La flamme d'un amant généreux et sincère" (5.7.1961–62) ("give Valère . . . the wedded happiness which is his due").

Tartuffe is reminiscent of the cynical barbarian, knowing no higher law than his own desires, who, in Freud's reconstruction, was the ultimate nemesis of the precivilized male: the all-powerful, invulnerable invader who might one day descend on him, drive him from his home, and seize his goods and his women (95–96). Surely, this is the essential meaning of Orgon's incredulous remonstration to Tartuffe: "Comme aux tentations s'abandonne votre âme! / Vous épousiez ma fille, et convoitiez ma femme!" (4.7.1545–46) ("How soon you wearied of the saintly life— / Wedding my daughter, and coveting my wife!"). In this updated version of Freud's primal dispossession scene, tyrannical force has been replaced by the intellectual, bourgeois vices of contrivance, fakery, and trickery. At the denouement, the terror of Tartuffe's victims is dispelled, their doom is reversed, and the day is saved by the descent on the scene of a godlike *rex ex machina* (Nelson 116–17), whose Supermanlike X-ray vision pierces, miraculously, to the heart of the matter:

> Un Prince dont les yeux se font jour dans les coeurs,
> Et que ne peut tromper tout l'art des imposteurs.
> (5.7.1907–08)

> A Prince who sees into our inmost hearts
> And can't be fooled by any trickster's arts.

Laughter and Difference in *Tartuffe*

Andrew J. McKenna

The character of Tartuffe would seem to present no enigma for students. He appears to be a religiously devout man to Mme Pernelle and to Orgon, her son, who has introduced him into the household as a model to be admired and imitated; but to the rest of the household Tartuffe appears as he is made to be seen by the spectators: a fraud. In an effort to disabuse his brother-in-law of this imposture, Cléante elaborates this difference thematically and programmatically by contrasting "l'hypocrisie" and "la dévotion," "l'artifice" and "la sincérité," "le fantôme" and "la personne," rounding off his lecture on appearance versus truth with the metaphors of true and counterfeit money (1.5.329–38).

Molière's play is indeed about difference but not of the kind between false appearance and essential, underlying truth that is expressed by Cléante and in which he and we, the public at large, routinely invest for our understanding of human relations. The difference between deceiver and deceived is essentially tragic, not comic; it corresponds notionally and ethically to the difference between victimizer and victim, and there is nothing funny about that. It is because Orgon engages in a complex strategy of self-deceit that we can laugh at his excesses and learn something about ourselves from their portrayal. Our laughter is proof against all kinds of differences on which we nominally rely, including our overconfidence in the difference between us and the arch-deceiver Tartuffe. Cléante wants to teach Orgon—and us—about virtues and values, but Molière, through his characters' relations with one another, teaches us something of incommensurately greater benefit, which is to laugh when we take ourselves too seriously.

If Tartuffe does not appear onstage until the third act, it is because the play is not essentially about him but about Orgon's apparently blind infatuation with him. Cléante evokes it as a "charme," as some sort of seductive spell: "Et se peut-il qu'un homme ait un charme aujourd'hui / A vous faire oublier toutes choses pour lui?" (1.5.263–64) ("Are you so dazed by this man's hocus pocus / That all the world, save him, is out of focus?"). Cléante also tells his brother-in-law that he is mad: "Parbleu! vous êtes fou" (1.5.311) ("Good God, man! Have you lost your common sense . . ."). It is commonplace hyperbole, but it takes on telling resonance when Mariane's maid, Dorine, elaborates Orgon's seemingly amorous enthrallment with Tartuffe as a kind of idolatry, which we understand as a travesty of religion, the worship of an image in the place of an authentic divinity:

> Enfin il en est fou; c'est son tout, son héros;
> Il l'admire à tous coups, le cite à tout propos;

Ses moindres actions lui semblent des miracles,
Et tous les mots qu'il dit sont pour lui des oracles.
(1.2.195–98)

In short, he's mad; he worships him; he dotes;
His deeds he marvels at, his words he quotes,
Thinking each act a miracle, each word
Oracular as those that Moses heard.

Orgon's madness is not literal—that would be simply and inextricably tragic —but metaphorical, *madness* in this instance serving to designate a person who does not know his own mind. In following just how the play conjugates or correlates these notions of seduction, madness, and idolatry as metaphors of one another, as variants of an essential delusion, we can help our students grasp something in Molière's comic vision that constitutes a veritable theory of human relations, in which travesty, make-believe, or imposture is everywhere.

Laughter thrives on difference. In the theater, it often erupts in the gap between our own discernment and one character's or several characters' lack of it. We experience this gap, for instance, in Orgon's first appearance onstage, where his mention of Tartuffe registers like an invocation or a ritual incantation. He inquires obsessively, "Et Tartuffe?," while being informed of the indisposition of his wife, Elmire, and then, following Dorine's description of Tartuffe's robust gluttony, he solemnly intones, "Le pauvre homme!" (1.4) ("Poor fellow!"). Though we are not conscious of its precise structure, our laughter is a function of the perceived contrast between what obviously deserves sympathy and what just as obviously does not. The viewing or reading public is acutely aware of the disparity, to which Orgon appears indifferent, oblivious. It is the play of difference and indifference on- and offstage, textually imagined or empirically viewed, that provokes laughter.

The philosopher Henri Bergson's definition of laughter is instructive here. He describes it as a response to witnessing "du mécanique dans le vivant," the machine inside the living ("Le rire" 423), such that we are regaled with the spectacle of a sentient being behaving in an automatic fashion that is rigorously contrary to its purported nature. But we have to plumb deeper into the implications of this anomaly to appreciate Molière's comic insights. At the very outset, his play stages our difference from Orgon and, to be sure, from Tartuffe, though the logic of his characters' interactions proceeds to undermine it.

Students will immediately understand that Orgon's blindness to the evidence recounted to him is buffoonish; it is so mechanical and compulsive that we assume that if he is not an insanely deluded—that is, tragic—character, then there is a method to his madness. This method is just what we learn in his discussion with Cléante, where he explains the value he places on Tartuffe:

Oui, je deviens tout autre avec son entretien;
Il m'enseigne à n'avoir affection pour rien,
De toutes amitiés il détache mon âme;
Et je verrais mourir frère, enfants, mère et femme,
Que je m'en soucierais autant que de cela.

(1.5.275–79)

Yes, thanks to him I'm a changed man indeed;
Under his tutelage my soul's been freed
From earthly loves, and every human tie:
My mother, children, brother, and wife could die,
and I'd not feel a single moment's pain.

Orgon aspires to godlike indifference to human affection. Cléante's immediate rejoinder—"Les sentiments humains, mon frère, que voilà!" (280) ("That's a fine sentiment, Brother; most humane.")—concisely summarizes Orgon's bid for transcendence of his human and social condition.

This ambition is essentially metaphysical. It bears on nothing real in the world but, rather, aims to renounce ordinary human relations for a supposedly higher ideal. Orgon expresses it again when, in the face of his daughter Mariane's passionate plea not to be forced to marry Tartuffe, he intones "Allons, ferme, mon coeur, point de faiblesse humaine!" (4.3.1293) ("Be firm, my soul. No human weakness, now.") Here, the word *humaine*, as that which he is striving to deny in himself, deserves extra emphasis. Orgon is struggling against his own common humanity, and that is just what makes him indelibly human, as he personifies Pascal's observation about our species: "Man is neither angel nor beast, and it is unfortunately the case that anyone trying to act the angel acts the beast" (no. 678).

As paterfamilias in the hierarchical society of seventeenth-century France, Orgon enjoys unquestioned authority over his household. As Mariane complains to Dorine about his decision to marry her to Tartuffe, "Contre un père absolu que veux-tu que je fasse?" (2.3.589) ("What good would it do? A father's power is great."). But Orgon is not satisfied with his traditional role. He does not repudiate it; on the contrary, he exaggerates it, taking it too seriously and himself as its embodiment. His dissatisfaction takes a form—religious devotion—that in other Molière plays has other forms for other characters as they foolishly strive for ascendancy. In *Le misanthrope*, it is honesty, or sincerity, for Alceste; in *Les femmes savantes*, learning is the leverage of Philaminte's power struggle. Argan's hypochondria in *Le malade imaginaire* makes him the center of his little world no less than Arnolphe's attempted domination of Agnès in *L'école des femmes* represents the superiority he seeks over other members of his widely cuckolded sex. Throughout his work, Molière's interest for us does not consist in the creation of peculiar types of individuals whom we can classify apart from our own behavior and sensibilities. On the contrary, it is precisely because the desire to stand apart from and above others can take any form or fashion that his theater abides as an important instrument of cultural interpretation. At this level, his plays are primarily not an object of study but a dramatic agency of real knowledge about our dealings with one another.

By imposing Tartuffe on his family as a model of thought and conduct, Orgon would be the uncontested source, the originating principle, of all authority and value—a god, in sum. Now that is ridiculous in our eyes and would be so to Orgon were it proposed to him in so many words. But Tartuffe offers a way for him to impose his will not in so many words but indirectly, under the guise of renouncing it in the name of absolute values—though such values are not an end in themselves but a means of exercising absolute power. As such, he is a caricature of the very king who saves him from his own folly in the last act of the play.

This tyrannical ambition is epitomized in his response to Mariane's resistance to declaring Tartuffe as her choice in marriage:

> MARIANE.   Il n'en est rien, mon père, je vous jure.
> Pourquoi me faire dire un telle imposture?
> ORGON.   Mais je veux que cela soit une vérité;
> Et c'est assez pour vous que je l'aie arrêté.
> (2.1.449–52)

> MARIANE.   But, Father, that's false, you know.
> Why would you have me say what isn't so?
> ORGON.   Because I am resolved it shall be true.
> That it's my wish should be enough for you.

Orgon expresses a will to truth as a function of the will rather than of the truth. In this respect he embodies a specifically modern form of moral tyranny. He is a prototype of ideological despotism perfected in our century, a prototype that, in the name of uncontested values, subordinates all consciences to the whim of a single master. Though history has taught us the baleful consequences of such a project when it is aided by modern technology and bureaucracy, it reflects for Molière a fundamentally comic illusion about a unified will that his play demolishes at every turn.

No such preposterous ambition as becoming a god is present in Orgon's conscious mind. Indeed, such self-aggrandizement is inconceivable to his pious self-image, but this image is just what Molière questions in this play and throughout his theater: the deluded image of an autonomous self that would be origin and master of its words and its wishes. Along with the Cartesian *cogito*, the notion of a sovereign and unified subject is emerging in seventeenth-century France as one of the central myths of modern Western culture. Orgon makes us laugh, though he is only a caricature of our own sense of personal identity and zealous mission, of our romantic sense of substantial difference from others, along with our concomitant belief in the difference between person and persona, man and mask—all themes of Lionel Gossman's enduring analysis of Molière's theater as relevant to the playwright's time and ours as well.

Sovereign individuality represents for us a genuine conquest of modern thought. It is held up as the source of myriad personal gratifications and of universally legitimate ethical claims. But its very universality entails a fundamental contradiction, that of generating rival claims to moral and social ascendancy. This is what Molière's theater has to teach us about spurious claims to authority still raging among us.

Orgon would evade this contradiction in the name of the transcendent values embodied in Tartuffe, to whom he subjects himself along with his family. He holds up Tartuffe as an icon, as a covert means of controlling the consciences of others, of ruling them from within. He has no interest in penetrating Tartuffe's mask since he himself is wearing it. He must therefore set an example to his family and pay obeisance to the god whom he has enshrined in his household, paradoxically defeating his own project of mastery by becoming slavishly devoted to his servant.

The irony of the would-be master-of-all enslaved to his protégé reflects the contradictory nature of Orgon's desire: to compel the free will of others. He cannot advertise this desire without inspiring rivals to imitate him, and the more they imitate him, the more he will imitate their imitation and persist in this desire, which is no longer his alone but one shared by those around him. In this aspect, Molière's theater thoroughly demonstrates René Girard's anthropological theory of mimetic or imitative desire, which argues that desire necessarily copies other desires in pursuit of its objects. We derive from others the image of what we claim for ourselves, and this unconscious imitation, or mediated desire, is the basis of the many rivalries that govern our behavior (see bk. 3, chs. 1 and 2 of *Things Hidden*). "Le mécanique" inhabiting Bergson's "vivant" is the other's desire. In Molière's social imagination, this interdependence results in a kind of universal theater. He envisions a world in which everyone plays a role; for each of us, the role is not one we choose on our own—that, presumably, is Tartuffe's specialty—but one in which we are unwittingly cast by others.

This vicious circularity—or, rather, comic reciprocity—is concisely dramatized in the scene following Tartuffe's attempt to seduce Orgon's wife, Elmire. Mimetic desire fuels Orgon's obstinacy in the face of his family's opposition to Tartuffe. The more they resist, the more he persists in his efforts to overcome their resistance, for their resistance functions as a model for his desire to overcome it. When Damis protests against his father's plan to marry Damis's sister to Tartuffe, Orgon all but confesses this causal connection:

Oui, traître, et dès ce soir, pour vous faire enrager.
Ah! je vous brave tous, et vous ferai connaître
Qu'il faut qu'on m'obéisse et que je suis le maître.
(3.6.1128–30)

Yes, and this very night, d'you understand?
I shall defy you all, and make it clear
That I'm the one who gives the orders here.

Everything Orgon does in this scene to show he is the boss shows that he has utterly lost control of the situation, which is ruled instead by the pattern of rivalry he has installed in his household.

This battle of mimetic desire, masking to all concerned a war of wills, is destined to focus on Orgon's son, whose violent temperament is literally, textually modeled on his father's own and serves in turn as a model for his father's rage. Damis opposes his father most violently because he resembles him most in his obdurate wrath, as is already evident in act 1 when he expresses his feelings toward Tartuffe in terms that bristle with filial rebellion: "Non, voyez-vous, ma mère, il n'est père ni rien / Qui me puisse obliger à lui vouloir du bien" (1.1.55–56) ("Ah no, Grandmother, I could never take / To such a rascal, even for my father's sake"). We thus find Damis using the very same words to denounce Tartuffe—"Et la bonté du Ciel m'y semble avoir conduit, / Pour confondre l'orgueil d'un traître qui me nuit" (3.4.1023–24) (". . . Heaven, in order to confound the pride / Of this great rascal, prompted me to hide [in the closet]")—as Orgon uses to defend him:

Mais plus on fait d'effort afin de l'en bannir,
Plus j'en veux employer à l'y mieux retenir;
Et je vais me hâter de lui donner ma fille,
Pour confondre l'orgueil de toute ma famille.
(3.6.1123–26)

Ah, but the more you seek to drive him away,
The more I'll do to keep him. Without delay,
I'll spite this household and confound its pride
By giving him my daughter as his bride.

The identical language here reveals a fundamental symmetry that most often goes unnoticed by the subjects involved: we always want to confound others' pride, though that pride itself is the model for our desire to do so. Instead of being offered an exemplar of individuated sovereignty in this scene, we are witness to a contest of duplicate ambitions. The duel of rival wills composes to Molière's comic imagination a self-perpetuating duet of imitations, a comic because unconscious mimicry. As our laughter erupts from a collapse of difference, we subtly learn the rule of comedy: one plus one equals one. "Plus ça change, plus c'est la même chose," as the French say: the more things change, the more they stay the same, which is just what Orgon says—"plus on fait . . ., Plus j'en veux. . . ."—though without a clue to his self-contradiction.

At the end of the next scene Orgon again unwittingly expresses this causal circularity of imitations. In a crescendo of self-assertion that is at the same time an abyss of self-effacement, he all but endows Tartuffe with his wife as well as his fortune, just to spite his household:

> Non, en dépit de tous, vous la fréquenterez.
> Faire enrager le monde est ma plus grande joie,
> Et je veux qu'à toute heure avec elle on vous voie.
> Ce n'est pas tout encor: pour les mieux braver tous,
> Je ne veux point avoir d'autre héritier que vous.
> Et je vais de ce pas, en fort bonne manière,
> Vous faire de mon bien donation entière.
>
> (3.7.1172–78)

> No, you shall not, whatever they may say.
> It pleases me to vex them, and for spite
> I'll have them see you with her day and night.
> What's more, I'm going to drive them to despair
> By making you my only son and heir;
> This very day, I'll give to you alone
> Clear deed and title to everything I own.

The dynamics of mimetic reaction rather than of self-assertive action, such as we find celebrated in Corneille's theater, are explicit as Orgon moves from explaining his decision as "en dépit de tous" to "pour les mieux braver tous." The semantic confusion or conflation of motivations, the negative "in spite of" becoming the positive "in order to," testifies against any notion of independent action or intent. Orgon's last words in this scene—"Et puisse l'envie en crever de dépit!" ("Then let them burst with disappointed greed!") point directly to the hidden rivalry with his family that governs his folly and that Gossman detects everywhere in Molière's comic characters' relations with one another.

These characters are not fully conscious of this rivalry. They have values and ideals behind which to disguise it, even to (especially to) themselves. This is the enduring theoretical significance of Molière's theater, as it offers us a good working definition of the unconscious: a pattern of rivalry, of identification with others' desires, that is everywhere denied in the name of individual differences or ultimate values and that is nonetheless manifest everywhere in word and deed. Our laughter is the dividend of this self-contradictory enterprise (see Girard, "Perilous Balance").

This pattern presides over the lovers' quarrel that takes place between Mariane and Valère. The scene miniaturizes the struggle for recognition that is wracking the household. The two young lovers engage in a literal duel of words, reminiscent of stychomythia in Corneille, in which each withholds the expression of desire in the expectation that the other will disclose it. "Sottise des deux parts" (2.4.775) ("You're both great fools"), notes Dorine, marking their symmetry, and she further concludes from their self-perpetuating misunderstanding: "A vous dire le vrai, les amants sont bien fous" (2.4.787) ("I tell you, lovers are completely crazy"). The lovers' madness reflects the same structure that Orgon's rivalry with his household does. In this scene, each is a prisoner of the other's desire, and as they imitate each other's demand for a declaration of love, they demand a confirmation that their very demand precludes. Madness is the metaphor for self-inflicted wounds, for self-defeat generated by the delusion, the postulate, the imposture, in Molière's terms, of an autonomous self clamoring for deference.

For Molière, as for Pascal (*Pensées*, no. 688), the self is a fiction; in rhetoric we call it a figure, whose comic potential is that there is no proper, literal, or substantial reality underlying it. Molière humors us with this difference, but if we overinvest in it, the joke is on us.

For it is by playing on the difference between literal and figurative that Tartuffe eludes the evidence of his attempted seduction of Elmire. He exploits the dualism built into the structure of language itself, according to which any term can serve as the figure or metaphor of another, any metaphor being the proper term of another metaphor. He openly declares his own baseness in a statement that is literally true—"Oui, mon frère, je suis un méchant, un coupable, / Un malheureux pécheur, . . ." (3.6.1074–75) ("Yes, Brother, I'm a wicked man, I fear: / A wretched sinner . . .")—but Orgon seizes on the declaration as a figure of humility. Orgon opts passionately for the figure because his own patronage of Tartuffe is a figure, a mask for his desire for absolute domination. Orgon's deafness to the literal truth of what he hears is propelled by his aspiration, his comic addiction, to a figural, metaphorical, hyperbolic reality, that of unquestionable sovereignty.

The same confusion of literal and figurative ultimately governs Tartuffe's behavior and our frequent misunderstanding of it as well. When Tartuffe undertakes the seduction of Elmire, he uses the language of idolatry, the adoration of the image in the place of its maker:

> Et je n'ai pu vous voir, parfaite créature,
> Sans admirer en vous l'auteur de la nature,
> Et d'une ardente amour sentir mon coeur atteint,
> Au plus beau des portraits où lui-même il s'est peint.
> (3.3.941–44)

How could I look on you, O flawless creature,
And not adore the Author of all Nature,
Feeling a love both passionate and pure
For you, his triumph of self-portraiture?

The language of amorous courtship is by definition idolatrous, being the
application of superlative or absolute terms not to the divinity, as properly
intended, but instead to one of his creatures. And Tartuffe slips into this
language, as it were, naturally. It is fruitless to ask whether Tartuffe is sincere
in these and other lines, whether "calculated scheming" is the proper intention
to apply to this lover's discourse. Alfred Simon astutely remarks that at this
point Tartuffe no longer knows who he is (134). How could he, since he is
mostly an invention of Orgon's, a fiction of Orgon's tyrannical devising? The
strict undecidability between seducer and seduced on Tartuffe's part constitutes the comedy of this scene as he promises to Elmire "une dévotion à nulle
autre pareille" (3.3.986) ("[a]n endless hymn, an infinite hosanna")—whereby
he replicates Orgon's devotion to him.

Up to a certain point, we can say that Orgon hides behind religious values to
mask his metaphysical ambition and that Tartuffe hides behind these same
values to mask his physical appetites. But this thematic opposition ultimately
misses the profound irony of the play by persisting in crediting differences that
the work insistently challenges. And credit, credo, belief, is just what the play
is all about: Orgon's belief in Tartuffe, but also Tartuffe's consequent,
contagious belief in himself as the master that Orgon has made of him, namely,
a master of disguise who can manipulate his mask at will.

Tartuffe's duplicity is undone by the delusion he entertains that he is the one
who controls it, that he is its unified source and director. This fallacy is
concisely belied by Elmire when she states a kind of universal law governing
self-deception, which pertains as much to Orgon as to Tartuffe: "Non; on est
aisément dupé par ce qu'on aime. / Et l'amour-propre engage à se tromper
soi-même" (4.3.1357–58) ("No, amorous men are gullible. Their conceit / So
blinds them that they're never hard to cheat").

In sum, Orgon's strategy of self-deception is sufficiently thorough to fool all
those around him, who honestly seem to believe that he is fooled by Tartuffe.
He even fools Tartuffe, who thinks he can get away with absolutely anything,
like seducing Orgon's wife right under his nose. As he says of Orgon to Elmire,

C'est un homme, entre nous, à mener par le nez;
De tous nos entretiens il est pour faire gloire,
Et je l'ai mis au point de voir tout sans rien croire.
(4.7.1524–26)

> . . . one can lead him by the nose.
> To find us here would fill him with delight
> And if he saw the worst, he'd doubt his sight.

This supreme self-confidence is the necessary and sufficient condition of Tartuffe's unmasking that eventually leads to his downfall. For only at this point, when Orgon's self-deception is thematically asserted by his idol and rival, when his mastery is denounced by the instrument employed to achieve it, does he come out of hiding to confront Tartuffe. Orgon's claim that he had long doubted his protégé (4.8.1547) is laughable but not entirely unbelievable; it indicts his earlier willful self-deception but is a comically persistent instance of it as well, being a refusal to renounce the sovereign self-image of himself as master.

It is the ubiquity of self-deception that explains the outside intervention of the king at the end of the play. The denouement postulates a transcendent authority endowed with the quasi-divine power to see into others' hearts (5.7.1907–08) and so to distinguish unequivocally between the true and the false; between the thing itself and its simulacrum, its sign. As undisputed sovereign, the king is in principle immune to rivalry (if not in fact immune, for in *Amphitryon* Molière stages a god's benighted rivalry with one of his subjects for the possession of the subject's wife). This necessarily offstage prince is a fiction that stabilizes differences for which there is no underlying foundation. By the very artifice of this conclusion, Molière confirms Pascal's essentially comic insight that it is better to have a divinely anointed fool sit on the throne than to have all and sundry fighting over it (*Pensées*, no. 94).

Tartuffe was virulently attacked in its own time for holding religious piety up to ridicule, though that is not really what the play is about. What can make the play immediate for students is the recognition that it concerns instead the contagious dynamics of self-deceit and self-defeat to which few of us are immune. For Molière it is not religion but truth that is a laughing matter, as truth exhibits itself in the roles we cast for ourselves and for others, in the fact that there are no essences or self-grounded individuals but only relations and relations of relations. It is not persons but patterns and personae that preside among us. This truth doubtless persuaded Molière to conclude his "Lettre sur l'imposteur" defending the play with the commonplace image of *theatrum mundi*, declaring all our participation in "la grande comédie qui se joue sur la terre entre les hommes" (*Œuvres* 1: 1180) ("the great comedy played out on earth by all mankind").

Molière's Precious Women in Context

Faith E. Beasley

In *Les précieuses ridicules* (1659) and *Les femmes savantes* (1672), Molière depicts the salon movement in seventeenth-century France, a subject that has profited from the recent critical attention given to women's roles during the age of classicism in France. In particular, literary scholars and historians have opened new interpretive avenues for these plays by bringing to the forefront women's participation in the "empire of letters." Studying these plays as representations of their social context allows students to appreciate the complexities of the literary scene in seventeenth-century France, especially the power of worldly society as exemplified by the female-dominated salons. These plays are much more than satires of "ridiculous" women, for they explore the debates surrounding the "law" in this intensely patriarchal society, the conflict between ideological and political order and disorder, as well as the laws governing literary criticism.

In what follows I outline an approach to teaching *Les précieuses ridicules* and *Les femmes savantes* that focuses on the status and role of women as authors and literary critics during the period and on the general concept of power—literary and social—central to these plays. To create a dialogue between Molière's plays and the literary and social scene, I have developed a dossier comprising a selection of key texts that detail the salons, the *précieuses* and the status of women in general. By using this collection of texts, teachers can give students a sense of the context surrounding the plays, focusing through primary sources on the works' vocabulary and argumentation. The dossier was designed for an advanced undergraduate senior seminar on the evolution of literary criticism and the changing role and function of the critic from the fifteenth through early eighteenth centuries. The underlying themes of the course are the influence and roles of women in this evolution, the concepts of literary "taste" and standards, the identity and status of the literary critic, the function of literary criticism in society, and the interpretive role of the historian (that is, the "fact" and "fiction" of histories and their ideological content). This approach—which may be adapted to a variety of levels and is useful for introductory literature courses, survey courses, and cultural studies, as well as women's studies—creates a dialogue between Molière and his period that allows students to see that *Les précieuses ridicules* and *Les femmes savantes* are not direct mirrors of his society but representations of it. Not everyone considered the *précieuses* or the *femmes savantes* to be "ridiculous" social aberrations who needed to be brought into line. Molière's portraits in fact underscore just how strong an influence women were perceived as having in the seventeenth-century literary realm, so strong that it constituted a very real source of power, provoking many to try to control it or even erase it altogether.

I begin the study of these two plays with a brief introduction to the history of salons and a literary history of women writers in the seventeenth century, focusing on the figure of Madeleine de Scudéry. Citing the work of Joan DeJean, Dorothy Backer, Carolyn Lougee, and Ian Maclean, I stress the antimarriage stance advocated by many of the participants in salon culture; the refinement of language; the role of such poets as Vincent Voiture; and two literary influences developed in Scudéry's *samedis* and in her novels, the conversation and the literary portrait. I also present the "Carte de Tendre," (a map developed by Scudéry to teach gallantry; see DeJean, *Geographies* 56), a survey of the development of the novel and memoirs, and the works of authors such as Scudéry, Lafayette, Montpensier, and Villedieu.

The first text in the dossier is Scudéry's *harangue* entitled "Sapho à Erinne," from her *Les femmes illustres* (1642). In this short text, in which Sapho urges Erinne to pick up the pen, Scudéry expresses some of her female contemporaries' desires to transgress the nonintellectual roles society has scripted for them. Not only is Scudéry inventing history, imagining a speech to fill the voids of the past, but she is also addressing her contemporary public through the authoritative voice of Sapho. The fiction is more transparently a reflection of seventeenth-century society when one knows that Scudéry herself was called the Sapho of her time. Scudéry uses the *harangue* to question the gender-specific "natures" of man and woman and to stress that they are defined by a male-dominated society. This discussion is especially enlightening when read in conjunction with Molière's plays because the "natural" sphere of women's activities as well as the "natural" paternal order are at the heart of *Les précieuses ridicules* and *Les femmes savantes*. Scudéry's text offers an opposing argument as she critiques the "ridiculous" components of the very concept of male and female nature, instead of satirizing those who violate "natural" laws.

One passage illustrates particularly well Scudéry's central concern and her method of argumentation. Throughout the text, it is apparent that Sapho seeks especially to convince Erinne that women were not placed on earth merely to serve as beautiful objects. She argues that it is natural and indeed essential for women to enter the intellectual realm traditionally viewed as reserved only for men. Sapho explains that those who would separate the feminine preserve of (physical) beauty from the masculine preserve of fine arts, literature, and science are "far from both justice and truth," for if this separation were valid, all women would be born beautiful and all men would have a propensity for learning; on the contrary, the existence of feminine ugliness and masculine stupidity puts the lie to this nostrum (424).

Here and throughout "Sapho à Erinne," Scudéry undermines a cliché derived from the natural differences between women and men, using clear and "natural" logic. The contrasting tone created by her use of direct vocabulary at the end of an elegant exposition—"laideur" ("ugliness"), "stupidité"—is both humorous and decisive and invites the reader to confirm her logical conclusion that defies the "natural" spheres of the two sexes. This argument further underscores that women can successfully participate in the world of the philosophical and aesthetic imagination.

Concomitant with Scudéry's emphasis on reason as a natural quality of women is her praise for women's judgment. Scudéry maintains that women can judge and valorizes such evaluations. Her emphasis on women's ability to judge plunges her work into the intellectual debates of the seventeenth century, when the validity of women's judgment, especially in literary matters, was heatedly contested. This subject recurs often in the texts of the dossier, as well as in Molière's plays. In each case, it is interesting to identify what qualities each author associates with judgment. Scudéry highlights imagination, *esprit* ("wit"), and *mémoire* as essential characteristics of the process of evaluation. Many authors associate these traits with women when describing the salon milieu, opposing them to the supposedly more valuable "male" sphere of reason embodied by the *doctes* ("learned"). In contrast, Scudéry praises these qualities, which she also views as female and uses them to advance the theory that women are naturally good arbiters.

From her discussion of judgment, Scudéry turns to the concept of the learned woman. To dispute the *bienséances* ("mores; sense of propriety") that prohibit women from pursuing knowledge, she argues that they are not God-given laws but societal practices established primarily by men. This argument elicits questions of why and how such laws are constructed and prevail, questions that are fundamental to Molière's plays. Scudéry underscores that *connaissance* ("knowledge") and writing are powerful weapons that men prefer to withhold from women. Her text may be seen as a call to arms to all women to take up the pen in order to combat the oppressive stereotypes that limit women's participation in society. Through her character Sapho, Scudéry appeals to her contemporaries to follow her lead and write, constructing their own image of their sex for posterity. Sapho implores Erinne, "[F]aites avouer à nos communs ennemis, qu'il nous est aussi facile de les vaincre, par la force de notre esprit, que par la Beauté de nos yeux" (440) ("[M]ake our enemies admit that it is as easy for us to conquer them by the force of our mind as by the beauty of our eyes"). Only writing will show that "notre sexe est capable de tout ce qu'il veut entreprendre" (436) ("our sex is capable of all that it would undertake"). Scudéry maintains that only through literature will the stereotypes that have guided society for centuries be eliminated.

The rest of the texts in my dossier are designed to delve deeper into the debate over the salons and women's creativity. The second text is one of Scudéry's *"conversations,"* set pieces that first appeared primarily in her novels and then were excerpted and published collectively in the 1680s. These conversations may be viewed as historical constructions of salon activities. I focus on one entitled "De la tyrannie de l'usage" because it addresses the issue of *bienséance* so central to both "Sapho à Erinne" and Molière's plays. In this text, Scudéry also makes specific reference to society's tyrannical control over "les ouvrages de l'esprit" (69) ("works of the mind"). There is a lengthy and serious discussion of word usage that provides an interesting contrast to Molière's satirization of women's obsession with words (70). This conversation illustrates that the same elements ridiculed by Molière were treated seriously by other authors.

The literary representation of the phenomenon of the *précieuses* and the salons and the agenda behind these often contradictory narratives are evident when one compares Scudéry's discussion of the issues with excerpts from two authors frequently considered to be authorities on the *précieuses*, the Abbé Michel de Pure and Antoine de Somaize. Orienting the class with Hayden White's thoughts on the role of narrativity in representing reality, I examine the writings of Pure and Somaize not as historical sources that reveal the truth about the *précieuses* but as literary constructs containing their views of what is characteristic, provocative, and transgressive about the movement. In *La prétieuse ou le mystère des ruelles*, Pure creates a *ruelle* ("salon") that re-sembles superficially the milieu of Scudéry's conversations, but to very different ends. To complement the study of Molière, I first choose an excerpt in which Pure stages a debate on how literary works are evaluated in the salon milieu and what qualities the most valid female critic should possess (3–36). In a later passage, he classifies women as types to specify the nature of a *précieuse*, distinguishing her from the rest of women (52–65). The principal occupation of Pure's *précieuses* is the judgment of literary works. In an argument between the two women over how this can best be accomplished, Agathonte "aime mieux être douce que sévère" (19) ("prefers to be gentle rather than harsh") because modesty and goodness are more fitting not only than rudeness but also than "le grand savoir" ("great knowledge") or some "fière habilité" (20) ("proud ability"). Agathonte, clearly favored by Pure, thus remains faithful to the stereotypes scripted for women. In contrast, Melanire pardons nothing and appears as a direct affront to *bienséance*, her critical stance motivated by an overwhelming desire for power. She explains that she derives extreme pleasure from elevating herself "en autorité sur l'ouvrage d'un homme d'esprit," comparing such males with prisoners in her courtroom, awaiting her life-or-death sentence. Molière's characters in *Les femmes savantes* use similar vocabulary to describe their activity as arbiters of literary value. In both works, this position of power is undermined by the author's contextualization.

One need only glance at Somaize's works to perceive his intention to mock the movement and eliminate any power it may have possessed. For his *Clef de la langue*, in the *Dictionnaire des précieuses*, I include the preface and letters A through H (xxxix–xlix), where he translates common words into "precious" language; for example, under the entry "eau" one finds "un verre d'eau: un bain intérieur" (xlvi) ("a glass of water: an internal bath"), and under "forêt," "un agrément rustique" (xlviii) ("a charming rustic place"). Molière satirizes the same language in both *Les précieuses ridicules* and *Les femmes savantes*. Instead of concentrating on the actual lexicon—most likely highly exaggerated, if not invented, by Somaize and Molière—I focus the students' attention on the fact that the salons and the *précieuses* were criticized or satirized for being arbiters of language. I ask the students to reflect on what it means to control language and on why this behavior could be considered subversive, drawing parallels to the Académie Française's dictionary project so that students gain a sense of the importance, both political and literary, of the question of language during this period.

Somaize's *Dictionnaire des précieuses* raises many of the same issues present in Pure's text. I include the preface in which Somaize outlines his intent (7–16) and a few of the entries (21–48). Many of his entries are portraits of specific people, reflecting and, at the same time, mocking a subgenre that reached its apogee in the sketches produced by Scudéry and Montpensier precisely when Somaize was composing his *Dictionnaire*. Like Pure, Somaize is especially against "ces sortes de femmes appellées précieuses" holding the pen, since those creatures who previously lurked in the "shadows" and only judged literature in secret have now, he rants, gone public and "usurped" the status of absolute judges over all writing, increasing their power until, "non contentes de juger" ("not content to judge"), they turned (Somaize uses the transgressive verb *se mêler*) from passive evaluation to active generation of "les productions de l'esprit" (22). Like Pure, Somaize tries to conquer this "empire" and draw these women back into "acceptable" norms.

All four texts included in the dossier reflect the state of literary affairs that surrounded Molière's theatrical productions. His preoccupation with the same questions that inspired these texts reveals that *Les précieuses ridicules* and *Les femmes savantes* are reactions to and commentaries on the gendered component of literary politics. When presenting the plays, I seek not to determine Molière's personal polemical stance, feminist or antifeminist but rather to detail his dialogue with the issues. In the dossier I also include two twentieth-century analyses of this literary scene by Domna Stanton ("Fiction") and Alain

Viala that discuss the importance of the salons for the reception of a literary work and trace the lines of the debates in the seventeenth century.

After we analyze the literary and social context, I have the students discuss *Les précieuses ridicules* and *Les femmes savantes* separately, weaving in the threads of the previous discussions, and then compare similar scenes in the plays. Molière's preface to the 1660 edition of *Les précieuses ridicules* is especially interesting in the light of Pure's text, since both authors reflect on the potential danger of the written word. Molière devotes most of his preface to an explanation of why he did not want the play to appear in print, indicating apprehension that readers will not have the same favorable reaction the spectators did. He seems to agree with Pure's Melanire, who warns that a written text can be reread and reinterpreted. Molière attempts to arrest this expansion of interpretation, stating that "le succès . . . dans la représentation était assez beau pour en demeurer-là" (*Œuvres* 1: 263) ("the production's success was such that things should be left at that"), perhaps because he fears that a group of readers, the *précieuses*, or worldly society in general will be offended if left to interpret the play without the "ton des voix" ("tone of voice, inflections") and other features of theatrical representation. The second part of the preface controls the interpretation of this specific group by establishing a now-canonical distinction between the "vraies précieuses" and the "fausses précieuses." Molière specifies that "les véritables précieuses auraient tort de se piquer lorsqu'on joue les ridicules, qui les imitent mal" (*Œuvres* 1: 264) ("the true *précieuses* would be wrong to take offense when the ridiculous creatures who imitate them badly are made fools of"). Molière's concern over the *précieuses*' reaction reveals their influence in the literary world. When viewed in the light of their historical context, Molière's fears would seem to be well founded, for while the play exaggerates the *précieuse*-salon milieu for comedic effect, it nevertheless may be interpreted as an attack on the social phenom-enon of *préciosité* and, more generally, on the very real power the salons and women exerted in the literary realm.

During the analysis of *Les précieuses ridicules*, I focus the class discussion on the following questions: Leaving the notion of "true" and "false" *précieuse* aside, how does Molière represent this social movement? What characteristics does he underscore? What light does the very existence of this play shed on the status of women, women writers, and women critics in seventeenth-century France? How is power depicted in these plays?

The play opens with a discussion of marriage, and this issue is paramount from beginning to end. Drawing on the insights of Maclean, DeJean, Lougee, and Backer, I ask students why marriage was such a prominent issue during this period, emphasizing that Magdelon's and Cathos's perception of marriage is derived from the novels they devour, particularly the heroic novels of Scudéry. Given that the heroic novel was associated with women writers, Molière's dis-cussion can be viewed as a critique of women's influence in the literary realm.

Women's power as writers and, more specifically, as critics is Molière's primary preoccupation in *Les précieuses ridicules*, where the erstwhile *précieuses*, like those of Pure and Somaize, wish to control language and literary norms. His final word in the play is a condemnation of the female literary movement, whose power is suppressed as Magdelon and Cathos are completely fooled. The absolutist voice of the author, the father figure, brings order back to a chaotic state by pronouncing the condemnation of this *monde à l'envers* ("topsy-turvy world") in an aside addressed to the audience: "Et vous, qui êtes cause de leur folie, sottes billevesées, pernicieux amusements des esprits oisifs, romans, vers, chansons, sonnets et sonnettes, puissiez-vous être à tous les diables!" (sc. 17) ("And you who are the cause of their folly, your hack-brained absurdities, pernicious pastimes of idle minds, novels, verses, songs, sonnets, and moonets, may the devil take you all!"; trans. Frame). It is interesting to reflect on the relation between this "vous" and the one in Scudéry's *harangue*. *Les femmes savantes* ends with a similar return to order, voiced once again by the father figure. Chrysale demands, "Allons, Monsieur, suivez l'ordre que j'ai prescrit, / Et faites le contrat ainsi que je l'ai dit" (5.4. 1777–78) ("Come, come, Sir, it is time your task was through; / Draw up the contract just as I told you to"). Women are once again relegated to silence as the social contract is reestablished.

In many respects, *Les femmes savantes* is a more refined and sophisticated version of *Les précieuses ridicules*. In studying the two plays together as commentaries on women's participation in literary affairs, I bring together parallel scenes so the students can appreciate their construction as texts, in addition to understanding their meaning within the historical context. In both comedies, Molière is preoccupied with satirizing certain key traits of women drawn to intellectual, literary pursuits: the relation between marriage (representing the social order in general) and these women, their desire to control language, and the critique of literary works and establishment of critical standards. There is no question of "true" and "false" intellectual women in *Les femmes savantes*, in which the author's commentary is more artful but less veiled than in *Les précieuses ridicules*. I have students first discuss the overall structure, whose underlying theme is the quest for a stability—seen as inherent in marriage—amid the chaotic goings-on of a household seemingly overrun by misguided female intellectuals. Of particular interest is act 1, scene 1, during which Molière opposes the traditional Henriette, who wants nothing more than to marry Clitandre, with Armande, who is following her mother's lead in adopting a life of the intellect. Dissecting this scene allows the class to examine how the two life choices are portrayed and to juxtapose them with Scudéry's text and the general concept of *bienséance*. The power of the female intellectual is shown to be in conflict with stable society. The play is a search for a return to order, a reestablishing of power that makes women intellectuals social outcasts with utopian feminist visions. I find it useful to have the students examine the composition of the play to see how Molière guides his audience toward a specific response. Is the public indeed free to accept or reject the general condemnation of this female intellectual world?

With this question in mind, a reading of act 2, scene 6 illuminates Molière's position in the debate over the control of language previously seen in scene 6 of *Les précieuses ridicules,* for in both scenes servants are reprimanded for not conforming to the absurd linguistic demands of their mistresses. I also pair act 3, scene 2 of *Les femmes savantes,* in which women critique Trissotin's literary "enfant tout nouveau-né" (3.1.720) ("infant"), with its counterpart, scene 9 of *Les précieuses ridicules;* I have the students read both passages aloud because the oral juxtaposition makes the similarities and differences especially apparent and gives the students a much deeper appreciation of Molière's art than does passive reading. One of the major differences between these two depictions is the role of the poet. In *Les précieuses ridicules,* the poet figure prompts the women to react in certain ways, thus dominating the scene, whereas in *Les femmes savantes* the women's judgment requires no such prompting. Their taste is much more established and potentially subversive. Philaminte highlights this dangerous taste by speaking at length of her desire to found an academy, one that would clearly be in opposition to the Académie Française. This scene leads to a discussion of the role of the academy, the development of the dictionary, the desire to set critical standards, and the relation among the academy, literature, and royal power. The salon women as depicted by Molière present a threat to this relationship.

When juxtaposed with other texts that depict the salon movement and the *précieuses,* Molière's *Les femmes savantes* and *Les précieuses ridicules* may be interpreted as one writer's historical representation of questions fundamental to his society. It is important to underscore that Molière's vision has in a sense become history. His depiction of the *précieuses* and the salon milieu may be exaggerated, but many scholars have traditionally accepted it as accurate and indeed have included the same characteristics in their own descriptions. The study of these plays in conjunction with other texts allows one to question why Molière's portrait became critical coin, what the ideological content of literature and history is, and what role literature plays in society. Why indeed has posterity adopted Molière's depiction of this literary and social power struggle? The "champ littéraire" ("literary field") of seventeenth-century France is becoming more and more cultivated as scholars delve into its complex set of forces, political and ideological, and include less well-known texts in their analyses. Reading Molière's plays as products of and reactions to this literary field allows students to appreciate the atmosphere of debate and interrogation of France's classical age and in fact draw many parallels with their own time as well.

"Yes, but What Does It Mean?":
Dom Juan and Rhetorical Perspective

Bruce Edmunds

The title of this volume is a paradox; if teaching, as it is commonly conceived among university students, reduces to the conveying of information, one cannot "teach" literature. We have long known that no work of literature can be exhausted by a simple cataloging of "themes" or "morals," that the metaphor of transmission cannot begin to account for what happens in the classroom. Yet students expect to be "taught" literature. After struggling for a time, patiently, they will demand the bottom line, the answer to the question "What does it mean?"

The problem is that until the late twentieth century critics largely accepted the canonical virtues of classical literature—clarity, simplicity, harmony—that derive from and support the idea that language is neutral, a mere envelope to be discarded once the contents have been delivered. How could they then fail to accede to the insistent demand that the teacher transmit, and without delay, the "real meaning," the "true interpretation" of a given classical text? Cherished critical dicta fostering the illusion of mastery have survived across the centuries; they support a myth proper to classicism, one that is gratifying, self-serving, and tenacious: the idea that classical works represent an unsurpassable literary achievement in their marriage of form and content. The teacher's task is to help students grasp the (aesthetic) wisdom great works contain. Teaching divests itself of any historical dimension as it devolves into the eternal repetition of eternal truths, as teachers become anonymous pitchers and students become anonymous vessels.

Language "constates," period. I borrow J. L. Austin's term (*How to Do Things* 1) only to suggest that his work provides ammunition to attack this Cartesian notion of language. Austin's conceptual complement of the constative, the performative (4), underpins a rhetorical approach exceeding the scope of his own work, an approach that would encourage students to ask questions richer and more pertinent to current literary concerns than those arising from the classical conception of language, which is for us today a received, uncritical conception.

Sketching the history of rhetoric and filling in its current renewal in more detail would be a good way to establish the necessary context for this approach. A brief discussion of the role of rhetoric in education and textual production from the Middle Ages to the Renaissance would prepare students to understand how its decline was linked to "the development, in various domains, of a mode of discourse conceived as neutral, nonpositional and transparent" (Bender and Wellbery 7–8). Some description of Descartes's contribution to this development and of its critical and literary repercussions would be indispensable. I suggest distributing the table of contents and a few key passages from Antoine Arnauld and Pierre Nicole's *La logique ou l'art de penser.* The meticulous division of the material suffices to suggest an attempt to codify exhaustively and thereby control figurative language, as does the specific title of part 1, chapter 15: "Des idées que l'esprit ajoute à celles qui sont précisément signifiées par les mots" ("Ideas the mind adds to those precisely signified by words"). For instructors using these materials, Sara Melzer's book *Discourses of the Fall* should prove helpful in establishing the linguistic context of classical writings. An equally important, though delicate, task would be to show how faithful "commonsense" views on language are to the antirhetorical spirit. That we may describe them as common sense attests to the success of Cartesian modes of thought.

Indeed, many students reside in a Cartesian world, so the challenge facing the teacher who would present Molière within the perspective of "rhetoricality" (Bender and Wellbery 25–39) is to dislodge them. Students will be familiar with some of the thinkers who have played important roles in the dismantling of the classical conception of language, and one would do well to refer to them. Few do not know about Nietzsche, even if their familiarity is limited to the ubiquitous graffito " 'God is dead'—Nietzsche; 'Nietzsche is dead'—God." There is no need to explore here the connection of the death of God, the transcendental signified, to Nietzsche's philological program; one could simply point out that for Nietzsche rhetoric is never reducible to simple "ornament" but is in fact the essence of language, much as Austin concludes, despite himself (perhaps!), that language is never reducible to "constation." When students are confident that the rhetorical approach, which rests on a principle that will be counterintuitive to many, draws from the work of seminal thinkers whose names they recognize, I believe they will be willing to give it a fair hearing.

Returning, then, to the development of the classical conception of language, one would point out that even as some thinkers were busily erecting the notion of transparency, others were tearing it down. In other words, the classical *epistémé* does not, Foucault notwithstanding, represent the "horizon" of thought, the limit within which all thought in this period must occur. Pascal "deconstructs" Port-Royal linguistic theory (Melzer 30–40). Mme de Lafayette "problematizes" representation (Lyons 170–78). Molière above all, particularly in *Dom Juan*, opposes the stance Bender and Wellbery call "antirhetorical" (7).

To help students recognize Molière's position, one might first lay out some of the problems associated with representation in *Dom Juan*, since the principle of the neutrality of language has as a key corollary the invisibility of the process of representation. One would do well to point out that this, too, is the legacy of Descartes's dream: to achieve in the reading of the world and in the communication of that reading the absolute clarity, neutrality, and indubitability characteristic of geometry. When perception and principle are thought to differ—take, for example, the distorting visual effect of water—

some additional principle may always be found to explain and measure the distortion. In this way Descartes protects the claim that specific cases "represent" general truths. The world still speaks to Descartes the language of geometry, and this is the language he uses to transmit his knowledge, to represent his thought.

Just as water in a glass distorts the image of a spoon, court society generates a discrepancy between misleading appearance and reality. Descartes would argue that some principle or principles exist to account for the discrepancy, allowing one to find the path leading reliably from the appearances to the "true state of things." The spoon is not "really" bent, nor is human seeming "really" true. The science of optics allows one to reckon with the (apparent) bend in the spoon, but how is one to understand an appearance of virtue given the apriori "reality" of vice and corruption? There are many ways, of course, including Pascal's "double nature" and La Rochefoucauld's "self-love." At this point the teacher should encourage the student to ask if there is a corresponding principle of rectification in Molière.

Court society in classical France is theatrical through and through; in it a gap between private and public, between psychological reality and appearance, is the very foundation of social order. No courtier would deny the importance of what Pascal calls the "pensée de derrière" ("deeper motive") (*Pensées*, nos. 1, 90, 91) or be ignorant of the need to project to others a certain socially defined image that selectively reveals the inner "truth." If the court of Louis XIV loved the spectacle and the costume ball so ardently, perhaps it is because they enact in extreme form the pervasive distinction between "être" ("to be") and "paraître" ("to appear"), a distinction necessarily and uncomfortably murky in the affairs of daily existence. Believing we can recognize a mask as a mask reassures us.

The most salient theme of *Dom Juan*, hypocrisy, might well have an equally reassuring effect. In hypocrisy, it is true, the disjunction of appearance and reality is unmarked as such, at least theoretically. Dom Juan cloaks himself with the demeanor of fidelity to seduce women, with that of piety to seduce his father. If the social order rests on the *être-paraître* distinction, one is nonetheless terrified to think of being duped by it. But hope is not lost; Molière obliges the reader by creating a bad hypocrite. Piety and hypocrisy are, then, distinct, each connecting to a sign or signs in a reliable way, and the privileged connection between appearance and reality is restored. We need not fear Dom Juan.

Such a characterization of hypocrisy in *Dom Juan* is readily grasped and reassuring but not altogether satisfying, for one senses that the problem of representation cannot be made to disappear so easily. Dom Juan is no more convincing a hypocrite than Tartuffe. The masks that both wear are full of holes. In giving us a means to distinguish between the hypocrite and the truly pious individual, however, Molière hands us a double-edged sword: if the other characters do not see the obvious holes in the mask, if they are duped, we cannot help wondering about them. Their complicity reveals the importance of the receiver of the message. If it is true that the objects of Dom Juan's seduction, his father included, wish to be deceived, then for Molière language implicates not intellect so much as desire.

This realization troubles students in a salutary way. They come to understand that if the *être-paraître* distinction leaves intact the metaphor that guides their thinking about language, that of transmission, Molière's insistence on the importance of reception and the receiver destabilizes the distinction itself. Desire blinds Dom Juan's victims, as it surely must "blind" us, readers-victims of Molière. We can no more be empty, featureless vessels into which Molière would pour moral truth than Dom Juan's father can be the neutral recipient of his scrambled message of conversion. Dom Louis himself says as much: "Ah! mon fils, que la tendresse d'un père est aisément rappelée, et que les offenses d'un fils s'évanouissent vite au moindre mot de repentir" (5.1) ("O! my son, how easily a father's tenderness is revived, and how quickly a son's offenses vanish at the least sign of repentance"). The rest of Dom Louis's speech is filled with superlatives that juxtapose the extent of Dom Juan's past crimes ("tous les déplaisirs que vous m'avez donnés" ["all the unhappiness you have caused me"]) with both the abruptness and the totality of his own transformation ("tout est effacé" ["all is forgotten"]). The father's joy provokes a state bordering on madness: "[J]e ne me sens pas" ("I am beside myself"). Dom Louis's desire prods him to weigh more heavily a handful of words ("moindre mot de repentir . . . les paroles que vous venez de me faire entendre" ["least word of repentance . . . the words you have just communicated to me"]) than a lifetime of misdeeds. When we consider the role desire plays in Dom Louis's assessment of his son's "conversion," what appears to be a simple case of hypocrisy is far more troubling. In showing how the receiver's history, network of relations, and, above all, desire impinge on the process of representation, Molière subverts the principle of the neutrality of language, a key feature of the antirhetorical stance, one that became so influential in the seventeenth century that it persists even today.

In Molière's plays the source of the utterance is no more neutral than the receiver, which suggests a purpose other than the mere communication of truth. Molière's characters generate power by allowing themselves to be "ventriloquated," or inhabited, by an authoritarian discourse (Riggs 9–14); to the extent that Dom Juan, Tartuffe, and Orgon convincingly cast themselves as oracles—connect themselves to a divine, incontestable source—they cannot be stopped by human agency. Their use of language is a product of their de-stabilizing desire to avoid exchange, reciprocity, relation, and all the attendant risks, chief among them error and humiliation. To consign Orgon to the lowest circle of hell, one need only laugh at him. It may seem strange to group Dom Juan with Tartuffe and Orgon, but ultimately he "is as monologic and as opposed to real surprise as any of the other types" (Riggs 70).

If these authoritarian figures succeed at all, it is because their victims accept their neutrality, their (projected) status as implements of a higher and unquestionable source, God. This is why the show of piety must be unconvincing. The abruptness of the change in Dom Juan's father strikes us as highly implausible. We are led to question not only the neutrality of the receiver, as we have seen, but also the veracity and good faith of the oracle: is Dom Juan really inhabited by divine language? By focusing on the desire of the oracle no less than on that of the receiver of the message, Molière undermines the concept of transmission, which posits a provisional inhabiting of a neutral, nonpositional source.

Shoshana Felman (*Scandale*) and Barbara Woshinsky put it somewhat differently, arguing that Dom Juan succeeds because he and only he understands that no ontological principle underpins the connection between words and things. The issue of representation provides the terms of the debate. Pierrot states, "Je te dis toujou la mesme chose, parce que c'est toujou la mesme chose; et si ce n'étoit pas toujou la mesme chose, je ne dirois pas toujou la mesme chose" (2.1) ("I always say to you the same thing, because it always is the same thing; and if it weren't always the same thing, I wouldn't always say the same thing"). As Woshinsky points out, this view of representation, in which "discourse corresponds to a pre-established objective referent," leaves "no room for equivocation or rhetoric" (401, 402). The philosophical antithesis speaks itself through Sganarelle, addressing his master: "Assurément que vous avez raison, si vous le voulez; on ne peut pas aller là contre. Mais si vous ne vouliez pas, ce serait peut-être une autre affaire" (1.2) ("Certainly, if that's what you want, you are right; one can't contest it. But if you did not wish it so, that would perhaps be a different matter"). On the one hand, this statement may be nothing more than an instance of hypocrisy: Sganarelle believes Dom Juan to be wrong, but his fear of a beating prevents him from saying so. If, on the other hand, it is taken as a statement of principle concerning language, one arrives at a rhetorical conception in which "language has no pre-ordained relation to the world; rather its relation is to the speaker" (Woshinsky 402). Dom Juan, the " 'new' linguistic man," understands this and so is able to dupe the other characters (408).

It is a dangerous power to exercise. Spectacle, we recall, comforts us because it marks the mask as a mask. Likewise, it quells our discomfort by encouraging us to believe that a mask donned to convey a certain appearance can be doffed at will. Again, Molière pricks our bubble. Sganarelle, like Dom Juan, is inhabited, but in a way that suggests another point and forces us to nuance the image of Dom Juan as "new linguistic man." When, at Dom Juan's command, Sganarelle disguises himself as a doctor, he is carried away by the language, costume, and, above all, by the authority of medicine: "[C]et habit me donne de l'esprit, et je me sens en humeur de disputer contre vous" (3.1) ("[T]his frock lends me intelligence and puts me in the mood to argue with you"). Also, the distinction he draws between "disputes" and "remonstrances" reveals an uncharacteristic pedantry (Woshinsky 404). The discussion ends as Sganarelle falls to the ground while attempting to urge a variation on the ontological proof of the existence of God. This bit of physical buffoonery allies Sganarelle with Pascal's freethinker, who would like to believe but cannot; Sganarelle represents an interesting twist on Pascal's discourse on "the machine." There Pascal claims that producing signs of piety may ultimately produce the state associated with them, reversing the more typical pattern in which the signs issue from, or are produced by, that state of inner grace. Like Pascal, Molière shows that the Cartesian notion of representation, which posits a substantial self as the origin of the signs, is not adequate to account for the human relation to them, since it is just as likely that the signs are the origin of the self. This observation highlights the danger of attempting to maintain a distinction between *être* and *paraître* for the purpose of manipulation. Sometimes the mask wears the man.

Dom Juan's conflation of erotic and pious language in his dealings with Elvire has the same effect. The admixture of discourses controls Dom Juan as much as he controls it. One thing leads to another as explanation and justification shade into seduction in such a way that he is no longer in control. Whatever the benefits of this ersatz *enthousiasme,* it poses a danger distinct from that of expulsion from the community: the attempt to enthrone the self through ventriloquation paradoxically entails the dispersal of that self. Dom Juan is carried away, then, not so much by his libido as by the languages that compete to speak themselves through him: pious, erotic, aristocratic, and even geometrical. From this point of view, his Cartesian credo has no special privilege, and they err who consider it to represent Molière's personal philosophy. As with Sganarelle, so with Dom Juan: sometimes the mask wears the man.

Perhaps we should reexamine that last statement. Language, it turns out, cannot even name. For what exactly is Dom Juan? "[U]n enragé, un chien, un Diable, un Turc, un Hérétique . . . qui passe cette vie en véritable bête brute, en pourceau d'Epicure, en vrai Sardanapale" (1.1) ("a madman, a dog, a devil, a Turk, a heretic . . . who lives his life as a truly brutish animal, an Epicurean hog, a real Sardanapalus"). The long list of epithets emphasizes the impossibility of assigning to Dom Juan a single name that would capture his essence. Things and words do not exist in one-to-one correspondence. In addition, Molière underlines the problematic nature of reference by introducing the notion of heterogeneity through the concluding epithet of Sganarelle's description: Dom Juan is a "grand Seigneur méchant homme" (1.1) ("a great Lord of a mean man"). He flies to the rescue of Dom Carlos (3.3) because he is a gentleman, but, as Dom Louis's remonstrance indicates, this gesture does not suffice: "Apprenez enfin qu'un gentilhomme qui vit mal est un monstre dans la nature" (4.4) ("Know that a gentleman who lives badly is a freak of nature"). In using the term *monstre,* Molière draws from the range of possible meanings two key attributes: Dom Juan is a warning (in Latin, *monere,* "to admonish"), and Dom Juan is a mixed being, part man, part animal, as Sganarelle's earlier description reminds us. The problem of defining *gentilhomme* is apparent in many texts of this period for the historical reasons Jean-Marie Apostolidès explores in *Le prince sacrifié.* One reason is connected to the status of the promise in feudal society, and the promise, in addition to being Dom Juan's tool, is the focal point of the debate concerning the performative-constative distinction. If Molière wanted to highlight problems associated with the referential function of language, he could hardly have chosen a better tale. For the story of Dom Juan focuses on the loose threads of the classicist identity as it is rapidly coming unwoven: class affiliation, the sacred character of the promise, the attempt to protect the transparency of language.

What, then, does *this* mean? In the context of the "new rhetoric," students cannot uncritically accept the classical conception of language associated with Descartes and the Port-Royal grammarians. In exploring the nature of representation and reference, in connecting them to context and desire, Molière points the way to a sustained critical enterprise that may greatly enrich students' experience of literature by encouraging them to consider not just what the text means but also how it works to produce a range of effects. To the extent that they participate in this exploration, students will be contributing to the current renewal of classicist studies—and to our liberation from the constraints imposed by the myth of classicism.

Pedagogy, Power, and Pluralism in Molière

Larry Riggs

Teaching Molière can and should be a challenging, dramatic experience because Molière has much to say about teaching. First of all, there is Molière's particularly rich version of the idea that comic theater entertains *and instructs* its audience. The preface to *Tartuffe* is eloquent about comedy's role in maintaining the cultural and political health of society as well as the behavioral health of individuals. Molière is keenly aware that a culture is a network of influences and that, therefore, pedagogy in all its guises is always a vital issue.

In the plays themselves, the *ridicules* (ridiculous types) are often, in effect, Molière's rivals as teachers. The word *leçons* is frequently on their lips. In *Les femmes savantes*, *L'école des femmes*, and *Tartuffe*, teaching is treated explicitly. In many of the other plays, it is important by implication. Dom Juan, as his servant Sganarelle says, speaks "tout comme un livre" (1.2) ("just like a book"); his discourse always defines him as the proprietor of superior knowledge. We must admit that in *Le bourgeois gentilhomme* Monsieur Jourdain's motives for seeking "knowledge" are closely related to what we advertise as the reasons for getting a good education. Modernity defines education as a means to upward social mobility. Desire for higher status is linked to knowledge and didacticism in all the major plays.

The *ridicules'* power-mad, univocalist pedagogy is undermined by Molière's dramatic, pluralist influence. Their regarding others as objects for a pedagogical enterprise is a vital part of what makes them ridiculous. Nearly all the plays have interesting implications for teaching. In this piece, I focus primarily on *L'école des femmes*, *Tartuffe*, and *Les femmes savantes*.

The opportunities and drama inherent in teaching Molière go well beyond the plays' themes. If we take those themes, and Molière's conception of comedy, seriously enough, our own teaching becomes an object of thematic awareness: the plays' relation to us becomes a pedagogical concern. The playwright's treatment of his characters' pedagogical absolutism is, I believe, part of his effort to influence the development of French culture, in the largest sense, at a key point in its evolution. Molière sees and challenges the rapidly gathering forces of what we call modernity. He stands at a kind of cultural crossroads, and his perceptions are valuable for us because we are, to a large degree, the inheritors of the culture and the pedagogy he criticizes. The values he opposes to the ones represented by his *ridicules* are useful to us in our attempts to escape some of the constraints of our own conception of knowledge and teaching.

We belong to a culture that, since the invention of mechanically reproduced print, has been counting on literacy and text-based knowledge to obliterate difference and establish comprehensive mastery. In his plays, Molière dramatizes the relations among textual authority, the desire for mastery, and the psychological and social sclerosis that has always been serious comedy's principal target. Our culture identifies knowledge with coherence, prediction, and control. What is outside the world defined by those values is ignored, vilified, or destroyed. Molière teaches us to treasure surprise, to value the leaks, or gaps, in our control. He also teaches us to ask, "Whose mastery?" and "In whose interest is this mastery achieved and exercised?" Molière's kind of pluralism is a useful value in a society groping for a more inclusive, tolerant epistemology and pedagogy.

One of comedy's traditional functions is to undermine rigid categories. It has always done what postmodernism tries to do: to prevent closures, to leave gaps in meaning that force the reader or spectator's involvement, to study the motives that drive representation, to make language itself a focus of lucid attention. As long ago as Aristophanes's time, comedy has often ridiculed characters who brandished written documents to silence opposition. Suspicion of "textualism" was all the more appropriate in Molière's time, when the power of writing was being multiplied by printing. Marginalizing and silencing unorthodox voices, including Molière's own, was very much on the agenda of some powerful seventeenth-century figures. Centralizing and standardizing language and culture at the expense of pluralism later became goals of the revolutionary government and of modern education, as well as of the monarchy. For us, in particular, it is important to notice that pedagogy is often an issue for Molière.

Texts tend to be antidialogic; Molière's comedy is relentlessly dialogic, or pluralist. Perhaps, in our experiments with things like "cooperative learning," we acknowledge a need for a more pluralist pedagogy. We cannot teach Molière in an authoritative, univocal way without becoming somewhat ridiculous. We cannot study his plays honestly without seeing our foibles ridiculed in them.

The relation between comedy and the comic type is similar to the one Freud posited between the unconscious and the ego: like the unconscious, comedy undermines pretensions to unity and mastery. There is a "negative" knowledge, that of the unconscious or the comic, whose complexity mocks the claims of comprehensiveness made for positivist knowledge. As Molière's plays make clear, the credibility of such claims depends on an epistemology and a pedagogy of enclosure, on a paranoiac obsession with excluding what cannot be controlled. Comedy reminds us that a teacher is a voice, not a text, and thus that a classroom is a dramatic social situation, not a static image of objective knowledge. The fundamental problem of modern pedagogy is the difficulty of reconciling plurivocality with text-based knowledge and the myth of objectivity. Like the absolutist state, the *ridicules* try to impose fear as if fear could do the work of respect and loyalty, advertising coercion as service and stupefaction as education. Like the absolutist state, and like the modern culture of definitive knowledge, they are ruled by fear. Fear of discursive pluralism is a typical motive for efforts to achieve excessive control. Molière relentlessly negates his types' efforts to make themselves into central subjects, custodians of cultural legitimacy and political power.

In his superb study of Molière, Max Vernet agrees with my contention that the comedian is a dissenter from the orthodoxy of modernity that was being consolidated in the seventeenth century. I just used the term *pedagogical absolutism* to evoke the *ridicules'* ambition, and I think it is important to recognize the pedagogical concomitants of political absolutism: such a program was social and cultural engineering in the fullest sense, and it subjected language itself to the prescriptions of state-sponsored institutions. Absolutism was instrumental in the advent of modernity: after all, it theorizes France as an abstraction, as an administrative space wherein the standardization of language, culture, and law is to make the inhabitants into objects of the one sovereign subject, whose discourse they must learn in order to speak meaningfully.

Vernet argues that *L'école des femmes* is the archetypal Moliéresque play, that Molière's reaction to the emerging modern culture is first comprehensively sketched in that play. I agree, and I think it appropriate to begin this detailed look at pedagogy in the plays with an examination of *L'école des femmes*.

In this play, Arnolphe certainly exemplifies the pedagogy of enclosure that serves his paranoid epistemology: for him, the purpose of knowledge and teaching is to control another person so as to make surprise, which he identifies with a wife's unfaithfulness, impossible. His "regime" is a would-be domestic absolutism whereby others must be creatures of his control. His conception of the proper education for his ward, Agnès, is a combination of imprisonment and infantilization. Arnolphe embodies what Shoshana Felman calls the illusion of the self-possessed proprietor of knowledge (*Jacques Lacan* 84).

Arnolphe's original plan was for Agnès to be kept from learning anything at all. The infantilizing intention of his project is made clear when he says that she inspired his love "dès quatre ans" (1.1.130) ("when she was four"). When enclosure in his house and in "une ignorance extrême" (1.1.100) ("an extreme ignorance"; my trans.) fails to prevent contact with erotic stimulation, Arnolphe resorts to moralistic precepts and texts. At this point, the critique of textual authoritarianism that will be a central theme in Molière's works really begins. Agnès's prison-cloister becomes a classroom, and Arnolphe tries to make her into a speaking puppet of his mastery as that mastery is defined in *Les maximes du mariage*.

Arnolphe's intention is clear in his injunction to Agnès, as he tells her to read the *Maximes*: "[I]mprimez-le-vous bien" (3.2.678) ("And listen to my every word with care"). He wants to form her subjectivity to his specifications by colonizing her with texts embodying his absolutist pedagogy. If Arnolphe has his way, Agnès's personality will be a library of canonical texts and precepts. She will correspond to his abstract idea of the good wife, having no spontaneous experience of her own. She will be a living monument to the efficacy of Arnolphe's pedagogy.

Like the other megalomaniacal pedagogues in Molière's plays, Arnolphe finds himself in a world that is far too complicated to be controlled by his reductionist, paranoid "knowledge." The "school" of comedy, which is synonymous with Moliéresque *nature*, easily breaches Arnolphe's architectural and textual walls. His clearly Cartesian ambition—he speaks of his approach to education as his *méthode* and says of Agnès that "[C]omme un morceau de cire entre mes mains elle est" (3.3.810) ("She's like a lump of wax, and I can mold her")—is mocked by chance, irony, and surprise. Arnolphe's idea of his relationship with Agnès reflects Descartes's claim that his own method will make man the master and proprietor of nature. Arnolphe views education as the inculcation of an authoritarian model for subjectivity.

This play's treatment of pedagogy makes another point that remains vital in the later plays I consider here: because the teacher is, despite pretensions to the contrary, a voice rather than a text, pedagogy is linked to desire or motive. Arnolphe's knowledge is a function of his desire for control and security. The school of Moliéresque comedy teaches that the order of the social world is always linguistic and that language always expresses desires. Molière dramatizes tension between speech, or drama, and text. He understands the temptation to use words as privileged signifiers to establish power for the self over the other and to disguise the desire for power as devotion to principles. Arnolphe's expectation that moralistic texts will accomplish his goal while hiding the fact that it is *his* prepares the way for Tartuffe's hypocritical discourse of *dévotion* (devoutness). Molière reminds us that teaching is performative; it is an effort to influence, not a transparent disclosure of truth or a direct transfer of "objective" knowledge.

Arnolphe's system of architectural and textual walls is intended to create and preserve his power over a woman. He sees education as normalization and "feminization," as a process for creating—imprinting—her subjectivity. He sees others with whom Agnès might come into contact as rival teachers. In berating her for her "infidelity," he says "Il faut qu'on vous ait mise à quelque bonne école" (5.4.1497) ("Someone must have put you in a good school"; my trans.). Here, Arnolphe inadvertently admits that he really understands the relation between desire and moralism. Arnolphe speaks like a moralizing book because he knows univocal control is threatened by rival discourses.

Tartuffe begins with the issue of normative pedagogy in the foreground. In the first scene, Mme Pernelle is preaching to her family. She reproaches them for ignoring her teachings: "Dans toutes mes leçons j'y suis contrariée" (1.1.10) ("I offer good advice, but you won't hear it"). In this play, and in the long controversy surrounding it, the largest political and cultural implications of pedagogy are exposed. The would-be domestic absolutism of Orgon and his mother, Mme Pernelle, is justified and buttressed by Tartuffe's moralism. In his preface to the play, and in his appeals to the king to lift the ban on its production, Molière speaks of the relation between moralistic didacticism and power in the real France of his time. He thus tightly links the play's themes to the world outside the play.

In the preface, Molière argues that it is comic theater's historic task to attack the pretentious discourses that depend on what we might now call a fetishism of words. He evokes this worship of words by saying that his enemies reproach him "d'avoir mis des termes de piété dans la bouche de mon Imposteur" (*Œuvres* 1: 885) ("with putting pious words in the mouth of my hypocrite"), as if the words themselves were the inviolable repository of devoutness. In the first written appeal to the king, Molière says that Louis XIV himself has been the victim of this phenomenon: according to the comedian, the king's own piety has been exploited by real hypocrites to perpetuate the ban. Molière prepares us to appreciate the play's treatment of the way desire motivates and shows through language by saying, in the preface, that his enemies "ont couvert leurs intérêts de la cause de Dieu" ("have hidden their interests behind God's cause").

Tartuffe is a fascinating study not only of power and pedagogy but also of pleasure. Tartuffe himself is a crude figure whose physical appetites are obvious. He is fat and sleek. He eats and drinks greedily. He uses the language of devoutness to pursue sexual ends. The play dissects the power-pleasure nexus on a more profound and more subversive level, however. Speech, both in itself and as a means of reducing others to silence, is a source of pleasure for the absolutist pedagogues. Beginning with Mme Pernelle in the first scene, they constantly interrupt and pontificate. First Orgon and then Tartuffe himself are brought low by their excessive desire to express their power in language. Speech and texts are means of penetrating and consuming others. Competition for the privilege of manipulating signs is an extension of more physical conflicts.

The point here is that if speech itself is both an expression and an extension of pleasure, then the ultimate hypocrisy is to preach asceticism to the silenced other. *Tartuffe* adds to the implications of *L'école des femmes* the perception that, in addition to being an instrument of desire, discursive dominance is itself a source of pleasure. Here, Molière's long battle against the univocal forces in seventeenth-century France is at its most intense. The lust being unmasked is not merely that of a seedy, hypocritical buffoon; it is that of all authoritarian moralism.

Like his mother, Orgon uses the word *leçons* to underline Tartuffe's importance in the house: "Qui suit bien ses leçons goûte une paix profonde" (1.5.273) ("To keep his precepts is to be reborn"). Tartuffe functions for Orgon and Mme Pernelle like a sacred text (Tobin, "*Tartuffe*"). He helps them realize their ambition while enabling them to pretend it is not theirs. His seeming expertise in using the language of self-abnegation legitimates their lust for control by covering it with a veneer of impersonality. The quasi-textual nature of Tartuffe's moralism is emphasized by the mention of *Les fleurs des saints* ("Flowers of the Saints"; my trans.), heavy in-folio books of moralism (1.2.208; see also *Œuvres* 1: 1341).

In his preface, Molière emphasizes comic theater's religious origins, implicitly setting up a rivalry between heavy, text-based discourse and the plurivocality enforced by comedy. Orgon's desire for authoritarian, univocal dominance over his family is clear when, in act 2, scene 1, he literally tries to "ventriloquize" his daughter, Mariane. He tells her what he wants her to say in response to his announcement that he intends to marry her to Tartuffe. The connection between Orgon's domestic tyranny and real absolutism is made explicit when Mariane says to the servant Dorine, "Contre un père absolu que veux-tu que je fasse?" (2.3.589) ("What good would it do? A father's power is great").

Tartuffe corresponds rather well to the Church as legitimator of absolutist hegemony and to Louis XIV's militantly orthodox Jesuit counselors. The battle for discursive dominance in Orgon's household reflects the one going on in France. Tartuffe provides both a source of religious discourse slanted to Orgon's advantage and a flattering mirror or double reinforcing Orgon's conception of himself as analogous to God. Both within the play and outside it, political centralization is abetted by a pedagogical imperative. Tartuffe, however, proves to be a palimpsest: his devout discourse thinly veils strong, earthy desires. *Dévotion* is a disguise for physical desire and social ambition.

Here again, then, Molière shows that teaching is performative and that univocalism is a fatal distortion of dramatic, dialogic social reality. Orgon is released from his fascination only when he hears Tartuffe's voice as a voice expressing desire. Hidden under a table, Orgon cannot see his idol and so is no longer mesmerized by what he has taken for a flattering reflection of himself. His teacher-double is revealed to him as a rival.

Tartuffe's concern with spurious transcendentalism and fetishized words is given further expression in *Les femmes savantes*, which exposes the ladies' textual world as a palimpsest: their lust for power, prestige, and artificially intensified sexual enjoyment constantly shows through their discourse, and their discourse is relentlessly didactic. In the first scene, Armande uses the word *guéri* (cured; my trans.) to evoke the effect that her kind of knowledge would have on her sister's frank desire to live a physically pleasurable life.

Les femmes savantes examines the way personal motives and physical desires can be disguised when one transforms them into normative language. The ladies' system is a method for acquiring power and prestige. They present it as an ascetic aspiration toward "higher" consciousness and an evangelical zeal to bring this consciousness to others. The ladies join in the classicist-*précieux* effort to control eros by encoding it in Logos—to domesticate desire by controlling linguistic expression. Molière mocks this ambition as both unrealistic and hypocritical: language can only disguise desire. It cannot transcend it. Normative language can hide, and serve, the pleasure of controlling others' access to pleasure. The learned ladies define resistance to their knowledge and pedagogy as defectiveness.

This purported mastery of emotion is part of classicism's effort to mask the consolidation of political power as cultural and psychological progress; it disguises oppressive mastery as a liberating education. To communicate meaningfully is to accept penetration and colonization by an officially sanctioned discourse. This supposed "progress" toward mental control of physical impulses was both an instrument and a justification of some people's growing hegemony over others. Molière, like other writers from Rabelais to Orwell, is aware of the way language habits are used to validate political hierarchies. He was involved in hard, serious battles for cultural, and therefore political, influence.

The play's second and third acts make clear what is at issue in the ladies' battle for discursive dominance. In act 2, scene 6, Philaminte, the "queen" of the *savantes*, announces that she is firing the cook. Her reason is the latter's bad grammar, language that "en termes décisifs condamne Vaugelas" (2.6.462) ("which Vaugelas deems unworthy to be heard"). Philaminte clearly counts on the authority of texts to buttress her hegemony: the mention of Vaugelas connects the play with the actual cultural evolution in France, which featured the elevation to special status of linguistic technocrats like Vaugelas. Moreover, an even more portentous trend is evoked here: a plurivocal world, in which everyone speaks his or her mother tongue, is being replaced by one in which a synthetic language taught in schools by specialists is the only one taken seriously. Molière here shows us that "meaningful" knowledge and discourse must not be identified with a particular set of interests.

That power is the *savantes'* real preoccupation becomes clear in this same scene when they begin to use words like "lois" (2.6.499) ("laws") to refer to what they have been trying to teach Martine. The therapeutic justification of their enterprise is emphasized by their use of "récidive" (483) ("recurrence"; my trans.), "cervelle indocile" (480) ("ineducable brain"), and "âme villageoise" (496) ("simpleton's mind"; my trans.) to define her alleged inadequacies. Martine's devaluation to the status of defective is necessary to justify the "operations" the ladies want to perform on her. In the end, her resistance leads them to expel her from their "school."

Making themselves into mistresses of a school—or, as they refer to it, an *Académie*—is, in fact, just what the *savantes* have in mind. In act 3, scene 2, their conception of education and its consequences are explored thoroughly. Here, it becomes clear that the ladies share with Orgon and his mother a fetishism of words, an identification of "higher" things with certain language and of themselves with that language. The ladies understand that pedagogy is power in a culture that makes teachers the arbiters of legitimate language use: Bélise says, "Vous verrez nos statuts, quand ils seront tous faits" (3.2.920) ("You'll see our by-laws, once we've worked them out"). Armande adds, "Nous serons par nos lois les juges des ouvrages; / Par nos lois, prose et vers, tout nous sera soumis" (922–23) ("By our high standards we shall criticize / Whatever's written, and be severe with it"). The ladies will be elevated to the highest status by a pedagogy whose purpose is universal application of what they take to be their standards. Proprietorship of what is defined as knowledge will guarantee their hegemony.

At the moment when the ladies are evoking their hallucinatory academy, the play has already shown the real nature of the didactic enterprise they are involved in and the actual consequences of their determination to live in a world of words. In act 3, scene 2, the ladies' Tartuffe, the hack poet Trissotin, has presided over a quasi-religious ceremony. The *savantes* lovingly repeat the lines of his poetry, making ritual, talismanic objects out of his hackneyed words and phrases.

In addition to demonstrating that the "knowledgeable" ladies are really serving as consumers and broadcasters of someone else's language, the scene shows that the language is itself merely a system of clichés and that the entire enterprise is motivated by desire rather than devotion. The ladies' worshipful reproduction of Trissotin's rhetoric (3.2) takes place within a context defined by their expressions of desire for and pleasure in the relationship with him. His words are called "repas friands" (3.1.716) ("delicious meals"), and the poet is asked to "hât[er] nos plaisirs" (718) ("to bring on our pleasure"; both my trans.). Trissotin himself refers to the poem as an "enfant tout nouveau-né" (720) ("infant"). Combined with their use of language that betrays their fascination with power and social status, these phrases that show the physical basis of their *lust* for knowledge and the sexual implications of their relationship with Trissotin completely demolish their transcendentalist and therapeutic pedagogy. Like Orgon, they want to live triumphantly in a world of words. Molière obliges us to acknowledge two dangers in this ambition: first, discourse hides the desires or motives of its users; second, and more important, the didactic or therapeutic view of the world inherent in a discourse and the pedagogy employed to inculcate it eventually become a cultural environment in which real people must live.

Like the learned ladies, Dom Juan speaks like a book. Much of this play's comedy and much of its meditation on power turn on the linguistic differences between Sganarelle and Dom Juan. Sganarelle resembles Martine, the cook in *Les femmes savantes*. He is superstitious, and he uses language like a peasant, while his master speaks the language of rationalism. To speak like a book is to reproduce orally the conventions of a written code. This mannerism gives to speech the air of having a source "above" the level of personal, dialogic communication and desire. One's voice seems to be a text and thus has authority no one would be willing to accord to a mere personal voice. Power's service to appetite is again disguised as normative discourse. In Dom Juan's case, the reality of power is always discernible under the pretense of reason.

Dom Juan is not really rational: others' acceptance of his "arguments" depends on his status in the social system, not on his persuasiveness. His intelligence and reasonableness are no more at issue than is his personal attractiveness. In terms of both sex and language, he trades on his advantages. Molière thus suggests that rational communication is in a problematic relation with the exercise of power. He would agree with Jürgen Habermas that real community will be realized only when there is unlimited speech, free from constraint by the dominance of ideology or neurosis (*Legitimation* xvii).

Dom Juan's major characteristic—and the essence of speaking like a book—is, then, his refusal of dialogue. Sganarelle's speech is deformed in at least two ways by his master's discourse of power: first, Sganarelle consciously avoids the kind of coherence that would make him Dom Juan's discursive rival; second, his oral, folkloric discourse is unable to match Dom Juan's bookishness in a society that has already decided to sanctify the superstition of reason above all others. Sganarelle is thus obligated to pretend to be more ignorant than he is. Dom Juan's dominance has nothing to do with possessing "truth"; it suffices that he possesses power. No satisfactory dialogue can develop in this situation. Being and drama can reassert themselves only through Dom Juan's complete destruction. The univocal subject-position must be obliterated.

The marginalizing, or silencing, of plurivocality is an extremely important issue in *Dom Juan*. Molière's own voice was silenced by powerful figures in seventeenth-century France. The servant's obligatory inarticulateness and caution in expressing appropriate thoughts mirror Molière's own situation. Dom Juan refuses to listen to Sganarelle's indirect warnings, and his refusal has disastrous results. The nobleman resembles the powerful in France who tried to silence Molière rather than heed his warnings about their abuses. Molière, who played the part of Sganarelle, speaks through the character. From inside his partial disguise as Sganarelle, then, Molière meditates on the effects of discursive tyranny. He offers the pluralist lessons of comedy.

Molière thus denounces discursive monopoly. He carefully, "inarticulately," mocks his masters as he plays the part of a servile but worried valet whose discourse is interrupted, distorted, and silenced by a master who ignores sensible warnings and indulges in a secular form of a popular genre: preaching. Dom Juan does, in effect, precisely what Molière's enemies did by banning *Tartuffe*. Like Sganarelle's disjointed speeches, this play says what the interdiction of *Tartuffe* prevented Molière's saying more directly.

Hegemonic power always undermines its own bases by destroying the mutuality that, finally, even the most powerful need if their power is to have any real meaning. Molière attacks the univocalism of French absolutism and of modern epistemology and pedagogy. His own difficulties were a direct consequence of the period's increasing moral and cultural authoritarianism.

Molière shows us that ideological worlds, including those within particular definitions of knowledge and styles of teaching, have their origin in, are constructed in order to realize, desires. The comedian's ridiculous domestic absolutists are a critique of and warning to real absolutists, in classrooms and elsewhere.

Oh, Those Black Bile Blues:
Teaching *Le misanthrope*

Louise K. Horowitz

Presenting the character of Alceste in the contemporary classroom requires moving beyond the two major critical positions. Students instinctively grasp that much in *Le misanthrope* mirrors late-twentieth-century discourses on power and the restriction of individual freedom. But if they wish to pursue this line of inquiry, they will not find much help in a long-standing tradition that derides Alceste for offering an "excessive" critique of seemingly anodyne social mores. They may, however, find considerable assistance in a second approach focusing less on Alceste's moral failure (his "démesure" ["excess"]) than on dissecting the tensions between the requirements of the absolute monarchy and those of the individual, especially the dissenting individual—even if much of this newer methodology is intended to demonstrate the realities of power in the age of absolutism, thus allowing that Alceste offers an originally conceived, if inherently impotent, challenge to the stifling conformity of his time.

We might, therefore, prefer to shift the focus away from the study of the plays as documents of Ludovician France and, while utilizing the sociopolitical path as a point of departure, question the reality of Alceste's, or any other character's, "originality." *Le misanthrope* occurs at a critical juncture in Molière's writing, following *Tartuffe*, with its challenges to orthodoxy (by both Orgon and Tartuffe) and preceding *George Dandin*, with its effective negation of any remaining power vested outside the monarchy. Alceste rebels in the name of an aggressive individuality, which he perceives as a radical and original challenge to existing social norms based on pleasingly polite social intercourse. Molière's play, however, demonstrates ultimately that the claims to independent thinking, precisely like the claims of the conforming adapters, are doomed to a listless and set repetition of preexisting rhetoric and "texts." In heralding an ostensibly "independent" cast of mind, Alceste, as the nexus of occidental civilization, can only repeat, echo, and finally predict the not-new and never old discourse of essential vulnerability and impotence, expressed through the metaphor of an aggrieved virility. The metaphor then both conceals and reveals the nature of a gripping crisis in Western life as institutional forces unite to diminish and finally wither (the discourse of) individuality.

In Molière's theater, apparently domestic or amorous situations allow the spectator or reader to focus on the particulars of individuals rather than on collective or political predicaments, thereby inviting critical judgment centered on the notion of excess. Characters are analyzed for their adherence to a standard of judicious restraint, one that the critic establishes as including recognition of human foibles but that ideally should remain free of the rage that marks so many of Molière's protagonists. This perspective, however, risks blinding us to a host of highly charged political terms that serve to refocus the real nature of the crisis.

In *Le misanthrope*, Alceste's heated reactions to Philinte's entreaties and to Oronte's sonnet are traditionally viewed as giving rise to great mirth. We readily perceive the familiar *démesure*, the gap between the trivial situation and the enraged reaction it engenders. One such seemingly anodyne semantic constellation is built around the notion of "bending." Philinte repeatedly urges Alceste to "bend with the times," while other words directly reinforce the concept of slackness: *lâche* in its etymological sense, for example. These terms are frequently contrasted with their opposites: *raide* and *raideur,* along with *droiture* ("uprightness") and *rectitude,* which signal Alceste's recourse to a constellation of hardness and rigidity in contrast to Philinte's moderating pliability. Similarly, the play returns manifold times to the term *complaisance*— that is, "compliance" with its clear dose of "pleasability." *Complaisance* appears often not only by itself but also in conjunction with the concept of softness, as in "les molles complaisances" (2.4.705) ("slack indulgence"). Alceste, it is to be understood, refuses to adjust to the demands of a social life that asks of him a conforming compliancy.

In fact, this terminology serves to define in large part the prevailing mode of "*l'honnêteté.*" (There is no true English translation for the code or system of aristocratic social comportment that came to dominate in the second half of the seventeenth century, commonly known as *l'honnêteté.* Its clear rules for conduct in noble society, especially concerning the art of conversation, were formulated by Antoine Gombaud, the chevalier de Méré, in his detailed writings regarding the status and behavior of principally the aristocratic male.) Alceste's outraged reactions to Oronte's sonnet and to Philinte's entreaties are conditioned by his ability to detect the explicit demands of the *honnête* code in otherwise innocuous vocabulary. Suzanne Relyea, following Domna Stanton, has analyzed the attempted rechanneling of aggressive instincts via this ostensibly aesthetic code. The advent of *l'honnêteté* in literature and essay and its absorption into the mental framework of large segments of the nobility and upper bourgeoisie reflect in Relyea's view an effort at achieving virile prowess and dominance in an urban rather than military culture (128).

Virility and dominance are indeed at issue here. But whereas Relyea sees the success of *l'honnêteté* in its role as a discourse of seduction, championing a "new" form of domination, Alceste views the entire system as precisely the opposite: a drastic denial and curtailment of male power and hence of power itself. Philinte's repeated exhortations to bend, along with the specific terms of Oronte's sonnet ("espoir," "attente," "complaisance," "désespère," "trépas"; [1.2.315–32]) signal to Alceste not personal losses in love but, rather, collective inertia and deprivation, offering a direct challenge to a past identity defined through aristocratic aggrandizement and shared power ("Si le Roi m'avait donné / Paris . . . " [1.2.393], ["If the King had given me for my own / Paris . . . "], chants Alceste in his "vieille chanson"). When combined with the dramatic and silly foppery of the two marquesses, such language communicates to Alceste a radically diminished stature for the nobleman, one that increasingly identifies him as that traditionally marginal figure in power terms: a woman. In Alceste's eyes the social conformists have acquiesced in their new and minimal role as decoration, as passive witnesses to the events of the age (Horowitz 71).

For it is not only the standardization of foppish clothes or the advent of long fingernails that has made Alceste so angry. Conformity per se becomes the sign of marginalized status, since it is increasingly identified with emasculation. Alceste thus rejects "une estime ainsi prostituée" (1.1.54) ("so promiscuous an esteem"), deeming the practice of mutual complimenting both feminizing and promiscuous. He mimics Clitandre's fashionable falsetto, ridicules the gownlike clothing, the long fingernails, and the blond wig, testifying concretely to his anxiety. And while it may seem as if Philinte, a typical Molière *raisonneur,* is a different breed from the inseparable dandyish marquesses, in Alceste's eyes his friend's vocabulary of compliance and his long-winded sermons on bending and loosening up are precisely the forerunner of an ominous decline. We should, therefore, read Philinte's verbose speeches not as "reasonable" responses to the ostensibly immoderate, "excessive" rage of Alceste. Rather, these entreaties are set pieces at the service of a specific ideology. (The term *ideology* is not too strong, although it is surely anachronistic.) As discourses championing an acquiescent acceptance of a radical denial of power, they have precisely all the value of a slogan, of an advertisement.

Philinte's words, which might be viewed as the dramatic adaptation of writings by the chevalier de Méré, find numerous echoes and supports in Eliante, his philosophical twin. In scene 5 of act 2, she readily seconds the *raisonneur* with her own set pieces, borrowed literally from Lucretius. And although Molière's work was subsequently destroyed or sold, according to Jean Chapelain, the playwright had previously translated much of Lucretius into French (Molière, *Œuvres* 2: 1337), thereby creating a two-stage derivation for Eliante's speech. Moreover, the "stolen" passage from *De natura rerum* is itself an encomium to the art of linguistic manipulation, describing the lover's will to twist the beloved's defect into a praiseworthy quality. Eliante's speech has always seemed contrived, even absurd. From this practically mute figure suddenly erupts a perfectly composed commentary on the capacity of language to mask, concealed within a borrowed set piece and thus itself a linguistic travesty. As she "plagiarizes" both Lucretius and Molière, she bears her decidedly unoriginal soul in favor of the continued worship of *complaisance.* Much like Philinte's repeated exhortations to bend, and thereby to conform and please, Eliante's exposition offers some derivative formulations in the service of the newly dominant mode. Both formally and thematically, she voices the "art" of conformity at the heart of *l'honnêteté.*

The scenes with Eliante, Oronte, and Philinte produce in Alceste a spurt of "black bile," which traditionally has been viewed as a demonstration of his temperamental flaw but which finally is best understood as an instinctive grasping of the crisis gripping the French nobility as the monarch's personal reign begins to take hold. To Eliante's appropriation of *De natura rerum*, wherein she praises the art of social dissembling and thus through both substance and style announces her own unchallenging acceptance of prescribed codes and prewritten texts, Alceste sputters, "Et moi, je soutiens moi" (2.5.731) ("But I still say . . .") before he is cut off by Célimène, who, wholly engaged in the affirmation of her social persona, fears hearing precisely the claims of the naked self. It is the very flatness of Eliante's words, their sheer unoriginality, like those of Philinte and Oronte, that has worn out Alceste, worn down Alceste, to the point of virtual madness. His twice repeated "moi," two syllables in a hemistich, is in fact the sole response possible to this agglomeration of cliché and slogan, a pastiche of texts buried in the literature and consciousness of Western life. "Moi," sputters Alceste twice. "I," alone am the answer; "I" alone the rebuff, in a direct challenge to the cancellation of an authoritative speaking subject, of "individual identity," as mandated by the norms of *l'honnêteté* (Relyea 145–46).

This ardent rejection of incorporation into speech and text also causes Alceste's fury in the first scene of act 1, as Philinte enthusiastically compares their quarrel with one of an earlier work:

> Ce chagrin philosophe est un peu trop sauvage,
> Je ris des noirs accès où je vous envisage,
> Et crois voir en nous deux, sous mêmes soins nourris,
> Ces deux frères que peint *L'Ecole des maris*,
> Dont . . .
>
> (1.1.97–101)

> This philosophical rage is a bit extreme;
> You've no idea how comical you seem;
> Indeed, we're like those brothers in the play
> Called *School for Husbands*, one of whom was prey . . .

Identified with the previous quarrel between Molière's own dramatic brothers, Ariste and Sganarelle, Alceste explodes—"Mon Dieu! laissons là vos comparaisons fades" (101) ("Enough, now! None of your stupid similes")—enraged that even his rage is without a grain of originality; for he is reminded no doubt that Philinte's recommendation to bend with the times perfectly echoes Ariste, while his own claims to virility, potency, and independence were formulated by Sganarelle a few years earlier in speeches deriding the emasculated conformity of the young. Thus Alceste fumes, while Philinte, Oronte, and Eliante —content, conditioned purveyors of old plays, old poems, and old prose—fit the mold.

Le misanthrope appears, then, to offer the disquieting but nonetheless morally uplifting claims to an aggressive individual distinctiveness—"Je veux qu'on me distingue" (1.1.63) ("I choose, Sir, to be chosen")—in the face of a pervasive authoritarian effort to repress. Alceste angrily contests the slogans and clichés mouthed by the Philintes and Eliantes, to say nothing of the foppish ways of the young marquesses, seeing in both the conditioned responses of a pacified aristocracy. Accepting at face value Alceste's assertions of unicity, we see in his hostile rage the reaction of one who simply refuses to join in the *honnête* game with its high investment in a stultifying conformity.

Yet Molière's play ultimately fails to provide the realization of an independent and original voice. Despite its surface image of individual resistance to the bores and hacks, *Le misanthrope* portrays the very failure of that challenge. Alceste, twin to his seeming adversaries, has merely appropriated other discourses, planting himself firmly in an anthology of "already existing metaphysical scripts" (Riggs 122). While they are different scripts from those of Philinte, Oronte, and Eliante, they are nonetheless preformed messages that Molière distributes throughout his play. He begins subtly. As early as the first scene, and almost immediately following his crazed response to Philinte's comparison of their debate to that of *L'école des maris*, Alceste unhesitatingly paraphrases another famous misanthrope. In describing his hatred of all men, of those who are "méchants" ("rogues") and then of those who traffic with the "méchants," Molière's misanthrope echoes Timon of Athens, as recounted by Erasmus in his *Apophtegmes* (Molière, *Œuvres* 2: 1333). For in Molière's play nothing and no one is "original." Alceste was a common appellation in the literature of the sixteenth and seventeenth centuries, and a character with this name is a hero of Molière d'Essertine's novel *Polyxène*, which recounts, in turn, a tale not unlike that of Alceste and Oronte. In *Polyxène*, a jealous Alceste engages in a quarrel with one Cloryman about a story he did not like, and a duel ensues. Similarly, an Arsinoé figures in Corneille's *Nicomède*, which Molière had produced. Finally, Philinte's name is not "new." "He" is already a character in Charles Sorel's *La suite de Polyxène* (Molière, *Œuvres* 2: 1331–32). This spiraling of borrowed names and texts, including of course that of Molière, is the ultimate hallmark of *Le misanthrope*.

Moreover, the many plagiarisms are free of any pejorative weight. Molière lifts his words and then triumphantly proclaims his "stolen" texts, while Alceste proclaims his uniqueness. Nowhere, of course, does his proposition sound more hollow than in the second and third scenes of act 4. Both scenes, particularly the third, offer little more than a direct incorporation of Molière's earlier work *Dom Garcie de Navarre*. Whole verses and entire speeches are placed verbatim in Alceste's mouth. These strange borrowings have been thoroughly discussed by Marcel Gutwirth, Michael Koppisch, and Larry Riggs. Alceste's wholesale appropriation of a quasi-tragic discourse, however, with its investment in virile-sounding "nobletalk" and its indictment of those who fail to live by the aristocracy's intrinsic standards, is, as we have seen, only one example of mimesis in a play composed largely of preexisting texts.

For like Philinte, Eliante, and Oronte, Alceste has appropriated for his "distinctive" claims a preformed discourse. *Their* texts systematically form extended propaganda in favor of the reigning *honnêteté*. *His* texts offer a ringing denunciation of that same code, in favor of a desperate appeal to a largely rhetorical "past," wherein power was defined and interpreted through a prism of aggressive maleness. "Je veux que l'on soit homme" (1.1.69) ("Let men behave like men"), declares Alceste, his cry echoing back and forth through the ages as he condemns the mores of his era as fundamentally emasculated. At the core of his discourse remains a controlling image of essential potency, lost "now," but whose elusiveness may yet be countered by the demonstration of the feminized soul of *l'honnêteté*. Fearing a vacuum at his center (Alcestis, after all, is one of Euripides's prominent *heroines*), Alceste "discovers" an age-old rhetoric, not "new" then or now, which attempts to strengthen an inner "male" core perceived to be in a state of drastic decomposition. Hence his recourse to the inevitable and all-too-familiar phallic metaphors, his obsession with "pliancy" at the expense of *raideur.*

In fact, Alceste's "text" is no more or less "original" than that of his adversaries. His case for originality, moreover, is scarcely furthered by Molière's having played Sganarelle in *L'école des maris*; Dom Garcie de Navarre in the play of that name; and Alceste himself, thereby creating another series of echoes, of both author and comedian, the one doubling the other, to the point of essential blurring and, precisely, radical indistinction. Attacking *la femme et le fat* ("the woman and the fop"), attempting to decenter and thus marginalize both (but Célimène, not Alceste, reigns, at least in her play court, and the dandyish marquesses, unlike Alceste, are present at *le petit coucher,* Louis XIV's formalized nightly ceremony of retirement, to which only select members of the aristocracy were admitted), an alienated Alceste can produce only the sounds of a perceived essential injury, all too familiarly lacing his discourse with an imagery of bold "independence." Larry Riggs has correctly seen that "Alceste is an empty costume agitated . . . by the 'wind' of a rhetoric that blows through him from out of a cultural vortex of previous performances stretching all the way back to Genesis" (152). Actually, all *Le misanthrope's* characters are "empty costumes" (hence Célimène's vanishing act at the play's end, her noisy self rendered mute as she simply vaporizes into the air), and while apparently differing rhetorics blow through them, in one fundamental fashion they are destined to play out ad infinitum the competing fictions of power in an ever-expanding void. The characters are left to "fight" it out through speech, castrating one another at the hemistich, in a losing battle not to "hear."

And when in fact they do hear, are forced to hear, they run to the courts, there to sue and hurl their slogans at one another yet again. Seeing the compulsive recourse to litigation as the classic sign of the dismemberment of individually conceived and expressed power, Molière strews throughout his play references to an unending series of lawsuits, whose causes are never explained. Their raison d'être, of course, is irrelevant; only their existence finally signifies in the whirlwind of accumulated discourse. When these suits fail to provide adequate distraction, Molière offers up the tribunal of the marshals of France, whose collective and shared identity ties them to both the king and the military and who are asked to hear Oronte's complaints concerning Alceste's refusal to approve his sonnet. The situation, of course, seems quite ludicrous, for the *maréchaux* are scarcely required to resolve such a petty quarrel! But just as Alceste "heard" in Oronte's poem a too-prompt obeisance to the code of enforced idleness and its concomitant despair, Oronte hears in Alceste's objections to his verse a direct challenge to this new mode of existence. Oronte's recourse to the marshals is therefore the correct political response to Alceste's subversive stance. Toward the end of the play, charges of sedition are amplified when the misanthrope is accused of having authored "un livre abominable" (5.1.1501), a libelous pamphlet depicting the political and moral climate of the early years of Louis XIV's reign. The courts and the marshals apparently listen to the various charges directed against Alceste, but he is never arrested and remains at large throughout the play. Philinte maintains that Alceste is not in danger because no one believes the charges. It may not matter, however, whether they are believed or not, for *Le misanthrope* is already at a distant point from *Tartuffe*. By now, the game is over and lost; "sedition," like *l'honnêteté*, is rhetoric, and Alceste, unlike Tartuffe, is a threat only to the conformists, not to the absolute monarchy. This perception of a game over and lost will cause another, final shift, from the melancholic mood of *Le misanthrope* to the depressing degradation of *Dandin*.

Restructuring a Comic Hero of Molière:
Le médecin malgré lui

Joseph I. Donohoe, Jr.

Turning from what is arguably the greatest comic trilogy ever created for the theater, comprising *Tartuffe* (1664), *Dom Juan* (1665), and *Le misanthrope* (1666), a student might well be tempted to overlook *Le médecin malgré lui*. This diminutive three-act comedy, hardly longer than a farce, presented for the first time some six months after the completion of the trilogy, has frequently been neglected. (The Georges Couton edition of Molière provides only three pages of introductory material for *Le médecin malgré lui* while allotting forty-nine to *Tartuffe*, twenty-eight to *Dom Juan*, and eighteen to *Le misanthrope*.) Following a long tradition, students may be inclined to see in this modest piece nothing more than a moment of respite for Molière after the Herculean labors of the three great comedies. They need to be reminded that *Le médecin malgré lui* also offers a unique opportunity to interrogate a disabused playwright at the height of his powers on the painful lessons learned about truth and justice in society during the protracted controversy over *Tartuffe*.

In the works preceding Molière's great comedies—especially in plays like *Les précieuses ridicules*, *L'école des maris*, and *L'école des femmes*—the hard-edged characterization of comic mania, set in relief by the irrefutable good sense of the *raisonneurs*, speaks to the relative serenity of the playwright's interaction with his public. Generally speaking, they jointly embrace a social ideal emanating from the dominant aristocracy and, along with that ideal, a common sense of what by definition constitutes the target of satiric laughter: variance from reasonable, decorous behavior. While success inevitably brought with it scattered criticism, founded for the most part on envy or bigotry, Molière was able to counterattack skillfully with the good-humored thrusts of *La critique de l'école des femmes* and *L'impromptu de Versailles*. Indeed, up to and including the putative three-act version of *Tartuffe* in 1664, Molière apparently continued to dedicate himself to the task inscribed in the motto of the Comédie Française, *Castigat ridendo mores* (that is, Comedy corrects public morals through laughter), there being no doubt about the standards to be invoked in the process. The unprecedented attacks on *Tartuffe*, however, coupled with a wavering of royal support, would soon bring about significant changes in the embattled playwright's view of social man as expressed in his theater and in his relationship to his public.

As early as *Dom Juan* and *Le misanthrope*, one notices that the comic identity of the protagonists has become more problematic, even ambiguous. Dom Juan, for example, seems neither all right nor all wrong, nor is it absolutely certain that he is wrong at all! (Doolittle 533). The same has often been said of Alceste, beginning with the famous letter of Jean-Jacques Rousseau. After *Tartuffe*, the norms shared by Molière and the *honnêtes gens* no longer seem adequate to cover the complexity and bitterness of the life experience with which the playwright has begun to fuel his theater. There are moments in *Dom Juan* and *Le misanthrope* when the comic heroes' criticisms of society could be unsettling for the spectator, but Molière, for reasons touching both the psychology of laughter and politics, never allows them to dominate. On the contrary, he acts to sustain the necessary (for the purposes of laughter) inequality of awareness between comic hero and spectator and, at the same time, to distance himself from the audience's potentially dangerous criticism by highlighting the manic comportment of the protagonist. It has long been observed by critics that Molière never confronted the public by rehabilitating or reconstructing his comic *aliénés* ("madmen") (Bailly 53). Robert Nelson in fact applauds Molière's shrewdness in not reforming his monomaniacs. To do so, Nelson tells us, "would take the spectator into affective and moral regions where the satiric purpose— laughter—might be compromised." Nelson also underscores the necessary inequality of awareness that the playwright must maintain to play's end between the spectator and a Dom Juan or an Alceste: "to make them share our superior view of their previous conduct would come dangerously close to identifying us with them in that previous conduct as well" (111). Molière is loath to attribute to spectators the same follies, dissatisfactions, and, on occasion, subversive reactions that his comic heroes demonstrate.

Nevertheless, in *Le médecin malgré lui*, Molière does take the unprecedented step of rehabilitating the comic hero, while projecting sotto voce the image of an amorphous world seemingly devoid of logic and reason. This complexity is concealed, however, not only by the opulent shadow of the trilogy but also by a frothy layer of wonderful nonsense beyond which few readers have had the heart to penetrate.

The play opens with a domestic quarrel between husband and wife, an opportunity for many students to exercise skills acquired during years of watching the soaps. Like most quarrels of its kind, this one is filled with noise and threats and gives little hint of the real issues dividing the antagonists. Sganarelle's opening speech—"Non, je te dis que je n'en veux rien faire, et que c'est à moi de parler et d'être le maître" (1.1) ("No, I tell you, I'll do nothing of the sort, it's for me to speak up and be the boss")—suggests that a struggle for dominance is going on in the household. Martine's rejoinder— "Et je te dis, moi, que je veux que tu vives à ma fantaisie, et que je ne me suis point mariée avec toi pour souffrir tes fredaines" ("And I'm telling you, I want you to live the way I say, and that I didn't marry you to put up with your nonsense")—confirms that supposition and indicates that the lady has no intention of being the loser.

Given the primacy of the paterfamilias in seventeenth-century society, one wonders initially about the strength and vehemence of Martine's revolt, but the answer is not long in coming. Sganarelle, it turns out, is a man who squanders his time and what little money they have in drunken idleness. He has even gone so far as to subsidize this way of life by selling off the family's worldly goods. Poor Martine! Sganarelle does seem to be rather subhuman, but what, after all, can she do? He is by force of law and custom head of the house. Besides, why marry such a clod in the first place? As for the quarrel, it is certainly not the first, nor does it promise to be the last. If the dispute accomplishes nothing else, one might conclude on a superficial level, at least it provides needed emotional release for the much-abused wife.

A closer reading of this scene, especially for students fluent in the language of the soaps, should bring to light several significant facts and at least one full-scale revelation. We are dealing with a woodcutter who quotes Aristotle, has had some Latin, served six years under a famous doctor, and who considers himself to be somewhat déclassé. "Trouve-moi," he challenges his wife, "un faiseur de fagots qui sache, comme moi, raisonner des choses, qui ait servi six ans un fameux médecin, et qui ait su dans son jeune âge, son rudiment par coeur" ("Find me a woodcutter who knows how to reason about things like me, who worked six years under a famous doctor, who learned by heart his basic subjects at a very young age"). Martine, who has heard it all before, is not impressed with her husband's vita. "Peste du fou fieffé!" ("A plague on the arrant fool!") she hurls back, eliciting from Sganarelle "Peste de la carogne!" ("A plague on the old hag!"). (Students, who may one day be faced with the same problem, will, however, be quick to note that in some measure the domestic strife in this peasant household is due to the "underemployment" of the husband.) After this latest exchange of insults, Martine intones a well-known lament for the choice she made of a husband: "Que maudit soit l'heure et le jour où je m'avisai d'aller dire oui!" ("Cursed be the hour and the day when I made up my mind to say yes"). When her husband replies disobligingly with an analogous complaint, Martine is frankly outraged:

> C'est bien à toi, vraiment, à te plaindre de cette affaire. Devrais-tu être un seul moment sans rendre grâce au Ciel de m'avoir pour ta femme? et méritais-tu d'épouser une personne comme moi?

> Of course, it's fine for you to complain! Should you let even a single moment pass without thanking God that you're married to me? And did you deserve to marry someone like me?

So certain is Martine of her interpretation of the facts that her question seems almost rhetorical. But Sganarelle, equally certain of his ground—or so it appears—counterattacks ironically without missing a beat: "Il est vrai que tu me fis trop d'honneur, et que j'eus lieu de me louer la première nuit de nos noces!" ("It is true that you did me a great honor, and that I had reason to be pleased with our wedding night!"). The protestations of both characters carry an undeniable accent of veracity, and the spectator has little sense of whom to believe as Sganarelle fires the second barrel of his riposte: "Hé! morbleu! ne me fais point parler là-dessus: je dirais de certaines choses . . . " ("Damnation! Don't get me started on that subject: I'd say certain things . . . "). What things? Martine would like to know, but Sganarelle is curiously reticent about the details: "Baste, laissons là ce chapitre. Il suffit que nous savons ce que nous savons, et que tu fus bien heureuse de me trouver" ("Enough, let's drop the subject. It's sufficient that we know what we know, and that you were extremely lucky to find me"). The discussion soon degenerates into violence. Sganarelle will begin to beat his wife—according, one suspects, to some recurring ritual. He picks up a stick and asks, "Vous en voulez donc?" ("So, you want some?")

It is clear from these exchanges that all Martine's criticisms are aimed at her husband's impossible way of life. Were he to stop wasting his time and make better use of their meager resources, her complaints might easily disappear. Such a change, however, does not seem likely, given the protests and lamentations emanating from Sganarelle. Who, after all, is the injured party here, and what precisely is it that keeps Sganarelle from changing his irascible ways? The only clue to an answer in the text—and here students may be quicker to the mark than the teacher—is the curious reference, heavy with irony, made by Sganarelle to the first night of their marriage ("Il est vrai que tu me fis trop d'honneur . . . ") whose resonance he prolongs with a threat to reveal some terrible secret ("[N]e me fais point parler là-dessus; je dirais de certaines choses . . . "). He concludes with a decisive: "tu fus bien heureuse de me trouver." If, playing with the irony implicit in the structure of Sganarelle's speech, we were to understand him as meaning "Tu me fis *trop de déshonneur*" ("You did me *a great dishonor*"), or, to put it another way, were we to posit that he had discovered on his wedding night that his bride was not the virgin he had supposed she was and that he had therefore become a sort of ex post facto cuckold, then certain details take on new significance. Sganarelle, cousin of the Sganarelle in *L'école des maris* and a true creature of Molière in that respect, would have seen himself as doubly dishonored, since he had both been wronged *and* fooled! What to do? Unfortunately, there is nothing to be done without exponentially increasing his dishonor by making it public. He is thus forced to swallow his shame and impotent anger, while over time making everyone—wife, children, and himself—suffer from his frustration. Now we can understand his reluctance, even in the heated exchange with his wife, to dredge up the awesome truth. We understand as well the reluctance of the wife to pursue the enigmatic utterances of her husband, for a discussion could lend substance to what she might otherwise allow herself to regard as mere suspicion on his part. No need here to emulate the mistake of Racine's Phèdre; some things are decidedly better left in the dark.

Sharing the couple's secret, we can now appreciate as well the implications of M. Robert's intrusion in act 1, scene 1. The beating that he thoughtlessly attempts to interrupt is, after all, part and parcel of the modus vivendi that the couple has evolved to deal with an otherwise unresolvable dilemma: Sganarelle relieves his anger and frustration by beating his wife, and she—although with less enthusiasm—receives the blows in acknowledgment of her guilt. "Et je veux qu'il me batte, moi" (1.2) ("And I want him to beat me"), she tells the astonished neighbor when he attempts to come to her rescue, and both she and her husband turn as one to cudgel the well-meaning intruder. For each has the best of reasons to keep the canonical beating a private family matter.

Although a cuckold quite literally in spite of himself, Sganarelle is obliged by an age-old, culturally induced reflex to view himself as without honor, as something rather less than a man. His way of life reflects and confirms this destructive image of the self: impaired by the loss of all self-regard, he has abandoned himself to the more primitive side of his nature. In spite of his vaunted education and talents, he gathers wood for a living, tyrannizes wife and children, and fills his days with drink and idleness. Should he pause at any point to examine his weakness, he is referred back, with the aid of a nagging wife, to its source, and the unholy cycle begins anew. One day, however, perhaps because of a crisis of frustration, a single blow too many, or too heavy, disturbs the equilibrium of their arrangement, awakening in Martine a heightened sense of injustice, which overrides her accustomed guilt and inspires in her, understandably, a thirst for revenge. For reasons more compelling perhaps than her own ironic explanation—"C'est une punition trop délicate pour mon pendard" (1.3) ("It's too delicate a punishment for this bum")—she has put aside thoughts of cuckolding her husband and, in a moment of inspiration, finds for him a perfectly proportioned punishment that will prove to be the salvation of each and both.

Thanks to a vigorous pounding by the servants of Géronte, administered at the behest of Martine, a bewildered Sganarelle soon agrees that he is indeed a doctor—at which point the play embraces a classic comic situation replete with young lovers (Léandre and Lucinde), a blocking character (Géronte), and the equivalent of the wily servant (Sganarelle), who works against Géronte to ensure the union of the young lovers. In the ensuing action, truth and falsehood, reality and illusion are interwoven to advance the causes of both the lovers and the peasant couple Martine and Sganarelle. Sganarelle, who is no doctor, embarks on the cure of a young woman who is not sick and, with the aid of an apothecary who really isn't one, brings about a complete cure, because he knows as much as any doctor of the period—that is, nothing! In the process, the counterfeit doctor acquires a reputation for healing that proves to be the perfect cure for his lack of self-esteem, the result of a mindless but operative view of cuckoldry.

In the final scene of the play, the individuals most deeply concerned make it clear that Sganarelle has been restored to honor and esteem by the dignity of his new calling. Martine claims—as well she should—her share of the credit for her husband's rehabilitation: "Puisque tu ne seras point pendu, rends-moi grâce d'être médecin; car c'est moi qui t'ai procuré cet honneur" (3.11) ("Since you won't be hanged, you can thank me that you're a doctor; because it's me who got you that honor"). And Sganarelle is willing to pardon the beating in favor of his newly found importance and a manifestly therapeutic self-esteem: "Je te pardonne ces coups de bâton en faveur de la dignité où tu m'as élevé; mais prépare-toi désormais à vivre dans un grand respect avec un homme de ma conséquence . . ." ("I forgive you the beating in view of the high rank to which you have raised me; but prepare yourself from now on to live in great respect for a man of my importance . . .").

In the ontologically problematic world of the *Le médecin malgré lui*, where the categories of illusion and reality apply only in the most idiosyncratic manner, where rules and logic do not pertain, and where the most serious efforts to cope may appear whimsical, Molière appears to delight in the spectacle of fate repairing its misdeeds in the interest of an authentic human response to adversity. The cruel revelation of his nuptial bed had plunged Sganarelle "understandably" into deep despair, leading him "logically," in his frustration, to abuse his wife who, while "justly" seeking to end her own humiliation, succeeded in reshaping her husband's psyche, the fate of Léandre and Lucinde, and her own fate as well. No *raisonneurs*, no privileged values, no grand moral schemes; rather, simple, bruised humanity expresses itself out of need—instinctively, authentically—and carries the day in a world otherwise emptied of justice and meaning. Here surely is the mark of Molière the champion of instinctual humanity as celebrated by Ramon Fernandez in the pages of his still remarkable biography (ch. 3, pt. 1).

Throughout the three great comedies preceding *Le médecin malgré lui*, in particular after *Tartuffe*, Molière seems intent on lacerating, albeit with a caution dictated by the number and power of his enemies, all misrepresentation, all twisted posturing, all defacement of the truth. The fantasyland of *Le médecin* offered an environment in which he might express his anger and frustration with a reasonable expectation of impunity. Molière did, in fact, take advantage of the opportunity to operate the first reconstruction of one of his comic heroes and in the process confirmed his definitively altered rapport with his audience. The criticism implicit in satiric laughter will henceforth be shared by the monomaniac with the ostensibly normal people who surround him, stand-ins for society at large. Having once established the axis for laughter, Molière will bend it subtly, against the laughers. What is more, two major comic protagonists, Jourdain and Argan, will receive, in the dizzying final moments of their plays, a kind of rehabilitation that, illusion for illusion, compares well with the fates of their would-be critics and exploiters. Finally, in the slide from certainty to skepticism hinted at in the evolution of his comic protagonists, Molière reaches out to Marivaux, whose Enlightenment comedy, in its effort to modify the views of his audience, will routinely reconstruct its comic heroes (Donohoe 180).

No painter is totally present in a single painting, but all paintings collaborate in the articulation of their creator's vision, and so it goes with a playwright and his theater. By approaching *Le médecin malgré lui* contextually and by remembering that the genius of its creator expresses itself in each of his works, students may enrich their appreciation of Molière and his dramatic imagination.

Le bourgeois gentilhomme in Intermediate and Advanced Language and Literature Classes

Clara Krug

There is a given among humanities teachers that we can understand various aspects of a literary text as we reread it over time. After the initial reading, we have only a limited appreciation. We may even dislike it. As we reread a text, however, our comprehension of it changes. The same is true of our students. To glean as much as possible from a literary text, they, too, need to read it several times at different developmental stages. Teachers can give students such opportunities to become more proficient readers by having them study a text more than once—at different stages in their academic career.

We need to be careful about the stage at which we first include each literary text. For example, in the second-year French curriculum, teachers often include one or more literary texts for detailed study. In a second-year class, however, students may not be proficient enough to understand, discuss, or write about a certain "texte intégral" without difficulty. For some, trying to do so would be demoralizing. Yet, arguably, those who will complete their foreign-language study at this "intermediate level" should experience literature, and those who will continue study would benefit from apprenticeship as literary scholars during this second year of course work. We need to incorporate literary texts in the second-year curriculum in a way that satisfies both audiences. Excerpts—such as a scene from Molière's *Le bourgeois gentilhomme*—can help us achieve that goal.

Students enrolled in intermediate French at Georgia Southern University meet M. Jourdain at the midpoint of the academic quarter. They devote a day and a half to one excerpt of *Le bourgeois gentilhomme*: M. Jourdain's lesson with the philosophy teacher (2.4) (Pucciani and Hamel 586–90). To study the excerpt, they use the "cognitive process" reading approach devised by Janet Swaffar and Katherine Arens. This approach to reading is based on eight fundamental assumptions. Three are primordial: authentic texts are preferable to specially edited versions or graded reading selections with English glossaries because the natural linguistic redundancies and language contexts in them aid readers; adult language learners need to read materials oriented toward adults; one should teach in the target language, relying on inferencing and logical strategies that the adult learners have in their native language.

With these assumptions in mind, Swaffar and Arens devised a reading sheet to help adult learners understand texts in a foreign language and distinguish between skimming and reading for detail. In addition, to assist them as they read for detail, the sheet includes tasks whose degree of difficulty increases according to the order of Benjamin Bloom's taxonomy of the cognitive domain:

knowledge, comprehension, application, analysis-synthesis, and evaluation (Bloom et al. 271–73).

Here is the cognitive process sheet that Jean-Paul Carton and I developed for the excerpt from *Le bourgeois gentilhomme*. It is in French; students complete it in French:

Reading Exercise for *Le bourgeois gentilhomme*, Molière

I.   Initial Contact
    A.   Read the text without consulting a dictionary.
    B.   What is the main idea?

II. Detailed Study
    A.   Make a list of the vocabulary related to school subjects.
    B.   Make a list of the details that seem comical to you. You may summarize certain passages.
    C.   Why are these details comical?
    D.   What is the moral of this story? Explain.

During class, in two steps, students complete the "Initial Contact" section. First, each student skims the excerpt for ten minutes and writes its main idea on the sheet. Then several students—volunteers, if possible—write their versions of that idea on the blackboard so that the entire class may proceed to the second step: examining, discussing, and comparing responses. In their initial examination and discussion of each response, students indicate whether or not it is, in fact, the main idea of the text. Then they compare responses to identify similarities and differences in information. Finally, focusing on form, they correct grammatical and spelling errors.

This entire prereading activity requires twenty-five minutes of class time. It prepares students for detailed reading by helping them identify the main idea—or ideas—of the excerpt. It also helps them realize that there is no one correct way to state that main idea. Instead of focusing on the teacher as the sole source of information, the activity focuses on the students as purveyors of information and the teacher as a facilitator who elicits that information. For homework, students need to read and study the scene to provide the information requested in the "Detailed Study" section of the reading sheet. In developing a list of vocabulary related to scholarly subjects, the students function at the knowledge and comprehension levels of the cognitive domain. When they determine which of the details related to those subjects are comical, they function at the fourth cognitive level, analysis. Item C also requires analysis, while identification and explanation of the moral make students function at the highest level of the cognitive domain: evaluation.

The next class is devoted to reviewing the "Detailed Study" section prepared by students and to introducing them to seventeenth-century France. The introduction begins as students enter the classroom; they hear the strains of Jean-Joseph Mouret's "Fanfares." I conduct the fifty-minute class session entirely in French and organize it according to the following plan:

1. While the music is playing, volunteers write on the blackboard their answers to items A, B, and C of the "Detailed Study." When they have finished, other students add items to each list. The entire class verifies the completeness of the lists. (15 min.)
2. Students discuss the comical details listed on the board. During the discussion, the teacher introduces the Bergsonian concept of the mechanical. (10 min.)
3. After discussion, teacher and students watch and discuss the "vowel scene" in Jean Meyer's film version of the play. (15 min.)
4. Students discuss the excerpt's moral. To be incorporated: What was a *bourgeois* in seventeenth-century France? A *gentilhomme*? (10 min.)

As in the "Initial Contact" section, students propose the answers and help one another understand which ones are valid. They correct grammar only after discussing content. Then, after viewing the vowel scene, students suggest additional sources of comedy: M. Jourdain's facial expressions, his gestures, his clothes. The most comical element of the scene is the sound of M. Jourdain's voice and the expression on his face as he pronounces the five letters, especially the "I, O, I, O . . . I, O, I, O" (2.4).

Again, the teacher serves as facilitator—with two exceptions. One exception is the introduction of Henri Bergson's idea of the comic value of repetitive actions that make human beings resemble machines:

> [T]he laughable element . . . consists of a certain *mechanical inelasticity* . . . a certain inborn lack of elasticity of both senses and intelligence, which brings it to pass that we continue to adapt ourselves to a past and therefore imaginary situation, when we ought to be shaping our conduct in accordance with the reality which is present.　("Laughter" 66–67)

After hearing the term *mechanical,* students nod in agreement. Some of them have already sensed that M. Jourdain's responses or comments during his lesson were comical because of their automatic, mechanical nature.

The second exception is a question that asks students to think about the difference between a *bourgeois* and a *gentilhomme.* In twentieth-century America, a member of the middle class may also be a gentleman. In late-seventeenth-century France, however, the two were mutually exclusive (Gaines 135–36). So could the bourgeois M. Jourdain become a gentleman? The students begin to understand the serious moral behind the play's sometimes farcical comedy: one should not aspire to upward social mobility in the society of Louis XIV.

During this class session, students listen to, speak, read, and write French as they unravel the excerpt. Twelve days later, they receive the two topics for their third composition of the quarter. Both appear in French on the assignment sheet. One is related to *Le bourgeois gentilhomme:*

The title *The Bourgeois Gentleman* is a contradiction: a "bourgeois" is a person who is not noble, and a "gentleman" is a man who is. When M. Jourdain, a bourgeois, aspires to be noble, he aspires to be what he is not.

There are also M. Jourdains today. They are called the "new rich" or "self-made" men and women. You probably know some. Identify a "self-made" man or woman of today. How does this person resemble M. Jourdain? In developing your thesis, consider the scene in which M. Jourdain has a lesson with the philosophy teacher. Why is it comical?

The students have approximately seven days in which to complete the composition; in the first two, they write a first draft in French. In individual compositions as in classroom discussion, the initial focus is on generating information. Then the writer moves on to a consideration of coherence and style. Only after writing the first draft should students begin to correct grammar. When pairs of classmates who have chosen the same topic exchange their first drafts, they have two days to provide comments designed to help each other improve the final draft. After receiving written peer comments, students spend two or three days on revision. When they submit the final version of this composition to the teacher for a grade, students have spent a significant amount of time reading and writing about *Le bourgeois gentilhomme*.

Second-year French students come into contact with the play a final time nineteen days after they have discussed the excerpt in class. A response related to it is an option in one section of an examination that they write in French. For the first time, students are asked to provide information about reading selections based on their own memory. It may be difficult for second-year students to remember the main ideas of all the texts they have studied. Therefore, they are not required to write about a particular text but may choose one from a number of options.

Study of this excerpt of *Le bourgeois gentilhomme* has been organized according to an approach that is normally associated with grammar study. The "spiral approach" to teaching grammar involves "several introductions and treatments of a given structure, first for concept control, second for receptive control, and finally for partial and then full productive control" (Liskin-Gasparro and Phillips 63). The spiral approach to teaching the scene from *Le bourgeois gentilhomme* involves several contacts with the excerpt over a twenty-day period, first for general comprehension, then for increasingly detailed analysis and evaluation. The goal is to help students become more proficient at understanding, discussing, and writing about literature in French. As students work with the scene, they focus on such functions (tasks) as defining, asking and answering questions, and explaining; they attend to the notion (content category) of a lesson covering part of a seventeenth-century play. They study realistic adult communication (Omaggio 213).

Some students study *Le bourgeois gentilhomme* again in French Baroque and Classical Theatre. Just before the midpoint of the academic quarter, they devote one hour to a prereading activity. They then read the play and spend the entire two hours of the next session discussing it. During the following session, they view and discuss the Jean Meyer film version. In general, students in this course are enrolled in a major or minor program in French and have already completed at least two third-year French courses. In these courses and in English classes, they have studied literature representing a variety of genres. Therefore, the goals of studying *Le bourgeois gentilhomme* in this advanced course are more sophisticated: understanding the play in its entirety; analyzing M. Jourdain; and evaluating the social and philosophical significance of the play. Students begin at the comprehension level in the hierarchy of Bloom's taxonomy of the cognitive domain, but they also perform tasks at the highest level of that domain, evaluation.

The prereading activity is based on the cognitive-process sheet that students complete when they read act 2, scene 4 of the play at the intermediate level. At this more advanced level, students spend fifteen minutes completing and discussing the "Initial Contact" section. Then they spend thirty minutes completing and discussing parts A through C of the "Detailed Study" section. Finally, they watch a film version of the scene to rediscover the importance of costume, gesture, facial expression, and voice as a source of comedy. Before the next class, they read the entire play, write a summary of it, and respond to two questions: "Quels détails dans la pièce sont comiques? Pourquoi?" ("Which details in the play are comical? Why?").

Their responses to the questions are the basis of the tenth class session. Students find two major sources of comedy: M. Jourdain's words and actions as he strives to become a *gentilhomme*; the words and actions of others who profit from his desire to become a *gentilhomme*. They find M. Jourdain's words and actions mechanical. So obsessed with becoming a nobleman is he that when he speaks to the other characters, he automatically turns the conversation to the nobility. The repetition of vocabulary items reinforces his preoccupation: "les gens de qualité" ("people of quality"); "(les) personne(s) de (votre) qualité" ("people of your rank"); "gentilhomme," "(les grands) seigneur(s)" ("lords"); "galant homme" ("man of honor"); "un homme de cette condition-là" ("a man of that status"); "marquis(e)"; "duchesse"; "comte"; "le fils du Grand Turc" ("the Great Turk's son").

To convince M. Jourdain to do what they want, characters need only attribute to him a quality or a title that the would-be gentleman associates with the nobility. When the tailor addresses him as "mon gentilhomme" and "monseigneur" (2.5), he uses two of his client's favorite words. When he adds "Votre Grandeur" ("Your Highness"), M. Jourdain is enraptured. The cumulative effect is to distract M. Jourdain completely from the upside-down floral print the tailor has used to make the bourgeois's new outfit. And to borrow two hundred pistoles for an unspecified purpose, the leech Dorante need only say, "[J]e parlais de vous encore ce matin dans la chambre du roi" (3.4) ("I was talking about you again this morning in the king's bedroom"). Finally, the bourgeois Cléonte and his valet profit from M. Jourdain's obsession. Early in their first conversation, the disguised Covielle refers to M. Jourdain's father as "feu Monsieur" ("the late gentleman") and "un fort honnête gentilhomme" (4.3) ("a very well bred gentleman"). The first half of the scene is taken up with this flattery of M. Jourdain's ancestors. The second is taken up with Covielle's flattery of M. Jourdain and his family. The "Grand Turc" wants to marry Lucile Jourdain and to make M. Jourdain "Mamamouchi" ("knight"); in so doing, he will ennoble both Lucile and M. Jourdain. The bourgeois has insisted on marrying his daughter to a nobleman and making her noble. His daughter's marrying the "Grand Turc" would accomplish this goal. In actuality, he is marrying her to a bourgeois.

Students decide that when the play ends, nothing in the social realm is different. No one's class has changed. Although M. Jourdain thinks that he has become a nobleman, he has not. A "Mamamouchi" and a "Grand Turc" exist only in his own mind. No one will marry a member of a social class that differs from his or her own. The marquise will marry the noble Dorante. M. Jourdain will remain a bourgeois married to another bourgeois. His daughter will marry a bourgeois. The two servants, Nicole and Covielle, will marry each other. This stasis reflects the values of late-seventeenth-century French society. A bourgeois is not and cannot become noble. Clearly, M. Jourdain is wealthy. Nonetheless, he is not noble:

> Only the superficial aspects of nobility are of concern to Monsieur Jourdain, for he cannot grasp that being and seeming are not the same thing. Naively he assumes that others are also unable to distinguish between counterfeit facades and essential traits.   (Gaines 157)

His mistake is believing that by changing his appearance he will become a gentleman. But this is simply not possible.

Philosophically, this social immobility is exemplary of man's place in the universe as expressed by Blaise Pascal: "Once that is clearly understood, I think that each of us can stay quietly in the state in which nature has placed him" (*Pensées*, no. 199). Man is neither the greatest nor the smallest unit in creation; nature has placed him somewhere in between. Powerless to change his intermediate position, he must remain there. M. Jourdain is a member of neither the greatest nor the least important social class in seventeenth-century France. Nature has placed him in the middle class, the bourgeoisie. Although he is assured as a result of his birth that he will not fall to the servant class, it is also certain that the nature of his birth will not allow him to ascend to the rank of nobility. He must remain where he is.

During the fourteenth class session, students take an hour-long written examination on three Molière plays: *L'impromptu de Versailles*, *Le bourgeois gentilhomme*, and *Tartuffe*. In the first section, they must write a summary of either *Le bourgeois gentilhomme* or *Tartuffe*. In the short-answer section, three of the ten questions are about *Le bourgeois gentilhomme*. In the essay section, students select one of three topics about which to write. One possibility: "Taking into account the text, explain why *The Bourgeois Gentleman* is the perfect title of one of Molière's plays."

Students' final contact with that play may be the examination. Or it may be the term paper that they write by the end of the academic quarter. They must select one of five suggested topics; all appear in French on the assignment sheet. Two are directly related to *Le bourgeois gentilhomme*:

1. In his analysis of *School for Wives*, G. Sablayrolles wrote of Molière: "Molière struggles against a rigorous ascetic morality. His sympathy for youth, his faith in life are evident in that play. He also favors the education of girls." Consider *The Bourgeois Gentleman* and *Tartuffe*. How do these two plays show Molière's sympathy for youth and his fight against a too rigorous ascetic morality?
2. The title *The Bourgeois Gentleman* is an antithesis: a "bourgeois" is, by definition, not noble, not a "gentleman." So when M. Jourdain, a bourgeois, aspires to be noble, he aspires to be something that he cannot be. How are his actions and his thoughts comical? That is, what are the sources of comedy in this play?

A rough draft of the term paper is due at the beginning of the twentieth class session. During the second hour of class, pairs of students who have chosen the same topic exchange their drafts and read and write comments about each other's work. At the end of class, they take their reviewed papers home. The final draft is due one week later, at the beginning of the twenty-second class session.

As at the intermediate level, the approach to teaching *Le bourgeois gentilhomme* here is the spiral approach. A student who selects a term paper topic related to the play begins studying *Le bourgeois gentilhomme* during the ninth class session and repeatedly returns to it until the twenty-second class. Students who do not select a term paper topic related to this play still need to return to it over five class sessions as they become acquainted with it, study it in detail, and then prepare to complete the written examination. In fact, this approach to teaching *Le bourgeois gentilhomme* extends back in time much farther than the ninth class session of French Baroque and Classical Theatre. Students actually reach back two years in their memory to recall their introduction to the comical M. Jourdain. This time, however, they become acquainted with him on a more profound level.

Visions of Nobility and Gallantry:
Understanding the Jourdains Historically

Orest Ranum

Is it socially acceptable or fair, teachers might ask their students, to ridicule a person, to laugh at what he says and at his lack of social grace, to make fun of his clothes? To us the ridicule that Molière constructed in the character of M. Jourdain seems cruel and unacceptable. If the great playwright had some sense of humanity, we might say, he would not have created a character to be laughed at to a degree so painful for the audience. Should we not, as students of the play, identify with M. Jourdain, to support him against his tormenters? All he wants, after all, is to improve himself, to catch up after the poor education of his youth, to gain social acceptance.

A knowledge of seventeenth-century French social and cultural history impedes us from being outraged by the ridicule meted out to M. Jourdain. Knowledge of history? Does history make ridiculing someone who is gauche more acceptable? On the contrary, the history of the social identities that Molière portrays and the histories of courtly culture and of marriage and gender relations enable us to discern that M. Jourdain's true attackers are not the people who make fun of him but the ones who flatter him. Also, the truly dishonest individuals who violate the behavior that society expects from people of their rank are, from a historical perspective, submitted to an opprobrium that makes the ridicule M. Jourdain suffers seem quite gentle.

Molière's comedies were written as ethical inquiry and social instruction about what the good life ought to be as it occurs among persons of different social ranks. The plays were also written, of course, to please and entertain both at court and in Paris. First presented in 1670, when Louis XIV and his court were residing at Chambord, the great Renaissance château of the Loire Valley, *Le bourgeois gentilhomme* examines the role of education in society and clearly delineates what ethical, or *honnête,* behavior ought to be.

The first issue explored is what we now refer to as the nature-versus-nurture question. Molière comes down clearly on the nurture or environmental side of the equation while remaining silent about the nature claims being made by nobles. M. Jourdain's talk about persons of *qualité* is obsessive; it refers to the widely held belief of the ancien régime that persons of noble birth were naturally superior to commoners. The word *quality,* as M. Jourdain uses it, has Aristotelian scientific connotations: in his day, persons with aristocratic blood had inherited superior qualities of courage, virtue, and honesty. The second estate, known as the *noblesse,* possessed social and political superiority as a birthright. According to this definition, M. Jourdain was not and never could be a person of quality.

The French monarchy had, for centuries, been granting nobility and the tax exemptions that went with it, but the noblemen newly created by such favors were not really accepted socially as part of the second estate. They were not *gentilshommes*, the rank accorded to nobles who were born noble. The commoner who bought his title from the king was not considered a "gentleman," but his sons and daughters would be accepted as true *gentilshommes* or *gentesdames*. The saying was "The king can make a nobleman; a *gentilhomme* is born."

M. Jourdain, a city dweller and property owner, enjoyed the privileges of bourgeois rank, the rank typically held by a cloth-merchant family like the one into which he was born. Being bourgeois was dignifying—and made one socially superior to thousands of more common city dwellers and millions of peasants—but it certainly was inferior to the status of a noble and a *gentilhomme*. Members of the bourgeoisie held municipal judicial and administrative offices reserved for persons of their rank and provided the city's general defense and police protection through militia service.

Throughout the sixteenth and seventeenth centuries, all ranks were becoming more and more specifically defined in royal legislation. Partly as a result of the courts' need for more precise definitions and partly as a result of the king's insatiable need for the revenue obtained from the fees charged for verifying noble titles, the hierarchical social orders of Molière's day were undergoing drastic changes as a result of civil strife and expensive foreign wars.

M. Jourdain's social crime is that he wishes to leap over the rank of mere noble and be accepted as a *gentilhomme*—if not by law, at least in his lifestyle and through his daughter's marriage. His plans for the love affair he is pursuing with Dorimène, a marquise, also constitute a dangerous leap of ranks. It is not social ambition as such that Molière condemns in the play but *exaggerated* social ambition.

Why does M. Jourdain want to make the leap? The answer is explicit throughout the play: others are doing it, and their rank is no higher than his. His vice—perceived then as a vice that was spreading throughout society—is his not explicitly stated but nonetheless evident belief that everything pertaining to social superiority can be bought, especially through improved education and influence at the royal court. M. Jourdain is rich and bourgeois, yet his belief in the omnipotence of money is shared by members of other classes. Because of social change in the seventeenth century, not just the bourgeoisie but the whole of society was very conscious of the power of money, and this power was frequently perceived as corrupting. Is M. Jourdain fundamentally right about his society? Can virtually every honor be bought? The new "friends" he has made and the teachers he has hired—and who dirty his house—all indicate by their flattery that outward social acceptance as a *gentilhomme* can be purchased. What pressures in society had created this challenge to the privileges reserved for persons of noble birth?

From the 1620s on, the military effort to repress Huguenot military power in the southern provinces and, later, to defeat Spanish imperial power drained the royal treasury of desperately needed funds to pay the troops. In the wars of the seventeenth century, victory or defeat depended on the availability of money. The investors who collected the excise taxes for the king and who lent him money—investors known as *partisans*—made enormous profits as a result of the royal treasury's desperate need for cash. The *partisans'* new wealth was not stowed away in the form of bonds or coins hidden in socks under the bedding. Instead, these men became passionate consumers of fine clothing, elegant new homes, jewelry, and works of art. The social rank of the *partisans* remained vague. None had the quality of birth required to be a *gentilhomme*, but their new wealth often enabled them to outspend *gentilshommes* on finery to wear at court, on receptions, and on the construction of prestigious residences. This disparity between the *gentilhomme* with little ready cash yet a claim to social superiority based on birth (and on military service) and the richly dressed *partisan* whose coffers overflowed with cash forms the social backdrop for understanding M. Jourdain's relations with Dorante, a *count*—a title that certainly indicates *gentilhomme* rank. The 15,800 *livres* that M. Jourdain has had the "honor" of lending Dorante represents the harsh social disparity between men of different ranks and qualities in an overtly and explicitly defined hierarchical society.

These disparities were articulated by education and consumer display. Without the courtly education movement, M. Jourdain and Dorante would simply have been a lender and a borrower. The philosophical background of the play began with the writings of the great Dutch and Italian humanists Erasmus and Castiglione. Dorante has obtained this courtly education (but perverts it); M. Jourdain seeks it.

The courtly education movement defined and redefined *honnête* conduct—that is, what the truly good person should be if he is to secure well-being, social acceptance, and political service. Broadly defined as a cultural movement that produced courtly or highly mannered persons, how-to textbooks about the education of adolescents had an enormous influence on European culture and social relations in the ancien régime. Ever commented upon, adapted, translated, readapted, and taught in schools as well as memorized at home, books on courtly manners had an influence that can scarcely be overestimated. These courtesy books provide the expertise for the various pedagogues engaged by M. Jourdain to teach him courtly manners. Ridicule and its coercive companion, snobbery, were (are) the principal instruments for inculcating courtly education.

Molière's plays are an adaptation and extension of this courtly literature. Many of Erasmus's and Castiglione's principles are obliquely incarnated in Molière's characters, who are updated and "Frenchified" without losing their universal ethical significance. As a result of the courtly education movement, the uneducated *gentilhomme* came to be recognized for what he was: a boor.

Similarly, the bourgeois with a courtly education, brought up to understand the principles of *honnête* conduct and to have good manners, could enjoy a certain acceptance in elite and courtly social circles.

Displaying sophisticated manners, acknowledging each person with the greeting (*révérence*) appropriate to his or her rank, dancing, fencing, writing poetry, playing the lute, wearing proper clothes, and conversing urbanely became the marks of the upright person. For Erasmus (who was the illegitimate son of a priest) and Castiglione, proper birth—that is, having noble ancestors—was an enhancement for the young person who wished to be accepted as *honnête*, but birth alone did not suffice, and its lack could not be overcome. Indeed, the word *honnête* also conveyed something of our word *honest*—that is, speaking truthfully and avoiding duplicity, theft, and other vices.

Dorante trades on his courtly education, just as he trades on having been born a *gentilhomme*: he violates fundamental ethical principles. His "friend-ship" with M. Jourdain is completely false, his expressions of respect are insincere, and his allusion to mentioning M. Jourdain in the king's chamber is tricky. He lets the uninformed infer that he has spoken to the king himself, but . . . his *malhonnête* conduct is exemplary when he talks of paying his debt to M. Jourdain. And, in his vague talk about "giving his word," Dorante completely betrays the principal tenets of what it was to be a *gentilhomme*. A promise kept, the *parole d'honneur*, was a matter of life and death for the upright *gentilhomme*. By allowing the audience to learn of Dorante's unethical conduct, Molière builds a hierarchy of values that makes M. Jourdain's ridiculous conduct far less scandalous than Dorante's. Strong doses of ridicule are certainly milder than outright opprobrium, and Molière trusts his audience always to draw the right conclusion.

The conduct of the music, dancing, and fencing masters, of the philosopher and the tailor, is not unlike Dorante's, for none lives up to the lofty ethical ideals of his education or profession. Some are more debased than others, but here the hierarchy of debasement follows an ethical program rather than a social one. Each cheats in his own way.

What did Molière think about the effects of money on social relations? As a moralist, he developed a far greater critical distance from the historically grounded personalities that he created than did any of his contemporaries. When he created society in a microcosm through constructing the relations among a handful of characters, Molière knew that the members of his audience could see themselves partially incarnated in not just one but all the characters in the play. No one was *honnête* by birth or by wealth, nor even by education.

As the great social equalizer, money continued to do its nefarious work. Always hard on philosophers who tried to discern truth by scholastic methods, Molière saw money as an integral part of social affairs and, as such, like language, no more and no less good or evil than other things. The play-wright is harsh on older males—in this case M. Jourdain and Dorante—be-cause they try to be something they cannot be and trade on appearances for

personal gain. The culture of appearances, an integral part of courtly education, contained within it the danger of illusion, like money. The power of
money, Molière may be saying, becomes more and more evident as persons
age. Dorante's conduct is a complete violation of every ethical principle
inculcated by a courtly education. He borrows money to buy gifts for
Dorimène and fine clothes for courting her. He lets M. Jourdain believe that
he is favoring his, Jourdain's, intentions of love for Dorimène. Molière's plays
are filled with genuinely sinister, morally reprehensible older males, and
Dorante is one of them. Still, it is not money itself that perverts the relations
between Dorante and M. Jourdain; it is failure to adhere to the principles of
courtly education.

The four great variables—young and old, male and female—intersect with
social rank and courtly ethical ideals to create in *Le bourgeois gentilhomme* a
society in microcosm. The courtly educational ideal rested on principles of
improvement, concentration, and learning from the experience of others,
which is what Molière's plays showed historically—and they still do. Castiglione
had distinguished between those persons who had grace and *sprezzatura* for
being upright, and it is evident that M. Jourdain has some of these skills, to a
limited degree. He knows that, in his own house, he should keep his hat on
before Dorante, and he knows how to compose a note expressing his love, but
these were rudimentary social graces. The courtly ideal rested on loftier ones:
internalized values, subtle conversation—saying things by not saying them—
nonchalance, poise, and obliqueness. M. Jourdain clearly does not possess
these skills and therefore cannot pervert them. Dorante possesses them and
uses them to dupe and condescend.

The persons who not only incarnate courtly ideals but seek to live by them
are Cléonte, the well-brought-up commoner who seeks Lucille's hand in
marriage, and Dorimène, the widowed marquise. Cléonte offers a nearly
perfect example of the young courtly male in love, but by complaining about
the lack of a *récompense* from his beloved, he too teaches the audience that
there is more to be learned if one is to be a perfect gentleman. This word
reduces the idealized love relation to a mere exchange, almost to money!
Cléonte might well expect something (a kerchief or a comb) from his beloved
in return for his affection, but he ought to have called this a *faveur*. In this play,
no one speaks courtly language in a completely ethical manner.

Dorimène almost incarnates the ideal. She seems unaware of what is going
on; her innocence is founded on ignorance. She does, however, admit to
aroused feelings as a result of the gifts she has received from Dorante. As a
widow she has greater freedom of action than Cléonte and Lucille. Her
honnêteté lies in her self-knowledge. She justifies taking Dorante as a husband
by claiming that, by this act, she can save him from financial ruin. Is Molière
suggesting, through Dorimène, that as they age women, too, become increasingly preoccupied with financial matters, rather than with matters of the heart?
It was not Dorante's expression of love but his gifts that aroused her feelings.

Molière tracks down noncourtly words and their relations to the passions, to make his plays part of this courtly educational program, not simply an account of it. And money can stabilize or destabilize relations.

By depicting all the good and less good features of human experience, Molière avoids the tendency of many moralists of his day, which was to create portraits of idealized, faultless persons. Through incorporating the less good and the good in individual characters, the playwright continued the great work of Erasmus, who believed that through reason all humans, regardless of their social rank, could clearly discern good from evil. By contrast, were not the eloquent fathers of the Jesuit order presenting idealized, completely ethical characters in their educational treatises? They carefully edited the works of the great writers so that readers would learn nothing scandalous. They saw human reason as untrustworthy and only minimally capable of judging right from wrong. In like manner, writers of history in the 1660s and 1670s tended to portray French kings as paragons of virtue and France itself as faultless.

By placing the characters he has imbued with deeply unethical features (Dorante, Orgon, Dom Juan, Alceste) in societies where individuals are *honnête* to varying degrees, Molière takes the position that society itself is upright and that, in one way or another, it generally has the power to bring the wayward into line. In some instances, if evil is too great, only the king or God can bring down the evil one, but this was not the case in *Le bourgeois gentilhomme*. We know that Dorimène will be able to keep Dorante on a short leash for the rest of his life. And that M. Jourdain will find himself back on his leash—which, for Molière, was what marriage as an institution was all about.

Teaching *Fête: Le malade imaginaire*

Claude Abraham

Legends die hard. There are two traditions in French literary history that, despite all the evidence and common sense to the contrary, persist. One insists on making of Molière a practitioner of "pure" comedy, uncontaminated by any nonliterary art. The other, more specific but no less silly, defies all medical facts by claiming that in his last years Molière was moribund, knew it, and made that knowledge a part—indeed an overriding theme—of his last plays. Molière repeatedly declared that he was interested in bringing music, dance, and other arts into his work; his contemporaries testified consistently to his love for and knowledge of music—some even suggested that he wanted the post of director of the Académie Royale de Musique et de Danse when it was first founded— but these oft-repeated testaments to Molière's interests and moods have never bothered critics and teachers whose minds are set in intellectual concrete: the stuff legends are made of, it would seem. And so they persist. I would nevertheless like to try, once more, to show that Molière, in his last year, was anything but a "moribond morose" and that his last play is a masterpiece of fantasy and mirth rather than a manifestation of the author's neurotic pre-occupation with his own impending death.

In 1908 Eugène Rigal called *Le malade imaginaire* a "défi jeté par Molière moribond à la médecine et à la mort" (2: 284) ("a challenge cast by the dying Molière against medicine and death"). Nearly eighty years later, Ralph Albanese still speaks of this "créateur moribond [qui] entreprend une gageure consistant à jouer la fausse maladie" (*"Le malade"* 3) ("dying creator who takes up the challenge of staging an imaginary illness") and who only manages to die offstage. Molière knew himself to be *pulmonique*, but many of his contemporaries were similarly afflicted, and many of them lived to a ripe old age, coughing and spitting but living just the same, and nothing written by Molière or anyone else suggests that Molière was overly worried about this illness. Nor does *Le malade* focus on this. Argan is a monomaniac, but the fear of death is not the focus; rather, his credulity in matters medical makes him prey to those who would instill such a fear in him. Many of Molière's adversaries thought him to be a hypochondriac. In 1670 Le Boulanger de Chalussay had portrayed him as such in his *Elomire hypocondre*. It is entirely possible that Molière accepted the label, but even such acknowledgment would not prove that it made him write an autobiographical play in which he foresaw his own death. The irony of his saying things such as "crève" ("croak") onstage and then suffering that fate is an irony perceptible only a posteriori. Rather than credit him with such improbable clairvoyance and thus see the play as concerning illness and death, we should recognize its primary subject as a man so in love with his body that any fear—including that of death—can so readily be implanted in him. Our response leads to laughter, not at death, but at his truly extravagant fear of it.

If one looks at the literary text—and only at that text—one may view this play as dealing with doctors and illness. But that is an unjustified reduction of the work. The staging of Molière's last comedy is so complex that its author reserved over ten weeks for rehearsals before the opening, an unusually long period in those days. The complexity of the staging and its lavishness were a constant source of worry (see La Grange's frequent references to the unusual expenses; e.g., 1: 144). Taken as a total spectacle rather than a bare literary text, *Le malade imaginaire* is readily seen not as a somber play about illness and death—or about the merchants of death, the doctors—but as a genuinely comic play about a monomaniac so wrapped up in himself that he is oblivious to all else, to everyone else. Argan's despotism, like his credulity, is a product of his monomania. M. Jourdain, by the very definition of his mania, needs society, *autrui*. A hypochondriac's concern is not these "others" but only his own physical self. Such self-centeredness is ideally served in a situation as absurd as it is elementarily logical: reliance on oneself not to cure—God forbid! —but forever to diagnose and medicate oneself. Such a solution needs a special atmosphere and a special world, which one may observe to be gradually established as the play progresses—but only when one considers the play as Molière originally intended it to be performed, as he created it with the help of Marc-Antoine Charpentier and Charles-Louis Beauchamp. It is the establishment of this other world, this other reality, this *fête*, that I examine.

First, there is a problem with the text that most students—and scholars—have on hand. Today's editions, including the so-called critical ones, follow the 1682 version, which has been shown by several critics (Powell and Hitchcock; Powell; Abraham) to be an impossible amalgam of earlier versions and a far cry from what Molière had authored. Only the "livret" edited by Powell and Hitchcock gives us a reliable basis for the study of this carnivalesque invitation to hilarity. All other texts can only mislead and perpetuate the misconceptions that have plagued the study and performance of *Le malade imaginaire*. It is this text, and only this text, cleansed of all the alterations perpetrated by self-styled lovers of Molière from Jean-Léonor Grimarest to modern-day editors, that allows us to see how Toinette leads Argan from his morose and anguished state to one of a euphoria in which everyone can join and find happiness. It is Toinette, not the "reasonable" Béralde (what is reasonable about reasoning with a madman?) who creates this *fête*, who allows this new reality to displace the old one, and only the text written by Molière and now restored to us in its purity will allow us to see that.

This authenticity is particularly important when we consider the prologue(s) and the *intermèdes*, which have suffered the most over the years. The two extant prologues raise many questions of interest only to the historian of theater or the biographer of Molière (Abraham, *"Le malade"* 86), but two considerations are capital. It is evident that Molière's heirs dropped the first prologue because of the costs it entailed and because it no longer seemed very useful. It is no less evident that the "other prologue," also composed by Charpentier—and whose words may already have been penned by Molière— maintained the integrity of the spectacle: it is not the brief ditty as may be suggested by the "literary" part of it but was "conceived in the rather formal style appropriate to [court festivities], with many repetitions and instrumental interludes [featured also in the *intermèdes*]" (Barnwell 12–13). These repetitions and interludes are what give this prologue its length and scope, just as the musical and balletic parts give this seemingly short three-act play a length sufficient to supply an evening's entertainment.

After this lavish and happy introduction, we are introduced to the dark and dreary interior of Argan's house. This contrast in moods is a jolt but, as we shall see, a deliberate one. The first *intermède* itself presents two seemingly unreconcilable moods, of which the more festive prevails. After a rapid *fantaisie*; a somewhat slower serenade; the problematic "Nott'e di" ("night and day"); followed in turn by "Zerbinetti," the witty and acid rejoinder of the old woman, with the music faithfully echoing the bite of the words; and the repetition of the "Air des archers" ("watchmen's song"), the *intermède* ends in a truly carnivalesque vein. There can be no doubt that Charpentier fully understood the play in which he had been asked to collaborate, since the music of these *intermèdes* carefully prepares the spectators for the dramatic expositions that follow. Thus do the strings in the second *intermède* sing a lively tune against a staid and pompous continuo, the initial 2/2 beat changing to an even jollier 3/4 beat, the musical conflict a clear foreshadowing of the dramatic one about to unfold in the following act. By the same token, the overture of the third *intermède* is a madcap one, perfect herald of the "cérémonie burlesque" that will end the performance.

The unfortunate metamorphoses imposed on some of these *intermèdes*— particularly the first one—have been amply studied by John Powell, H. W. Hitchcock, and me, and there is no need to go back over that ground. What matters here is that the reconstituted first *intermède*, in a stylized, balletic way, gives us in a nutshell the argument of the following act. Despite all the changes that Charpentier brought to the structure of that *intermède*, its function and tone were to remain constant until modern scholars decided to butcher it—when they did not eliminate it altogether.

These *intermèdes*, it should be added, are among the most burlesque in all of Molière's work. This tendency perforce weakens the unity of tone many critics would like to see in a work of art. As one editor of this play notes,

> [O]n voit le danger: celui de manquer d'homogénéité. *Le Malade imaginaire* est-il une farce où l'on trouve des scènes 'dignes de la haute comédie' (selon Voltaire), ou une excellente comédie de caractère où l'on trouve "quelques scènes qui se rapprochent de la farce" (selon Geoffroy)? . . . La psychologie la plus vraie côtoie la fantaisie la plus débridée. Cela peut gêner. Cela a beaucoup gêné surtout ceux qui ont négligé l'effort de synthèse pour ne considérer, par analyse, que les éléments constitutifs de la comédie.   (Bory 206–07)

> One sees the danger of a lack of homogeneity. Is *Le malade imaginaire* a farce where one encounters scenes "worthy of high comedy" (according to Voltaire) or an excellent character comedy featuring "some scenes that approach farce" (according to Geoffroy)? . . . The most realistic psychology lies side by side with the wildest fantasy. It can be disconcerting. It has especially bothered those who have attempted no synthesis, concentrating only on the internal elements of the comedy for their analysis.

This is true of the three acts, of the three *intermèdes*, and particularly of the entire play, in which way we may witness not a haphazard juxtaposition of disparate elements and tones but a deliberate progression, a supplanting of one by the other.

It is precisely because I see this progression, and the profound structural unity that results from it, that I cannot agree with Pierre Mélèse's categorical condemnation of the structure of *Le malade*: "Sauf la fameuse 'Cérémonie', les intermèdes sont moins des agréments qu'une surcharge. *Le malade imaginaire* n'est plus une comédie-ballet; c'est une comédie, et ce sont des ballets" (64) ("Apart from the famous Ceremony, the *intermèdes* are more of a burden than an embellishment. *Le malade imaginaire* is no longer *comédie-ballet*; the comedy is a comedy, and the ballets are ballets"). If one looks simply at the component parts of the play, as Jean-Louis Bory accused many of doing, then that is indeed the inevitable finding. Even if one goes a step further and looks (only) at the words of the acts preparing the ballets or the words of the ballet referring to the dialogues, then the relations among the various parts remain tenuous. For the first *intermède*, for instance, we have been told that

Polichinelle will be of use in the plot to save Angélique from her father's terrible plan to marry her off for his own sake. Nevertheless, there is a definite change at the end of act 1: "Le théâtre change et représente une ville." Polichinelle, announced by Toinette as her lover at the end of the first act, does indeed come to serenade but is prevented from doing so and eventually leaves without having done so. Consequently the next act begins, again in Argan's room—that is, in the "real world"—with the plot advanced no further than it had been before the interruption. Much the same can be said of the second *intermède*, whose participants are brought by Béralde to "disposer [le] chagrin" ("dispel the chagrin") of his brother, and it amuses us as well as Argan, but if one's concern is limited to the plot, the contribution of these intruders is, like that of their predecessors, tenuous at best. In this light, only the last *intermède*, the famous ceremony, is well integrated and absolutely essential to the advancement of the plot and the outcome of the play.

But why should the play be reduced to such a low denominator? Louis Auld says it well, and it is a pity that he has not been heard or heeded by all:

> "Structurally, . . . one can perceive in the interludes of that work a certain progression, which perhaps explains their character. Beginning with a typically pastoral prologue, completely opposed and unrelated to the bourgeois setting in which Argan appears, the author progressively brings the two opposites together, the first interlude being still very unlike the world of Argan, but announced in the text as existing somewhere outside the house; the second act brings into the house characters as absurd as a *commedia dell'arte* Polichinelle (Diafoirus); the following interlude is presented as entertainment in the house (in which dancers are not what they are: "Egyptiens déguisés en Mores," (gypsies disguised as Moors); the third act brings Argan into direct contact with a character quite as farcical as either the Polichinelle or the Diafoirus family; and the final mock ceremony shows him in just such a role himself. The two opposites finally dovetail as fantasy comes into the lives of ordinary people.   (226–27)

I would quarrel only with the final sentence, in that it does not go far enough: it is not fantasy that comes into the lives of ordinary people but people who leave everyday reality to escape into fantasy, into another, more bearable "reality."

This is very much what happens in *Le bourgeois gentilhomme*, where that movement is made even more manifest by M. Jourdain's invitation to all to come see his ballet, but an important distinction must be made between that play and *Le malade imaginaire*. In *Le bourgeois gentilhomme* we are in the presence of a "courtly" ballet, and the unity of that play and its central theme are enhanced in and by "balletic" scenes even where there had been no music. In both plays we can speak of a progression toward *fête*, toward carnival, but now these words take on another meaning or, at the very least, carry the meaning to another level, removed further than ever from theatrical norms. In *Le malade imaginaire*, the *intermèdes* prepare us for the final ballet in a process not unlike that of *Le bourgeois gentilhomme*, but the effect is quite different. Slapstick gradually invades the stage during the three acts and during the *intermèdes*—and, with it, burlesque. This development may surprise. After all, if Louis XIV included ballet as an art to be codified in and taught by the Royal Academy of Music, it was because he saw that it was one of the arts useful in the glorification of the state and its royal incarnation. Apparently, slapstick is the very antithesis of ballet, since it is violently boisterous horseplay detrimental to flow and decorum. And yet these two elements, ballet and slapstick, are precisely what Molière amalgamates so felicitously in these plays, producing a comic tension that yields some of the funniest scenes in all of his theater, and it is this amalgamation that makes the balletic representation so effective (for a full discussion of this process, see Abraham, "Farce" 172–78). By the time the final curtain falls on Molière's last play, we have witnessed the establishment of a truly madcap world. But there is no need to be surprised, for that is the ending made inevitable and predictable by many preparatory scenes. At the verbal level, we have witnessed Toinette's interruptions of her master (1.2) and also heard Argan and Diafoirus talking simultaneously, thus creating mayhem (2.6; for a fuller discussion, see Abraham, "Comedy"); slapstick elements abound, increasing in tempo and physicality, ranging from Louison's faked death, Argan's chasing Toinette, and her stuffing a pillow over his head, to the openly scatological scene in which Toinette makes the most of her master's fecal problems. In short, the carnivalesque atmosphere is the result of an evolutionary process. It grows as the play goes on, and in the last act, with Toinette masquerading as a doctor, the progression becomes extremely logical both in content and in form. The question is not, as it had been in *Le bourgeois gentilhomme*, whether there are "balletic" scenes within the acts but whether the ascension toward mayhem colors the structure as well as the characters and the plot, and the answer is a resounding yes.

In that sense the progression toward the culminating scene, the inauguration of Argan into the medical order, is extremely logical, perhaps even more so than its counterpart in *Le bourgeois gentilhomme*. In that play, when the Turkish scene is over, the play is ready for a resolution, a denouement. Here, when the indoctrination is over, everything is already resolved. The play was intended for carnival time, and there is a madness to celebrate, a joyful, beneficial madness. *Monsieur de Pourceaugnac* sings the praise of such a madness. *Le malade imaginaire*, with every word, with every gesture, and with every step, choreographed or not, celebrates it and invites us to join in that celebration.

The Paris theater public has been treated to some superb modern re-creations of *Le malade*—interestingly enough, thanks to the efforts of "outsiders" such as H. Wiley Hitchcock, John S. Powell, and William Christie. But not every French theatergoer reacted with joy to the efforts of these invaders from *"Outre-Manche"* ("Beyond the Channel") or *"Outre-Atlantique."* While Jacques Lonchampt welcomed the *"fastueux spectacle"* ("sumptuous spectacle") that re-created the play as Molière and Charpentier had intended it, deploring only the inability of the actors to live up to the high standards set by their musical counterparts ("Ah! le grand médecin"), Pierre Marcabru felt that the words and the music were like oil and water, destined never to fuse ("Une somptueuse contradiction"), and Pierre-Petit, steadfastly attached to Molière's text, only bemoans having to sit through all that music ("Ajouter au *Malade imaginaire* environ deux heures d'une musique somme toute assez uniforme" ["Adding to *Le malade imaginaire* about two hours of music that is, all things considered, rather uniform"] to enjoy Molière's language, forgetting entirely that this was precisely the music that Molière wanted and in whose creation he had even collaborated, to ensure that his language would not be misconstrued. Legends die hard, but this is one we should try to kill before it does any more harm.

Authentic Costuming for
Tartuffe and *Le misanthrope*

Stephen V. Dock

As Molière's comedies become available to North American audiences in an increasing range of film, video, and television versions, as well as stage versions, it is more essential than ever to take into account visual approaches to the plays. The physical appearance of a character stirs the imagination and sways the audience's sympathy before, during, and after his verbal performance. Yet this situation is hardly new, for the original seventeenth-century Parisian audiences came to the theater as much to feast their eyes on the marvels of costuming as to entertain their ears with well-turned couplets. The economics behind opulent costuming is deeply intertwined with the history of princely patronage and court entertainments; Louis XIV sometimes took a personal interest in sartorial details on- and offstage. Since theater is always a matter of showing off as well as recounting, students can profit enormously from an exploration of the visual fashions in which the playwright's texts are anchored.

It seems difficult to believe that issues related to costume could prevent a play from being produced, but such considerations in fact undermined productions of Molière's *Tartuffe ou l'imposteur* and of his *Dom Juan ou le festin de pierre*. History has recorded that Tartuffe's original costume, the one that he wore in the 12 May 1664 premiere during *Les plaisirs de l'île enchantée*, a fete celebrating the expansion of Versailles, incensed the religious community. According to *L'histoire du père de La Chaise* (1694), "the impostor appeared for the first time if not in Jesuit's robes, at least in cassock and in a hat with a wide brim" (Molière, *Œuvres* 1: 838). La Chaise's qualification is important: if Tartuffe did not in fact appear in a Jesuit's robes, he at least wore the familiar churchman's cassock and hat with a wide brim. In a late-seventeenth-century Nicolas Bonnart engraving titled "Abbé in Cassock" (fig. 1), we see the wide-brimmed churchman's hat, the small collar, and the top of the cassock, which was usually ankle-length. The bottom of the cassock resembles a choir robe, and the principal color of the entire outfit would have been black, with a small square white collar and white cuffs. (The ribbon decorations and the ruff sleeves in figure 1 are indications of this particular abbé's worldliness, elements that Tartuffe would not have adopted.) Georges Couton attests to the ecclesiastical air of Tartuffe's original costume without specifying what Tartuffe wore:

> His costume sufficed so that, at the moment of his entry, the first Tartuffe was catalogued: he was one of those postulants for ecclesiastical benefits, who have without doubt been tonsured and perhaps even received minor orders, and [who] have "launched themselves into reform."
>
> (Molière, *Œuvres* 1: 836–37)

Abbé en Sotttane

L'Abbé dans cette modestie   Aussy fait il bien sa partie
N'a rien de l'air d'vn desbauché   De paruenir à l'Euesché
        chez N Bonnart, rue S.t Iacques à l'aigle . Auec priuil. du Roy .

Fig. 1. Nicolas Bonnart. "Abbé in cassock." (Paris, Bibliothèque Nationale, Cabinet des Estampes)

LE TARTVFFE

Fig. 2. François Chauveau. Engraving for the 1669 and 1673 editions of *Tartuffe ou l'imposteur*. (Paris, Bibliothèque Nationale, Département des Imprimés)

Trying to appease those who objected to Tartuffe's original costume, Molière attempted to disguise Tartuffe as Panulphe, a pious man of the world. Molière describes his efforts at changing Tartuffe's image in his "Second Petition presented to the King in his camp in front of the city of Lille in Flanders," written shortly after the 5 August 1667 production of *L'imposteur*:

> My comedy, Sire, did not here [in Paris] enjoy Your Majesty's goodness. In vain I produced it under the title of *L'imposteur* and disguised the character in the attire of a man of the world; in vain I gave him a small hat, a lot of hair, a large collar, a sword, and lace all over the costume, [in vain] I incorporated mollifications, [in vain] I carefully removed everything that I judged capable of furnishing the shadow of a pretext to the famous originals of the portrait I wished to make: all that served for naught.   (*Œuvres* 1: 891–92)

The changes Molière made to his famous hypocrite's costume were to no avail: on 6 or 7 of August 1667, an interdiction of *L'imposteur* was delivered to the theater by a representative of the first president Lamoignon, and the archbishop of Paris threatened anyone presenting, viewing, or reading the play with excommunication (*Œuvres* 1: 845). Georges Couton argues convincingly that if we reverse Panulphe's worldly image (the small hat, the long wig, the large collar, etc.), we arrive at the vestimentary image of the pious laymen of the day who wore large hats, short hair, and small collars (1: 835–36). Such laymen were in fact known as *petits collets* ("small collars"). Antoine Furetière specifies that they actually wore small collars and that hypocrites wore them to affect piety:

> They call *petit collet* a man who has reformed himself through devotion because, for reasons of modesty, the men of the Church wear small collars, whereas the men of the world wear large ones decorated with needlework and lace. And sometimes it is said in a bad way of hypocrites who affect modest manners, especially by wearing a small collar.
>   (s.v. Collet)

Interestingly, this definition aptly summarizes the kinds of vestimentary transformations Molière probably effected in Tartuffe's costume between 1664 and 1667.

By February 1669, Louis XIV had permitted *Tartuffe* to reappear onstage. We do not know what sort of costume Tartuffe wore in the revival of February 5, but seventeenth-century engravings suggest that he wore worldly clothing with pious accessories. In one engraving attributed to François Chauveau (fig. 2), which appeared in the June 1669 and May 1673 editions of the play, Tartuffe's dark costume consists of a low round hat with a medium brim, a knee-length cape, a small plain white collar, a close-fitting buttoned doublet with small white cuffs, a rhinegrave (a pair of wide knee-length breeches, also known as petticoat breeches, attached at the knee and resembling a wide skirt with folds at the bottom; see my glossary in *Costume* 378), dark stockings, and flat shoes with small rosette decorations. Tartuffe's small collar and short hair suggest that he is a *petit collet*, but those elements contrast with the cape and rhinegrave which were worldly garments. In a detached engraving by an anonymous artist (fig. 3), Tartuffe wears an identical costume with some minor modifications: he holds his hat in his left hand, his collar is medium-size, the separation between his doublet and breeches is decorated with a line of ribbons, and he wears wide breeches with dark ribbon garters rather than a rhinegrave. In his 1682 engraving for *L'imposteur* (fig. 4), Pierre Brissart copies Tartuffe's costume from the original 1669 engraving, also with slight modifications: Tartuffe's hat is taller and has a wider brim, his collar is smaller and squarer, a white shirt protrudes from under the bottom of his partially unbuttoned short doublet in the fashion of dandies, and he wears breeches with large ribbon garters under his rhinegrave.

My research into Molière iconography indicates that it is of limited reliability. Most of the artists who illustrated Molière plays had probably not attended them, and their renderings of costumes came more from their knowledge of fashion and from their imagination than from fact (see Dock, *Costume* 351–52; Ranum). Of much greater reliability are the descriptions of nineteen of Molière's thirty-one costumes contained in the postmortem inventory of his possessions (Molière's *inventaire après décès*, or IAD; see Jurgens and Maxfield-Miller 566–73) and the vestimentary vocabulary that Molière uses in his plays.

According to Orgon's son Damis, Tartuffe is a boor, a *pied plat* (1.1.59) who is as unacceptable in society as a peasant wearing flat shoes. Dorine, Mariane's lady-in-waiting, adds that in fact Tartuffe had no shoes when Orgon took him in; furthermore, his clothing was not worth six deniers (1.1.63–64) or half a sou (James Gaines states that the *livre tournois* was equivalent to twenty sous and that each sou was equivalent to twelve deniers [20–21]; therefore, Tartuffe's shoes were not even worth half a sou). In his famous opening lines Tartuffe mentions his hair shirt and scourge to impress listeners with his religious zeal: "Laurent, serrez ma haire avec ma discipline" (3.2.853) ("[Laurent], Hang up my hair-shirt, put my scourge in place"). The ridiculousness of this line becomes apparent when one realizes that a truly devout person would never treat these objects as if they were no different from a hat and coat. Tartuffe's healthy physical appearance (1.4.233) plainly suggests that he would never have accepted flagellation or the wearing of a hair shirt.

Although the seventeenth-century engravings lead us to believe that, in his dress, Tartuffe combined the ecclesiastical with the worldly, the play suggests that he was once a poor beggar who therefore would have no taste. In a late-seventeenth-century engraving by Humblot entitled "The Hypocrite" (fig. 5), we see items that Tartuffe might have been more likely to wear: a large hat

Fig. 3. An anonymous engraving entitled "L'imposteur ou le Tartuffe" resembling Chauveau's (Paris, Bibliothhèque Nationale, Département des Imprimés)

Brisart d.   J. Sauve f.

L'Imposteur

Fig. 4. Pierre Brissart (1682). "L'imposteur." (Paris, Bibliothèque Nationale, Département des Imprimés)

L'hipocrite.

A ce dehors beat, à cet humble maintien,   Fuyez les faux devots, craignez l'hipocrisie
De ce franc charlatant, qui ne sera trompé   L'un et l'autre toûjours n'enfante que des maux
Il croit dupper le Ciel faisant l'horne de bien;   Et si vous vous plaignez de la sotte copie,
Mais levez son manteau po.' n'être pas dupé.   Que penseriez vous donc sur les originaux

Humblot excud.

Fig. 5. Humblot, "The Hypocrite." (Paris, Bibliothèque Nationale, Cabinet des Estampes)

with a fairly wide brim, a simple knotted cravat, a long buttoned vest with pockets, a knee-length cape, breeches with knee rolls, hose, and flat shoes with simple buckles. It is doubtful that Tartuffe would wear a wig or a sword like Humblot's hypocrite, but the Bible (or religious treatise) tucked under one arm, the rosary held in folded hands, and the small scourge projecting from one of the vest pockets are marvelous props for a hypocrite like Tartuffe. He probably would have worn a little collar in lieu of a cravat.

We know what Molière wore for his Orgon costume because it is described in his IAD (Jurgens and Maxfield-Miller 567). The expensive material (soft Venetian wool), the watered silk (*tabis*) lining of the mantle, the decorations of English lace on the mantle, the garters and shoes all clearly indicate Orgon's wealth. The seventeenth-century engravings do not create the image of the wealthy bourgeois suggested by the description in Molière's IAD. In the 1669 and 1673 engravings, Orgon, who has the white hair and beard of an old bearded man (a *barbon*), is just emerging from beneath the table where Elmire told him to hide (4.6), and we see only his collar, larger than Tartuffe's, and the left arm of a dark long-sleeved doublet. In the detached engraving (fig. 3), Orgon has emerged from beneath the table, and we see his costume. It consists of a simple white collar with a sawtooth edge, a dark long-sleeved doublet, a dark shirt, wide dark breeches, dark stockings, and shoes. We know that Orgon has a beard because Dorine, his daughter Mariane's lady-in-waiting, makes fun of it when he announces that he plans to marry Mariane to Tartuffe (2.2.473); the beard is supposed to be a sign of wisdom.

As for the women's costumes, they should be sources of delight and humor. Louis Béjart originally played the role of Mme Pernelle in drag (Molière, *Œuvres* 1: 1334), and, according to René Bray, he wore a mask (97). The writer of the *Lettre sur la comédie de L'imposteur* ("Letter Concerning the Comedy of the Impostor") (1667) states that Mme Pernelle prefers "the ridiculous austerity of past times" and that her clothing does less to indicate her importance than do the attentions of well-dressed members of Orgon's household (Molière, *Œuvres* 1: 1149). Mme Pernelle takes pleasure in deriding her daughter-in-law's stylishness, denouncing Elmire for being spendthrift and for going about dressed like a princess (1.1.29–32). We know that the cloth in Elmire's costume is indeed soft and probably luxurious. Tartuffe uses this excuse to put his hand on her knee—"Je tâte votre habit: l'étoffe en est moelleuse" (3.3.917) ("[I am] feeling your gown; what soft, fine-woven stuff!")—and to examine the needle-work on her garment (919). In his 1682 engraving for *L'imposteur*, Brissart adopts elegant late-seventeenth-century court styles: Elmire wears a décolleté, V-necked bodice decorated with lace at the top and a magnificent, full, floor-length skirt of embroidered material with *retroussis* (an outer skirt folded back up over the hips; see my glossary in *Costume* 377). Her narrow sleeves are tied with bands of ribbon, and there are large garnishes of ribbon in her hair.

As for the other women's costumes, Molière describes parts of Dorine's but refers only in passing to Mariane's. We know that Dorine wore a décolleté

Fig. 6. An undated circular screen attributed to Jean Lepautre. (Paris, Bibliothèque Nationale, Département des Imprimés)

dress. According to 1669 stage directions, Tartuffe takes his handkerchief from his pocket and asks her to use it (3.2.859–60) to cover her exposed bosom. Likewise, Dorine, a *suivante* (lady-in-waiting), probably dresses stylishly, as do Elmire and Mariane. Dorine remarks that Tartuffe's servant has chastised them concerning their ribbons, rouge, and beauty spots: "Il vient nous sermonner avec des yeux farouches, / Et jeter nos rubans, notre rouge et nos mouches" (1.2.205–06) ("He comes to reprimand us with fierce eyes, / And to throw away our ribbons, rouge, and beauty spots"; my trans.). Only monied women wore such stylish accessories. Tartuffe's own rage against such items culminates in his tearing up a lady's handkerchief that he finds in a religious book, charging that it is a crime to mix saintliness with the "parures" (210) ("vanities") of the devil.

An undated circular screen attributed to Jean Lepautre (1621–91) depicts four scenes from *Tartuffe*, copying the styles of some of the engravings already described and offering new insight concerning other costumes (fig. 6). In the bottom section of the screen, Dorine, Orgon, and Cléante discuss Tartuffe's health (1.6). Dorine wears an elaborate décolleté dress with billowy sleeves decorated with a lace-edged apron, and she has a muff on her right arm. Orgon wears a dark costume: a small round hat, a dark cape, a dark doublet, dark breeches, stockings, and shoes. Cléante, dressed like a dandy, wears a plumed hat, a long curly wig, a lacy cravat, a justaucorps (a long tapered coat with buttons down the front and large side pockets; see my glossary in *Costume* 368) with a large bandolier, very large lacy *canons* (starched lace decorations worn around the knees), and shoes decorated with large ribbons. In the right section of the engraving, Tartuffe offers Dorine a handkerchief with which to cover her bosom (3.2). He wears a tall dark hat, a small white collar, a dark cape, a dark rhinegrave, dark garters, dark stockings and shoes. Dorine wears the same costume as in the preceding scene. The top section of the engraving is the mirror image of the earliest engravings for *Tartuffe*: Orgon on the left under the table, Elmire in the middle, and Tartuffe on the right. Elmire wears an elegant décolleté dress with a V-necked bodice and billowy sleeves decorated with lace, the skirt has large *retroussis* embellished at the edge with ribbons, and the skirt itself has embroidery down the center and on the hem. Her hair is stylishly done up in ringlets, and she wears a pearl necklace (the most common accessories for elegantly dressed women in the seventeenth century were a pearl necklace and teardrop pearl earrings). Tartuffe wears the same costume as in the preceding scene but holds his hat in his right hand as he kisses Elmire's hand. As for Orgon, who is emerging from under the table, one sees only his plain white collar and his dark doublet. In the left section of the engraving, M. Loyal discusses his eviction notice with Orgon (5.4), who wears the same costume as in the bottom section. M. Loyal's costume is similar to Tartuffe's: a square white collar, a dark cape, a dark rhinegrave, dark stockings and shoes. According to the play, M. Loyal wears a black *jupon* or long doublet (5.4.1767). Since he is a *huissier à verge* or tipstaff (1742,1768), he might carry the staff that symbolizes his office. Such a staff is not, however, visible in Lepautre's screen. Damis and the other characters stand in the background. Damis's elegant costume consists of a low hat covered with plumes, a lacy collar, a billowy-sleeved shirt, a long cane, a knee-length justaucorps with a bandolier, wide breeches, large lace-edged *canons*, stockings, and shoes decorated with large bows. Another character, probably Cléante, stands to the left of Orgon wearing court attire similar to Damis's.

The costumes for *Tartuffe* must reflect Tartuffe's hypocrisy; Orgon's wealth, old age, and lack of taste; the ladies' wealth and stylishness (in décolleté dresses with stylish accessories); and the elegance of Mariane's lover Valère, who doubtless dressed like a *jeune blondin*, one of the young blond-haired dandies of the time (see Dock 72, 80, 93, 94, 154n8, 188, 210, 212, 340, 344–46; for visual images, see figs. 24 and 25).

By all appearances, *Le misanthrope* takes place on a much higher social scale than *Tartuffe*, and many of the upper-class characters were doubtless dressed like aristocrats. With the exception of Dom Juan, Molière does not describe his aristocrats' costumes in detail. Concerning Alceste's costume, Molière mentions only the pocket (4.2.1236) in which he keeps the letter to the marquis Oronte from the coquettish Célimène. In another such letter about the members of her coterie, Célimène describes Alceste as "l'homme aux rubans verts" (5.4) ("the man with the green ribbons"). An anonymous 1667 frontispiece (fig. 7) shows Alceste, who is seated, wearing a round hat with ribbon trimmings, long curly hair or a wig, a flat collar (*rabat*), a loose open vest with billowy slashed sleeves, large ruff cuffs, a small open doublet, a rhinegrave decorated at the belt with a frieze of ribbons, stockings, and high-heeled shoes with ribbon laces. We know that in 1667 it was stylish to wear ribbon trimmings—*une frise de rubans* (a frieze of ribbons)—at the belt of the rhinegrave (Ruppert 3:40), and we assume that in Alceste's instance those ribbons and the ones on the hat and shoes are all green. Molière's IAD (1673) describes a luxurious costume quite different from that of the 1667 engraving:

> *Item*, another box where one finds the costumes for the presentation of *Le misanthrope* consisting of breeches and a justaucorps of gold-striped brocade and gray silk, lined with watered silk, decorated with green ribbon, the vest of gold brocade, the silk stockings and garters, appraised at thirty livres.   (Jurgens and Maxfield-Miller 567–68)

The richness of this costume is outstanding. Dressed in such a handsome costume, Alceste is not out of style; moreover, it visibly exposes the hypocrisy of his own claim that he loathes everything about the court. Vests were stylish—as we shall see in regard to Oronte's clothing—and this is the first time a vest is mentioned in one of Molière's plays. Alceste's justaucorps is somewhat puzzling: although on 16 January 1665 Louis XIV had established the elitist *justaucorps à brevet*, a type of court uniform allowing direct access to the king (Wolf 273), the justaucorps itself did not supposedly come into full style until

Fig. 7. Anonymous frontispiece of the 1667 edition of *Le misanthrope*.

LE
MISANTROPE
COMEDIE
Par I.B.P. DE MOLIERE.

A PARIS.

Chez IEAN RIBOV, au Palais, vis à vis la Porte
de l'Eglise de la Sainte Chapelle,
a l'Image Saint Louis.

M. DC. LXVII.
AVEC PRIVILEGE DV ROY.

1670 (Boucher, *Histoire* 431). We conclude, therefore, that either Alceste is a forerunner of fashion or, as Tom Lawrenson suggests, that Molière updated this costume in 1670 and wore it in fourteen subsequent performances of *Le misanthrope* (167). Pierre Brissart's 1682 engraving for that play (fig. 8) shows Alceste wearing the splendid court styles of the 1680s, including the justaucorps: a round hat with a single ribbon decoration at the front and a turned-up brim, a long curly wig, large shoulder ribbons, a magnificent justaucorps decorated with embroidery and with small buttons about the opening and pockets, large cuffs, wide breeches embellished with loops of material at the bottom, stockings, and narrow high-heeled shoes.

The green ribbons that decorated Alceste's justaucorps have become a necessary decoration for the costume of any actor playing Alceste. Molière's troupe bought the famous actor Michel Baron green ribbons for his Alceste costume when he took over Molière's role on 24 February 1673. Green was Molière's favorite color; it is the prevalent color in his costumes and was also dominant in the furnishings for his living quarters (Jurgens and Maxfield-Miller 556–57, 560, 563–64, 566–70, 575–76). According to Alfred Copin, Molière's favorite role was that of Alceste, and he chose green ribbons to give that role a personal touch (118–20). There were apparently other implications relating to the use of green in costumes: Ludovic Lalanne cites several instances in literary history where green symbolizes folly or craziness in the people wearing it, including Don Quixote (125–27). In Molière's plays, his most famous *fous*, or crazy people, wear green, occasionally combined with golden yellow (*aurore*) (see Dock 171–72). When worn by Alceste, the green ribbons may symbolize his persistent melancholia and his foolish insistence on trying to reform society.

Although nothing is mentioned about Philinte's costume, in the seventeenth-century engravings we see him dressed even more splendidly than Alceste. In the 1667 engraving he wears a round, wide-brimmed hat decorated with large plumes, a long curly wig, a large collar decorated with lace, a loose open vest with short slashed sleeves, a shirt with large billowy sleeves and ribbon garters at the elbows, a fringed bandolier, a sword, rhinegrave breeches (the *rhingrave-culotte*), ribbon garters, stockings, and high-heeled shoes decorated with ribbons. According to Jacques Ruppert, the large lace-edged collar, the fringed bandolier, and the rhinegrave breeches were stylish in the period from 1660 to 1668 (40). In Brissart's 1682 engraving, Philinte's costume resembles Alceste's but surpasses it in magnificence. Philinte, who holds a large plumed hat under his right arm, wears a long curly wig, a large lacy cravat, large embroidered shoulder ribbons, a handsome justaucorps decorated with embroidery and small buttons around the low horizontal pocket and side vent, a sash with a fringed end, several large garnishes of ribbons on the cuffs, a sword, wide breeches decorated with large loops of material like Alceste's, stockings, and narrow high-heeled shoes. That Philinte should be dressed more elegantly than

Fig. 8. Pierre Brissart (1682). *Le misanthrope*. (Paris, Bibliothèque Nationale, Département des Imprimés)

Alceste fits his image as a person who intends to succeed in society by accepting its proprieties.

Although it is difficult to tell by reading the play whether or not Alceste's role—as played by either Molière or Baron—was humorous, it is certain that the petty fops (the *petits marquis*) and their costumes compensated for any lack of humor on Alceste's part. In asking Célimène why she esteems Clitandre so much, Alceste describes some of the items that fops wear: the blond wig, the big *canons*, the masses of ribbons, and the wide rhinegrave, adding the unique detail of Clitandre's long nail on his little finger:

> Est-ce par l'ongle long qu'il porte au petit doigt
> Qu'il s'est acquis chez vous l'estime où l'on le voit?
> Vous êtes-vous rendue, avec tout le beau monde,
> Au mérite éclatant de sa perruque blonde?
> Sont-ce ses grands canons qui vous le font aimer?
> L'amas de ses rubans a-t-il su vous charmer?
> Est-ce par les appas de sa vaste rhingrave
> Qu'il a gagné votre âme en faisant votre esclave?
> (2.1.479–86)

> Is it that your admiring glances linger
> On the splendidly long nail of his little finger?
> Or do you share the general deep respect
> For the blond wig he chooses to affect?
> Are you in love with his embroidered hose?[1]
> Do you adore his ribbons and his bows?
> Or is it that this paragon bewitches
> Your tasteful eye with his vast German breetches?

There is no proof that the stylish *marquis* wore a long nail on his little finger. Clitandre's long pinky nail may have had a functional purpose: like the *marquis* in *Remerciement au roi* (Molière, *Œuvres* 1: 632), he must know that it is stylish to scratch on doors rather than knocking, and he may have used his long nail rather than his comb. Molière has described the *marquis*'s wide *canons* and excessive ribbons in other plays (see *L'école des maris* 1.1.35 and *Dom Juan* 2.1), but this is the first time that he calls the rhinegrave by name. Clitandre's long fingernail, striking blond wig, and falsetto voice classify him as one of Molière's most effeminate *marquis*. Another young *marquis*, Acaste, brags to Clitandre about his ability to dress well (*se mettre bien*), thereby staking his own claims to Célimène's affections: "Quant à se mettre bien, je crois, sans me flatter, / Qu'on serait mal venu de me le disputer" (3.1.799–800) ("As for my dress, the world's astonished eyes / Assure me that I bear away the prize"). Visual images of the *petit marquis* appear in François Chauveau's frontispiece for the 1666 edition of Molière's works (Dock, *Costume*, fig. 18, in which

Mascarille is on the left), in Brissart's engravings for *Les précieuses ridicules* (fig. 19), and in *L'impromptu de Versailles* (fig. 31).

Another *marquis*, Oronte, who aspires to become a poet and society wit, apparently wishes to distinguish himself by wearing a vest; in Célimène's letter she refers to him as "l'homme à la veste" (5.4) ("the man with the vest"; my trans.). Although Alceste is unwilling to accept Oronte's poetry or behavior, he will admit that he admires Oronte's skill on horseback and with arms (4.1.1150).

The clothing of the other male characters in *Le misanthrope* indicates their station and suggests the power of their office. The guard who delivers a message from the marshals of France to Alceste concerning the latter's quarrel with Oronte wears an impressive garment, according to the servant Basque: "Il porte une jaquette à grand'basques plissées, / Avec du dor dessus" (2.5.746–47) ("It's a long tail-coat that this fellow wears, / With gold all over"). The magnificence of the tailcoat with the gilt pleated tails indicates the importance of the marshals of France. This splendor contrasts with the somber costume and mien of the bailiff, who later serves Alceste's valet Du Bois with a summons for Alceste's arrest. Du Bois is terrified by the bailiff, whom he describes as "noir d'habit et de mine" (4.4.1449) ("a man in a black suit, / Who wore a black and ugly scowl to boot"); consequently, Du Bois appears before Alceste and Célimène humorously attired in some sort of traveling attire, ready to escape (4.3.1435). Du Bois's ludicrousness makes Alceste angry (4.4.1436–37). According to Couton, Du Bois had dressed up like a postilion, ready to run to the border with Alceste to escape the police (Molière, *Œuvres* 2: 1343). The boots that Michel Laurent mentions are undoubtedly part of this ridiculous gear (Lancaster, *Mémoire* 118).

As for the female characters, the text mentions only their makeup. To give Alceste an example of the danger of telling the truth all the time, Philinte asks him if he would dare insult the elderly Emilie by telling her that her white makeup (1.1.83; undoubtedly similar to the *blancs* mentioned in the *Maximes du mariage* in *L'école des femmes* [3.2.761]) scandalizes everyone. Arsinoé, who is younger than Émilie, also wears white makeup in an attempt to appear beautiful (3.4.942).

There are two primary reasons for using authentic seventeenth-century costuming for Molière plays. The first is that Molière often uses vestimentary vocabulary specific to the seventeenth century, and the second is that a successful rendition of Molière's plays often requires an evocation of the era of Louis XIV and its sartorial elegance. This evocation is certainly essential to the production of *Le misanthrope*, with its aristocratic overtones. To some extent it is also necessary for *Tartuffe*, where the contrast between Orgon's dark bourgeois dress (although expensive) and the elegance of the clothing of the women characters and of the dandy Valère might be difficult to approximate with contemporary clothing. Both my own work on the period—including a style lesson about the fashions of the seventeenth-century French court (*Costume* 8–23; see also the glossary 354–80)—and Diana de Marly's *Louis XIV and Versailles* offer sufficient insight into the period to allow costumers and tailors to approximate period dress. (For a general costume history, I recommend Boucher.) Cost may well be the most important consideration for a producer who is deciding whether to attempt authentic costuming, which is doubtless considerably more expensive than settling for twentieth-century styles.

NOTE

[1]Although Wilbur's translation is masterly, *canons* were not embroidered hose. They were wide round ornaments of linen, often trimmed with lace, which were attached just below the knee to decorate the lower leg. See Dock, *Costume,* figs. 2, 18, 19, 24, 25 and color plate 2.

Performing Molière: *Le misanthrope*— Tragedy or Comedy?

Sara E. Melzer

Like many of Molière's plays, *Le misanthrope* opens in the middle of a conflict between two characters, pitting Alceste's values of authenticity against Philinte's belief in the necessity of accommodating oneself to the world's duplicities. The conflict is so intense that it forces the audience to side with one against the other. But unlike Molière's other plays, *Le misanthrope* does not clearly indicate which side we should choose. In teaching this play, I begin by asking my students which character they identify with and why. This question opens up the play in useful ways because it ultimately helps illuminate the nature of Molière's comedy.

Confronted with the competing logics of Alceste and Philinte, most of my students favor Alceste, assuming that he occupies the play's position of truth. But this choice presents a problem. If we consider that he is as truthful, honest, and sincere as his professed principles are, his character and situation become tragic rather than comic. And this perception is precisely what Alceste himself would want; he asks to be read as a tragic figure. For his character to produce a laughter appropriate to comedy, the play's position of truth would have to be reversed so that the audience views Philinte, and later on Célimène, as mature, "realistic" figures who, unlike Alceste, understand the complexities of social life. They puncture Alceste's "truth," making him a burlesque caricature of a tragic figure. To dramatize this point and to understand how this dynamic operates, I propose a method of teaching whereby the students perform a given scene both as a tragedy and as a comedy.

This approach is useful for two reasons. First, it enables students to explore the boundaries between these genres, dramatizing how a theatrical work is not inherently comic or tragic but depends on the manner of presentation. Molière's major plays seem to invite this kind of experimentation since they flirt with both genres. Thus these comedies have often been seen as tragic: Chateaubriand spoke of Molière's "tragic gravity," Stendhal wrote that in his time one no longer laughed at Molière, and many modern stagings and literary interpretations of his major comedies have brought out their tragic elements.

Second, this approach helps students appreciate the performative dimension of theater. Molière was an actor who wrote plays because he needed material for his acting troup to perform. In his note to the reader at the beginning of *L'Amour médecin*, he writes that his plays are meant to be performed and that the only people who should read them are those who can see beyond the written words to imagine "tout le jeu du théâtre" (*Œuvres* 2:95) ("the spectacle of theater"). The best way to have students discover this "jeu du théâtre" is by having them perform a scene.

One key to the "jeu" lies in understanding not simply what the characters say but also how they act toward and relate to each other in uttering their words. Thus, before students memorize lines and stage the action, I ask them to write a paper to help them discern the emotional logic of their character. This exercise quickly involves the students in a hermeneutic circle. Since people use words to say one thing and mean another, establishing the relation between the words on the page and the characters behind them is problematic. How is it possible to figure out an actor's character except in relation to what he or she says and does? (Here, the way a character uses language is an act.) And yet how is it possible to figure out how actors use language except in relation to our understanding of their characters?

Literary interpretations can tolerate a great deal of complexity and ambiguity in responding to this dilemma. But to perform a play, the actor has to make clear choices. To help my students capture the emotional logic behind their characters' words, I ask them to answer a series of questions that Uta Hagen, the stage actor, asked in preparing her roles. As an example, I will analyze the emotional logic behind Alceste's words and actions in the climactic scene 3 of act 4 from *Le misanthrope* by using Hagan's set of questions.

This scene occurs just after Alceste has been given a love letter he believes Célimène has written to Oronte. In a rage, he confronts Célimène with the "proof" of her infidelity. Célimène, refusing to be put on the defensive, counters, What if it were addressed to a woman? Incredulous, Alceste rails against her trickery but then gives in and asks her to prove it was addressed to a woman. She refuses, insisting it was addressed to Oronte. Alceste breaks down and expresses his passionate love for her. He begs her to pretend the letter was for a woman and says he will pretend to believe her faithful.

I ask the students to answer questions about this scene from both the tragic and the comic perspectives. I have space only to discuss Alceste's character, but a similar analysis would obviously be necessary for all the characters.

The Tragic Perspective

If we accord Alceste the position of truth, we must accept his words at face value and perceive him, the world, and the people around him as he does. Judging Alceste, then, on the basis of what he says, we would see him as a pure, honest soul. But in the world in which he lives, honesty is no ordinary character trait, as he presents it. It engages him in battle with the worldly culture that vehemently disdains sincerity and all the values he holds dear. To combat these forces requires an act of great courage and heroic strength. His honesty elevates him to a distinctive level of being: the noble stature of a tragic hero.

Alceste sees himself as inhabiting a Jansenist tragic universe characterized by a Pascalian or Racinian worldview. His sincerity constitutes both "la misère et la grandeur" ("the misery and the greatness") of his soul, to borrow Pascal's phrase. Alceste's sincerity constitutes his misery for it allows him to see what others blindly accept: the false values that govern human relationships. Amour propre leads people to indulge in flattering games of mutual self-deception, just as Pascal says. But Alceste's sincerity also constitutes his greatness because he refuses to yield and adapt to the miserableness of human social relations. Rather than engage in such emptiness, Alceste prefers to be alone, not craving the divertissements of salon culture, as do the Philintes and Célimènes of this world. His greatness is, however, what makes him tragic in the Racinian sense. It makes him unable to live in this world, for doing so would require accepting values that are untenable to the nobility of his soul. Like Racine's most noble and tragic characters, Alceste refuses to compromise with the values of this world. His noble attachment to the ideals of purity and sincerity is so great that at the play's end he severs connections with society to live in a desert.

Scene 3, act 4, highlights the conditions for tragedy: here Alceste sees just how wide the gap between him and Célimène really is. They speak a different language. Alceste speaks the tragic language of Racine's heroes caught in grand passion. The first line of this scene, "O Ciel! de mes transports puis-je être ici le maître?" (1277) ("Sweet heaven, help me to control my passion"), seems to echo Oreste's mournful cries. Throughout this scene, Alceste lashes out against "le Ciel en courroux" (1283) ("Hell's or Heaven's wrath"), "le poison qui me tue" (1318) ("your black and fatal spell"), "traîtres appas" (1320) ("treacherous charms"), and so forth. Like Racine's Phèdre, Alceste continually invokes a highly moral language of guilt and moral condemnation to persuade Célimène she should be ashamed (1286–1330). But Célimène, like all the other characters, refuses to accept his language, thereby underlining Alceste's separation from her world. Instead, she laughs and appropriates his tragic, moral discourse to mock and devalue his ideals. She ridicules him, suggesting that he adopts a moral language as a social ploy to grab attention.

The most truly tragic moment of the play comes in a sad twist on the Racinian tragic scenario. In a first moment of this scene, Alceste, aware of the ever-deepening chasm that separates him from Célimène, possesses the strength to reject her and her world. But then in a second moment, his resolve breaks down, and he is drawn by the irrational forces of love into her world. His tragic fate compels him to compromise his noble principles and adopt Célimène's corrupt values. When Alceste is given Célimène's love letter, he immediately grasps her deception. To this Célimène adds a second layer of duplicity: she claims the letter is addressed to a woman. And yet, although Alceste knows her assertion to be a vile subterfuge, he knowingly seeks to blind himself to this truth to prevent himself from losing her. His desperation leads him to engage in the kind of hypocrisy he most abhors: he begs her to pretend she is innocent, and he will pretend to believe her. What makes Alceste a tragic figure is his lucidity, his painful awareness of all the rational forces that drive him away from Célimène's world and of all the irrational forces that drag him back into it because of his inexplicable love for her. Like Phèdre, he possesses sharp insight into the destructiveness of his love, yet he is powerless to control it. Love tragically strips this man of his will, his principles, indeed his very self. Love reduces him to nothingness, forcing him to plead for the very thing he abhors.

The following questions help students understand the emotional logic of their character. Students should answer the questions as if they were Alceste. Here I sketch out some brief answers.

Who am I?   I'm a simple, honest being who wants simple, honest relations with others.

What time is it?   A time when my personal ideal of honesty conflicts with the social ideal of "l'honnête homme," which encourages conformity to the conventions of an inauthentic, polite society and not to the honesty of one's own feelings. This is a time in which I do not belong. It is the late seventeenth century, when society revolves around the court and the salon.

Where am I?   A place that conflicts with my social needs. I am in Célimène's salon in Paris, a place that forces people to socialize continually with one another and play meaningless social games.

What surrounds me?   Chairs: large, plush accommodating chairs, inviting the whole world to join Célimène.

What is my relationship to the other person in this scene?   I am irrationally in love with Célimène. I know my love for her is crazy. She embodies everything I hate. She has "l'humeur coquette" (1.1.219) ("coquettish ways"); she flatters others to gain their favor. She has a strange hold over me. I feel powerless before her.

What are the circumstances?   I've been trying to find out if she truly loves me. I've just discovered a love letter she wrote to Oronte. Now I see my error clearly. She doesn't love me. She's been deceiving me all along.

What do I want?   I want Célimène to leave her world and its false values to come live with me in my desert. Then she will learn to love me.

What's in my way?   Her treachery. Her deceptions. She says her letter is addressed to a woman but refuses to prove it.

What do I do to get what I want?   I accept the treacherous values of her world to get her to love me. I will do anything to get her love—even betray my deepest principles. This is how low I have sunk.

The Comic Perspective

The comic perspective works within the same double logic as the tragic does, but the position of truth is reversed. We reject Alceste's self-proclaimed truths and accept Philinte and Célimène's perspective, which deflates Alceste's tragic grandeur down to the size of comic buffoonery. From their perspective, Alceste's "lucidity" masks his true blindness. Philinte and Célimène see a double logic operating within Alceste himself, a gap separating Alceste from himself. His tragic language of morality and grand passion does not reflect his most deeply felt sentiments, as he would have us believe, but is, rather, a defense mechanism to prevent him and us from seeing what he is afraid to admit.

Philinte first tips us off to Alceste's blindness in the play's opening scene by puncturing his overinflated moralistic, tragic language, highlighting the discrepancy between Alceste's high moral tone and the mundaneness of the reality he describes. Célimène performs the same function in this scene. While writing a love letter to another man is far from laudable, it hardly qualifies as the crime Alceste says it is. Alceste describes it as follows: "Que *toutes* les horreurs dont une âme est capable / A vos déloyautés n'ont *rien* de comparable" (1281–82; emphasis added) ("I mean that sins which cause the blend to freeze / Look innocent beside your treacheries"). As Jacques Guicharnaud notes, Alceste speaks an excessive, all-or-nothing language unsuitable for the situation described (*Molière: Une aventure*). The more Alceste puffs up the tragic side of his character with his hyperbolic despair and self-delusional grandeur, the more ludicrous he appears. The comic effect intensifies as the discrepancy widens between Alceste's exaggerated language and the substance of what he is talking about.

Whereas Alceste construes his emotionally intense language as belonging to the tragic universe, Philinte sees it as indicative of what Alceste wants to camouflage. The play's subtitle *L'atrabilaire amoureux* provides the key to Alceste's hidden character. What motivates him is not his sincerity, as he would have us believe, but his anger—a deep-seated rage that dominates his whole being. But the question is, What is he so angry about? And why should it be funny?

Alceste's anger is one of the most primitive of human feelings. He is furious that he is not loved as he feels he should be. He wants to be preferred to the exclusion of everyone else; he wants the world to bend to his needs and desires and to revere him as an exalted, godlike figure. While there is probably not a soul alive who, at some level, does not share these feelings, most of us become socialized adults by recognizing such feelings as irrational. We learn to compromise and adapt to the complexities of living in society, where we cannot be the center of the universe.

Alceste's behavior becomes comic when we interpret it through the eyes of the more rational, adultlike character of Philinte. In this perspective, Alceste's behavior unintentionally betrays the emotional logic of a tyrannical child furious at a world that refuses to accommodate his infantile needs and desires. The comedy comes from a kind of comic timing—the speed with which the audience rejects what Alceste is saying. The audience suddenly perceives several contrasts that produce laughter. One contrast is between the high and the low, between the tragic grandeur of his adultlike pretensions and the pettiness of his childish impulses. This contrast leads to another: If we were to remain in the interpretive world of his tragic grandeur, Alceste's rage would appear harmful and threatening. But once his rage appears to result from his childish impulses, it becomes harmless and thus comic. The laughter stems from the abrupt contrast between the sense of harm his rage portends and its ultimate harmlessness. In addition, the more harmless and uncontrollable Alceste's rage becomes, the more comic he appears, especially since his need is to control others by his threats to do harm.

To gain a sense of Alceste in a comic mode, students should answer the same questions presented above for the tragic mode. In both modes, Alceste perceives himself as tragic. But whereas his perception is correct for the tragic mode, it becomes ludicrous in the comic. The comic perspective is complicated because it necessarily involves a dual logic. The play's director should stage the action to allow the audience to perceive Alceste's emotional logic but at the same time to perceive and identify with Philinte's interpretation of Alceste. I first sketch out Alceste's emotional logic. Then I present Philinte's perspective while transposing the play into contemporary college culture.

Who am I?   I'm a sincere, solitary soul. The wellspring of my soul goes so deep that no one feels things as profoundly as I do. And no one expresses these feelings as honestly as I do.

What time is it?   Time for me to leave. Nobody understands how noble and important I am.

Where am I?   In a foreign world, Célimène's world, where the most shallow values smother me.

What surrounds me?   The latest in Paris's deceitful, degraded, decadent fashion.

What is my relation to the other person in this scene?   I adore Célimène as no man has ever loved any woman.

What are the circumstances?   Célimène has betrayed me by writing a letter to an insect of a man, infinitely inferior to me.

What do I want?   I want her to come crawling on her hands and knees and beg me to take her with me to my desert island.

What's in my way?   Célimène's refusal to recognize that I alone am right and that she belongs in my world.

What do I do to get my way?   I tell her the awful truth: she is a lowly, unworthy creature no better than the rest, but I can save her. Then she'll be mine, body and soul.

Philinte, however, offers an alternative logic. What Alceste views as sincerity, Philinte sees as a defense mechanism. I present Philinte's logic using a scenario that relates Alceste's psychology to college campus life today. Alceste fears he is a nerd because people do not respond to him as the BMOC (big man on campus) that he would like to be. He can't compete with the campus athletes for Célimène's affections. To win her over, he redefines the rules of "coolness" so that he'll come out on top. The new rules that he proclaims as valid for everyone are that the NSM (new, sensitive male) is superior to the traditional macho type. According to him, only the NSM is in touch with his feelings and expresses them openly and honestly. These qualities constitute true courage and strength. Although Alceste sees himself as a genuine NSM, deep down he'd love to be a macho campus athlete, if only he could. But he can't. So he flips the existing values on their head and proclaims his superiority.

Alceste's love for Célimène also stems from a desire to control the world. He thinks he genuinely loves her. But what he loves about her is that she possesses what he lacks: personal power and the ability to command attention. He wants to be like Célimène but cannot admit it because of his fear of failure. In possessing Célimène, he can get indirectly what he cannot acquire directly for himself.

At the end of the scene, he fantasizes about her being destitute so he can re-create her and give her everything (1427–35). He will accept her only if she is totally dependent on him and sees in him her whole world. Célimène rightly questions and mocks this "true" love: "C'est me vouloir du bien d'une étrange manière!" (1433) ("This is a strange benevolence indeed!").

Comedy depends on our ability to gain lucidity and insight into a character's blindness. Our distance from Alceste allows us to see him as comic and to perceive immediately what he cannot. Comic distance is created only when Alceste's suffering does not have the resonance, the force, the reality that he thinks it has. Following Henri Bergson's theory of the comic, an actor should play Alceste not as a fully rounded and developed person but more as a machinelike creature dominated by a single obsessive characteristic: his anger, as fixed and unchanging as a mask. Like an unsocialized child, he is furious that the world does not automatically bend to his needs and desires. His response is to re-create the world and a system of values whereby his supposed superiority would become overwhelmingly evident to others so that he would get the recognition he feels he deserves.

What must have made this play highly comic for seventeenth-century spectators, an aspect probably lost on audiences today, is the way it parodies that period's conventions of tragic plots and language. This parody corresponds to ancient Greek notions of theater, which staged a "satyr" play after a series of three tragedies. The satyr play took the same material as the tragic ones but reversed it and played it as a comedy. In *Le misanthrope,* Molière is standing Racine and tragic discourse on their heads.

While this aspect of Molière's theater may be mostly lost, other forms of laughter are not. The laughter in this play corresponds to three of the traditional theories of comedy. The incongruity theory, based on Schopenhauer, suggests that laughter results from the sudden perception of a discrepancy between an image or concept and the reality. Our distance from certain characters allows us to see two things: how the characters see themselves and what they blind themselves to. It is the contrast between these two things that creates the comic. As the above discussion indicates, these discrepancies are brought to the fore only in the comic production of *Le misanthrope.* Whereas Alceste sees himself as plainfully lucid, we see this lucidity as false. Whereas he sees himself as noble and tragic, to us this tragic nobility is a defense mechanism to hide his petty, tyrannical nature. Whereas he sees himself as sincere, we see him as deceiving himself about his true desires. He hates Célimène's crowd and her world, yet he would love nothing more than to be exactly like her, with all her personal power. He thinks he loves Célimène, but his notion of love is one that would cripple rather than nourish her. This is love with a vengeance.

That we can see what Alceste cannot makes us feel superior to him and to other such fools. The superiority theory, based on Hobbes (ch. 7), suggests that laughter comes from the self-congratulatory experience of superiority over others. To the extent that Alceste appears blind, rigid, and mechanical, we can dissociate ourselves from his illusion of superiority. The more exaggerated he is, the more we feel protected against falling into the same trap. From the security of this distance, we can laugh.

Related to these theories is the relief theory, which postulates that laughter results when repressed feelings are suddenly unleashed. Alceste acts out the childish, narcissistic feelings that all people experience at a primitive level but control and deny in adult civilized society. The spectators achieve a purgative effect by experiencing unavowed sentiments and desires vicariously through Alceste. But at the same time, spectators can position themselves at a safe distance from Alceste by laughing at him as if these sentiments and desires are only his. Again, it is only from the security of this distance that spectators can laugh.

From Classroom to Stage and Back: Using Molière in Performance

James F. Gaines

To have a class learn about Molière's plays through acting them out is one of the most natural approaches imaginable to a type of artwork that was envisioned primarily as a social experience and only secondarily as a textual one. Moreover, it is certainly not a new approach, for teachers have been using dramatic performance for ages in a variety of educational contexts. The method is as old as the French theater itself: during the Renaissance, *collèges* often staged plays to teach rhetoric, grammar, and philosophy, as some of the earliest French and Latin plays of humanists like George Buchanan attest. Even earlier, in the medieval period, religious drama served a didactic end, teaching the faithful—in their own vernacular—about the lives of saints and the passion of Christ. Medieval comedy was also closely tied to the schools, since the *soties* (carnival satires) and some farces, like *Pathelin,* were rooted in the societies of law students clustered around the universities. Medieval and early modern teaching was itself intensely theatrical, with the professor's ex cathedra declamation serving at once as textbook, discussion, and hieratic revelation. Ironically, the formation of academies and eventually of centralized educational bureaucracies took drama out of the classroom; in our post-Gutenberg era, the electronic innovations of instructional television, video, and CD-ROM promise to restore drama to its original pedagogical importance.

Though the approach is old, little has been written about it. Perhaps it fell into the taxonomic cracks created by modern learning systems, since it can be viewed as too untextual for scriptocentric literature faculties and not sufficiently quantifiable for the behaviorist schools of education. Heavily reliant on "show" as well as "tell," performance-based teaching does not lend itself handily to learned journals eager to avoid the added costs of illustrations, although there are a few notable exceptions, such as *Theatre Journal.* In attempting to construct a theoretical framework for the use of performance in conjunction with literary studies of seventeenth-century French drama, it is useful to make a preliminary distinction between the importation of a stage performance into an otherwise literary classroom experience and the actual creation of a performance inside the classroom setting, using members of the class themselves as the actors. Since the latter process represents a more complicated situation (though not by any means the second choice for every class), I discuss it after examining imported theatrical experiences, ranging from television and video to live, out-of-class stage performance.

The same economic considerations that made seventeenth-century playwrights reluctant to print their creations have acted as a brake on the production and dissemination of twentieth-century video materials. Nevertheless, television broadcasting offers several advantages that are helping to overcome the theatrical phobia about offering the public alternatives to live performances. For one thing, the elevated economics of television can be alluring to traditionally cash-starved theater people, who may be tempted to allow cameras into the playhouse, provided that the producers can influence the timing of the broadcast to avoid a negative impact on ticket sales. Moreover, television producers may actually be able to finance complete stage productions never meant for live audiences, as in the case of Jonathan Miller's *The Shakespeare Plays*.

Now that VCR technology, joined with the satellite dish, facilitates taping and replaying of such programs, and now that videocassette and diskette technologies are making cultural materials such as play performances marketable on a global basis, teachers can take advantage of an increasingly wide range of recorded performances in the classroom setting. The introduction to this volume contains a list of available video-format materials, and that list is bound to grow exponentially in coming years. For productions of *Tartuffe* and *Le misanthrope*, several offerings are already available in both French and English. As the list of video plays grows, only the less commonly taught plays remain exclusively in the domain of the theater. (Could this be the reason that some of the outstanding French stage successes of recent years have been productions of *Monsieur de Pourceaugnac, George Dandin,* and *L'étourdi*?)

What, however, are the roles of video performance in the classroom? Its usefulness as a language learning tool is somewhat circumscribed since most French-language video performances are likely to be rendered at an acoustically fast pace, too fast for most who rate in the ACTFL novice or intermediate ranges to be able to seize much of the dialogue without already knowing the material. Further, a full five-act comedy is likely to achieve linguistic overkill, since it will contain much more material, either functional-notional or grammatical, than a beginner can absorb.

The attractiveness of Molière videos at the sub-advanced levels may lie in careful editing of scenes that can be reviewed and played back in conjunction with either memorization or "reader's theater" application in the classroom, especially if such scenes are selected on a functional-notional basis, so as to coincide with oral-proficiency-based approaches to language teaching. Units involving parts of the body could be integrated with scenes from some of the medical satires, such as *Le malade imaginaire* (1.5–7) and *Le médecin malgré lui* (2.3–4), and description of neighbors with the "portraits scene" from *Le misanthrope* (2.4) or the first scene of *Tartuffe*. Even in this controlled application, one should take care to gloss typically seventeenth-century elements of language beforehand, since any unintelligible phrase will seem like gibberish to the beginning student. The mnemonic value of material learned or reviewed in this way is enhanced for the same reason that other oral-proficiency, TPR (total physical response), or Rassias-method techniques are valuable, since bodily involvement creates a greater number of potential memory coordinates than does simple mental or oral repetition.

Success, however, involves more than just scholarly homework and preparation of vocabulary sheets. One of the great hidden resources of the performed text lies in its ability to unleash comedy from apparently uncomic constellations of words. Take the scene in Truffaut's *L'argent de poche* in which a lethargic class responds halfheartedly to the teacher's "magisterial" exposition of *L'avare* (4.7), only to burst into frenetic activity and high humor as soon as Mlle Petit, the official representative of culture, leaves the room and they feel free to dive into the dialogue, with abandon of classroom protocol and the wringing of throats. Once the extract has been selected and glossed by the prof, a minimum of control is in order, since spontaneous impersonation of the theatrical roles, even if it is linguistically or culturally somewhat "incorrect," is liable to yield greater long-term results and provide for better group dynamics than an intimidating form of cultural modeling. The free play of words by the actors who use them is certainly authorized by Molière himself, if one looks closely at such scenes as *Les femmes savantes* (1.4–6) and *Le bourgeois gentilhomme* (2.4).

Above the intermediate level, the extensive use of video performances is likely to yield more fruitful results, since many of the comprehension hurdles that stymie novices and intermediates will have been removed, while advanced learners are likely to have constructed a rudimentary "horizon of expectations" from the various instructional material they have picked up en passant. Though the most obvious use of a Molière video performance would be to teach about the seventeenth-century theater and classical notions of civilization, this is by no means the only or even the most appropriate application in an advanced-level classroom. For instance, culturally specific notions of the comic, which Molière certainly had some role in forming as well as "reflecting," are fundamental to many linguistic concepts as well as to a vast array of cultural domains. Sganarelle's "tobacco speech" from *Dom Juan* (1.1), for instance, makes an interesting example in a class working on style (particularly if one contrasts it with his "native speech" in other scenes), and the numerous "dépit amoureux" scenes, such act 2, scene 4 of *Tartuffe*, are wonderful instances of sarcasm, emotional shading, and misunderstanding based on ambiguity.

Even at the advanced level, there are certain advantages for delaying video exposure until the middle or later phases of discussing a literary work. In presenting *Le misanthrope*, *Tartuffe*, and *Le bourgeois gentilhomme* to my classes, I have noticed that early exposure to the video tends to have a deterministic effect on classroom attitudes toward the play, perhaps because of the unwritten cultural norm of our times that anything seen on a TV set must be true and definitive. In my experience, delaying the presentation of a video allows students a bit of critical space and permits them to evaluate the performance as one among many alternative ways of interpreting the text. I further encourage their critical analysis by asking for both oral and written evaluations of the strong and weak points of the performance seen in the video.

It is worthwhile to remember that English-language and French-language video performances have their respective merits: the former are not merely a watered-down pis aller to be used with students at the lower end of the comprehension scale. While French video materials have the tremendous advantage of presenting the original language, undistorted by translation and embellished by its full poetic force, English-language versions may actually have superior performance values to the French equivalent, and they cannot fail to enrich the viewing and learning process by providing a second frame of reference for comparison of different representations. Where time permits, the pairing of versions in both languages is highly desirable and may be the best alternative to the loathsome distraction of subtitles.

Taking any class to live plays is a more complicated procedure than utilizing videos, not only because there are obvious logistical difficulties in transporting the students and obtaining their tickets but also because the preparation process is necessarily different. Whereas videos provide for easy previewing and reviewing, involving only a quick adjustment of the VCR, live performances are generally one-time-only affairs. In fact, the previewing of a video in preparation for a live performance is an ideal exercise, usually resulting in a greater appreciation of the live actors' talents.

The easiest experiences of this type are in-house assignments to view campus productions of Molière, usually in English. Such productions are handy to all parties, and logistics may be simplified if the sponsors of the production are amenable to cross-disciplinary cooperation in such matters as ticketing and post- or preproduction interviews with cast members. The quality may vary wildly, from the most elementary theater-workshop interpretations of farces such as Le médecin malgré lui to full-blown, elaborately set and costumed versions of five-act comedies such as Le misanthrope (often in Richard Wilbur's rhymed couplets, which reward the skilled student actor but tend to show up the flaws in their less polished counterparts). Preparation for attending all such performances is essential, with a view toward providing for separate frames of reference. If students are led into the play from the beginning by way of a single interpretive strategy—especially that of local directors, who almost infallibly leave a firm imprint on the text—their experience may be flattened by lack of surprise. A gimmicky production is especially likely to turn the spectators into witnesses of a self-fulfilling prophecy. It may be desirable deliberately to work around, rather than through, the interpretive lines of a local production, building in video and textual slants that can be contrasted with it, such as acquainting students with Roger Planchon's radical staging techniques in anticipation of what promises to be a traditional production of Tartuffe or playing the no-nonsense Antony Sher version of the play to a group about to see Orgon loping around the suburbs in a sweater or Flipote played by a wolfhound.

As for professional productions, the most desirable are those that originate or tour in or near campus. Occasionally, French-language productions are available in this category, though less frequently now that Le Tréteau de Paris has stopped touring the United States and that shrinking budgets have restricted the activities of the Services Culturels. Nevertheless, English-language productions can be superlative stimulants to the study of Molière's comedies, as the recent Louisiana tour of Swine Palace Productions' *The Hypocrite* (*Tartuffe*) proved to be. Under the leadership of the former Royal Shakespeare Company director Barry Kyle, the troupe used Jeremy Sams's updated translation to build a production rooted in the Louisiana culture, with Mardi Gras serving as the backdrop for the struggles of Orgon's family and a title character who resonated with the tones of Jimmy Swaggart, Oral Roberts, and other figures familiar on the local spiritual scene. My association with Kyle had tipped me off to many but not all of his theatrical surprises; nevertheless, I deliberately chose to veil these surprises from my classes, centering preperformance discussion on such aspects as verbal and physical disguises and the temporal specificity (or lack of it) in Tartuffe's strategy. Thus when the students saw Elmire in a brothel girl's garters and Cléante in drag, Orgon's famous table transformed into a triumphant carnival float, and none other than the spirit of Huey Long delivering the Exempt's speech, their delight was unabated; yet they were prepared to appreciate these effects in much greater depth than could normally be expected. Having encouraged them to attend a postproduction reception for the actors, I was interested to learn myself that the same tension between careful fieldwork and pure creativity exists onstage as well as in class. Michael McNeal, the very effective Tartuffe, revealed that (to the irritation of Kyle, who had warned his actors against overt parody) he had one day slipped into the notorious local hotbed of religious devotion, Swaggart's Family Prayer Center. Impressed and surprised by the obvious sincerity of almost everyone present, he deepened his character by endowing Tartuffe with a strong consciousness of how firmly worshippers cling to their spiritual dreams.

Provided that the classroom experience does not become too dependent on a single stage experience, any playgoing can potentially stimulate interesting conversation and new understandings. I have often taken advantage of the National Theatre of the Performing Arts' bilingual productions, even though they are aimed primarily at high school students. Besides being able to remember that they are not removed by many evolutionary steps from those creatures, my own university students are prepared to evaluate the effectiveness on the target audience of the NTPA's broad acting style and tongue-in-cheek "replays" of scenes in a contrasting language, since we discuss physical buffoonery and the commedia dell'arte tradition beforehand. It is stirring to be exposed all at once to the majesty of classical verse, as I was one autumn evening in 1965 when my high school teacher heroically led a field trip to New York City so that we might see a Comédie-Française performance of *Le Cid*. But there is nothing to be lost by beginning at the other end of the spectrum and seeing a novice student actor struggling to impersonate Harpagon in word and deed. Like Shakespeare's Athenians in *A Midsummer Night's Dream*, who "recontextualize" the version of *Pyramus and Thisbe* served up by Bottom and his band, one can have a lot of fun and gain much understanding by appreciating each production in its own conjuncture.

Before one can stage Molière's drama within the classroom context, one must take certain variables into consideration: the size of the class and the pool of acting aptitude it contains; time constraints, since a fifteen-week semester is the absolute maximum interval of production in many cases; representation space, blocking, and property requirements; and finally workload, which may not leave room for learning extensive roles. All these factors interact to make the performance of full-length five-act comedies inadvisable unless the teacher-producer enjoys considerable facilities, students with flexible schedules, and a two-semester production interval.

Fortunately, the Molière canon contains a wealth of shorter entertainments, including *La jalousie du Barbouillé*, *Le médecin volant*, *Les précieuses ridicules*, *Le cocu imaginaire*, *L'école des maris*, *Les fâcheux*, *L'Amour médecin*, *Le Sicilien*, *Le médecin malgré lui* (the most compact of the three-act plays), and *La comtesse d'Escarbagnas*. *Le médecin volant* requires considerable acrobatic skill, which may be as out of reach for a student actor as it was for the middle-aged Molière, and *Les fâcheux* is one of the author's most topically dated offerings, making it perhaps less accessible than other plays to a twentieth-century audience. All the remaining titles present interesting opportunities and roles that are within the grasp of many classes. The most popular of them has so far been *Les précieuses ridicules*, which has been staged with considerable success by the students of Bill Mould at the University of South Carolina (along with *L'école des maris*) and of Thérèse Malachy in Israel, among many others. It is interesting that this one-acter works so well, since some of its original success must have been due to the audience's delight at seeing the combination of Molière and Jodelet together, which can only be compared with our seeing Billy Crystal onstage with Woody Allen or Dana Carvey with Dan Aykroyd, outstanding representatives, respectively, of two generations of comics. The ability of unknowns to provoke laughter with the same parts more than three hundred years later points out the structural strengths of this tightly knit comedy about disguise, exaggeration, and affectation. One possible disadvantage of the *Les précieuses ridicules* is that it depends to a large degree on period costuming, whereas *Le Sicilien* or *La comtesse d'Escarbagnas* may be staged in stylized or even contemporary dress without losing much comic effect. Like all the Sganarelle plays, *Les précieuses* places a considerable burden on one actor, while *Le Sicilien* and *La comtesse* distribute the lines more evenly among all characters involved.

The choice of a Molière text depends largely on the aims of the production and its place in the language or literature class. The more canonical status of *Les précieuses ridicules* has certainly contributed to its popularity on- as well as offstage. Yet it is possible to relate other one-act plays to five-acters that may be fixtures on the literature syllabus, illuminating *Le malade imaginaire* with

L'Amour médecin, for example, or *Le bourgeois gentilhomme* with *La comtesse d'Escarbagnas*. In the language classroom, furthermore, canonical status holds little importance, for a play is being used to foreground communicative concerns that have nothing to do with literary history or theory. *La jalousie du Barbouillé*, with its rudimentary stagecraft, broad humor, and down-to-earth lexicon, may be far more appropriate for an intermediate class than a few scenes from *Dom Juan*, and *Le Sicilien* may be as fitting for an advanced phonetics group as *L'école des femmes* would be.

Other, less fully dramatized exercises are more or less de rigueur in the preparation of a one-act production or in the production of selected scenes from longer plays. Such exercises include "reader's theater" and quick-line rehearsals, taping individual parts for phonetic review, and writing out brief "motivation papers" to explore how lines should be delivered in a particular situation. One of the most salient by-products of the production should be an emphasis on intonation and enunciation of whole phrases, as well as "micro-pronunciation." Just as French actors in the conservatoire study breathing in preparation for roles in the theater, the student actors should place great importance on grouping their phonetic output into units that are manageable, completely intelligible, logical, and as close to native-speaker usage as possible—not that emulating native rhythms means emulating native pace. Even in their native languages, most apprentice actors do well to slow down their verbal delivery, and this principle holds doubly true for second-language learners. Keeping in mind that a theatrical role is not a United Nations simultaneous translation marathon, they should remember that their target audience is likely to be far less familiar than they are not only with the acoustic symbols they are using but also with the meaning behind them. Indeed, in my experience this technique makes actors think deeply about their speeches, instead of barreling through material that they are reluctant to admit they misunderstand.

Participation in classroom theatricals gives a sense of linguistic competence that few other exercises can confer, while enhancing the status of those cultural artifacts, the plays, that make such an experience possible. It brings Molière out of the realm of the newspaper or the train schedule, where, some complain, the dominance of proficiency-based teaching strategies has consigned him and the rest of French classical culture. Provided that the acting classes also share their productions with other students less far along the path to fluency, it also imparts a confident response in the audience that they, too, can realistically reach the performance level of their older comrades. There is ample evidence that Molière himself conceived of the theater as a form of school, an *école* where one gains a command of *les moeurs*, or what we today would call cultural competency. Bringing the stage into the classroom can bring the classroom from the shadowy depths of erudition back out onto the resplendent stage of life.

CONTRIBUTORS AND SURVEY PARTICIPANTS

Following are the names and affiliations of contributors and of the scholars and teachers who took time from their busy schedules to respond to the questionnaire on approaches to the comedies of Molière. These responses and the information provided were invaluable to the editors of the volume.

Claude Abraham, *University of California, Davis*
Ralph Albanese, Jr., *Memphis State University*
Louis E. Auld, *Central Connecticut State University*
Susan Reed Baker, *University of Florida*
Faith Beasley, *Dartmouth College*
Alegria Bendelac, *Pennsylvania State University, Schuylkill Campus*
Philip Berk, *University of Rochester*
Jules Brody, emeritus, *Harvard University*
Marie-Florine Bruneau, *University of Southern California*
Biruta Cap, *Kutztown University of Pennsylvania*
Claire Carlin, *University of Victoria*
Elisabeth Caron, *University of Kansas*
Hugh H. Chapman, Jr., emeritus, *Pennsylvania State University*
Hugh M. Davidson, emeritus, *University of Virginia*
Gérard Defaux, *Johns Hopkins University*
Rafael Robert Delfin, *University of New Hampshire*
Stephen V. Dock, *East Carolina University*
Joseph I. Donohoe, Jr., *Michigan State University*
Bruce Edmunds, *University of Alabama*
Nina Ekstein, *Trinity University*
Perry Gethner, *Oklahoma University*
Elizabeth C. Goldsmith, *Boston University*
Michèle Gragg, *Rosary College*
Erica Harth, *Brandeis University*
Lyra Hekmatpanah, *Elmhurst College*
Eglal Henein, *Tufts University*
Ingrid Heyndels-de Saissey
Marie-France Hilgar, *University of Nevada, Las Vegas*
Louise K. Horowitz, *Rutgers University, Camden*
Clara Krug, *Georgia Southern University*
Donna Kuizenga, *University of Vermont*
Barry Kyle, *Louisiana State University*
Lise Leibacher-Ouvrard, *University of Arizona*
Janet T. Letts, *Wheaton College*
Philip Lewis, *Cornell University*
Richard Lockwood, *Rutgers University*
James Madison, *United States Military Academy*
Andrew J. McKenna, *Loyola University of Chicago*

Sara E. Melzer, *University of California, Los Angeles*
William Mould, *University of South Carolina*
Marlies Mueller, *Harvard University*
Buford Norman, *University of South Carolina*
Mary Anne O'Neil, *Whitman College*
Orest Ranum, *Johns Hopkins University*
JoAnn M. Recker, *Xavier University*
Larry W. Riggs, *Butler University*
Sylvie Romanowski, *Northwestern University*
David Lee Rubin, *University of Virginia*
Marie-Odile Sweetser, *University of Illinois at Chicago*
Ronald W. Tobin, *University of California, Santa Barbara*
Sylvia P. Vance, *Otterbein College*
Jean-Claude Vuillemin, *Pennsylvania State University*
Selma Zebouni, *Louisiana State University*
Eléonore M. Zimmerman, *State University of New York at Stony Brook*

WORKS CITED

Abraham, Claude. "Comedy and Linguistic Iconoclasm in Molière." *Papers in French Seventeenth Century Literature* 19 (1983): 767–86.

____. "Farce and Ballet." *Cahiers du dix-septième* 2 (1988): 171–79.

____. "*Le malade imaginaire* at the Court of Versailles." *Actes de Baton Rouge*. Ed. Selma Zebouni. Tübingen: Biblio 17, 1986. 81–91.

____. *On the Structure of Molière's Comédies-Ballets*. Tübingen: Biblio 17, 1984.

Adam, Antoine. *Grandeur and Illusion: French Literature and Society, 1600–1715*. Trans. Herbert Tint. New York: Basic, 1972.

____. *Histoire de la littérature française au XVIIᵉ siècle*. 5 vols. Paris: Domat, 1948–56.

Albanese, Ralph. *Le dynamisme de la peur chez Molière: Une analyse socio-culturelle de Dom Juan, Tartuffe, et L'école des femmes*. University: Romance Monographs, 1976.

____. "*Le malade imaginaire*, ou le jeu de la mort et du hasard." *Dix-septième siècle* 154 (1987): 3–13.

____. *Molière à l'école républicaine: De la critique universitaire aux manuels scolaires (1870–1914)*. Stanford: Stanford French and Italian Studies, Anma Libri, 1992.

Apostolidès, Jean-Marie. *Le prince sacrifié*. Paris: Minuit, 1985.

____. *Le roi-machine: Spectacle et politique au temps de Louis XIV*. Paris: Minuit, 1981.

Arnauld, Antoine, and Pierre Nicole. *La logique ou l'art de penser*. Paris: Flammarion, 1970.

Aubignac, François Hédelin, abbé d'. *La pratique du théâtre*. 1657. Ed. P. Martino. 2 vols. Paris: Champion, 1927.

Auld, Louis. "The Unity of Molière's Comedy-Ballet." Diss. Bryn Mawr, 1969.

Austin, J. L. *How to Do Things with Words*. 2nd ed. Cambridge: Harvard UP, 1962.

____. *Philosophical Papers*. London: Urmson, 1970.

Backer, Dorothy. *Precious Women*. New York: Basic, 1974.

Bailly, Auguste. *L'école classique française*. Paris: Colin, 1921.

Barnwell, H. T., ed. *Le malade imaginaire*. London: Grant, 1982.

Barthes, Roland. *Sur Racine*. Paris: Seuil, 1963.

Bender, John, and David E. Wellbery. "Rhetoricality: On the Modernist Return to Rhetoric." *The Ends of Rhetoric*. Ed. John Bender et al. Stanford: Stanford UP, 1980.

Bénichou, Paul. *Man and Ethics: Studies in French Classicism*. Trans. Elizabeth Hughes. Garden City: Doubleday, 1971.

____. *Morales du grand siècle*. Paris: Gallimard, 1948.

Bergson, Henri. "Laughter." *Comedy*. Ed. Wylie Sypher. Baltimore: Johns Hopkins UP, 1956. 61–190.

_____. "Le rire." *Œuvres*. Paris: PUF, 1959. 381–485.

Bloom, Benjamin S., J. Thomas Hastings, and George F. Madaus. *Handbook on Formative and Summative Evaluation of Student Learning*. New York: McGraw, 1971.

Bordonove, Georges. *Molière génial et familier*. Paris: Laffont, 1967.

Bory, Jean-Louis, ed. *Le malade imaginaire*. Paris: Hachette, 1965.

Boucher, François Léon Louis. *Histoire du costume en Occident de l'antiquité à nos jours*. Paris: Flammarion, 1965.

_____. *Twenty Thousand Years of Fashion: The History of Costume and Personal Adornment*. Trans. John Ross. New York: Abrams, [1967].

Bray, René. *Molière: Homme de théâtre*. Paris: Mercure de France, 1954.

Brody, Jules. "Amours de Tartuffe." *Les visages de l'amour au 17e siècle*. Spec. issue of *Travaux de l'Univ. de Toulouse-Le Mirail* (ser. A) 24 (1984): 227–42.

Brunetière, Ferdinand. "La philosophie de Molière." *Revue des deux mondes* 1 Aug. 1980: 649–87.

Butler, Philip F. "Tartuffe et la direction spirituelle au XVIIe siècle." Cairncross, *L'humanité* 57–69.

Cairncross, John, ed. *L'humanité de Molière*. Paris: Nizet, 1988.

_____. "Molière subversif." Cairncross, *L'humanité* 11–21.

Calder, Andrew. *Molière: The Theory and Practice of Comedy*. London: Athlone, 1993.

Carmody, Jim. *Rereading Molière: Mise en Scène from Antoine to Vitez*. Ann Arbor: U of Michigan P, 1993.

Chevalley, Sylvie. *Molière en son temps, 1622-1673*. Geneva: Minkoff, 1973.

Copin, Alfred. "L'homme aux rubans verts." *Le Moliériste* 1 (1879): 118–20.

Corneille, Pierre. *Œuvres complètes*. Ed. Georges Couton. 3 vols. Paris: Gallimard, 1980–87.

Corvin, Michel. *Molière et ses metteurs en scène d'aujourd'hui*. Lyons: PU de Lyon, 1985.

Dandrey, Patrick. *Molière ou l'esthétique du ridicule*. Paris: Klincksieck, 1992.

Deconstructions: Corneille and Molière. Spec. issue of *Theatre Journal* 34 (1982): 341–478.

Defaux, Gérard. *Molière, ou les métamorphoses du comique: De la comédie morale au triomphe de la folie*. Lexington: French Forum, 1980.

DeJean, Joan. "Classical Reeducation: Decanonizing the Feminine." *Yale French Studies* 75 (1988): 26–39.

_____. *Fictions of Sappho, 1546–1937*. Chicago: U of Chicago P, 1989.

_____. *Tender Geographies: Women and the Origins of the Novel in France*. New York: Columbia U P, 1991.

Dennis, Michael. *Court and Garden: From the French Hôtel to the City of Modern Architecture*. Cambridge: MIT P, 1986.

Dock, Stephen Varick. *Costume and Fashion in the Plays of Jean-Baptiste Poquelin Molière: A Seventeenth-Century Perspective*. Geneva: Slatkine, 1992.

Donohoe, Joseph. "Marivaux: The Comedy of Enlightenment." *Studies on Voltaire and the Enlightenment* 98 (1972): 169–81.

Doolittle, James. "The Humanity of Molière's *Dom Juan*." *PMLA* 68 (1953): 509–34.

Edelman, Nathan, ed. *The Seventeenth Century*. Syracuse: Syracuse UP, 1961. Vol. 3 of *A Critical Bibliography of French Literature*. David C. Cabeen and Jules Brody, gen. eds.

Elias, Norbert. *The Court Society*. 1969. Trans. Edmund Jephcott. New York: Pantheon, 1983.

Faguet, Émile. "Molière." *Les grands maîtres du XVIIe siècle*. Paris: Lecène, 1885. 105–28.

Felman, Shoshana. *Jacques Lacan and the Adventure of Insight*. Cambridge: Harvard UP, 1987.

____. *Le scandale du corps parlant*. Paris: Seuil, 1980.

Fernandez, Ramon. *Molière ou l'essence du génie comique*. Paris: Grasset, 1979.

____. *Molière: The Man Seen through the Plays*. Trans. Wilson Follett. New York: Hill, 1958.

____. *La vie de Molière*. Paris: Gallimard, 1929.

Ferreyrolles, Gérard, ed. *Molière:* Tartuffe. Paris: PUF, 1987.

Figuière, Abbé. *Tartuffe ou l'imposteur*. Paris: Poussielgue, 1882.

Freud, Sigmund. *Civilization and Its Discontents*. London: Hogarth, 1961. 57–145. Vol. 21 of *The Standard Edition of the Complete Psychological Works*. Ed. James Strachey. 24 vols.

Furetière, Antoine. *Dictionnaire universel*. 3 vols. La Haye: Leers, 1690. Paris: Le Robert, 1978.

Gaines, James F. *Social Structures in Molière's Theater*. Columbus: Ohio State UP, 1984.

Géruzez, E. *Histoire de la littérature française*. Vol. 2. Paris: Didier, 1861.

Girard, René. "Perilous Balance: A Comic Hypothesis." *MLN* 87 (1972): 811–26.

____. *Things Hidden since the Foundation of the World*. Trans. Stephen Bann and Michael Metteer. Stanford: Stanford UP, 1987.

Gossman, Lionel. *Men and Masks: A Study of Molière*. Baltimore: Johns Hopkins UP, 1963.

Goyet, Thérèse. "Tartuffe, parle-t-il chrétien?" *Mélanges offerts à Georges Couton*. Lyons: PU de Lyon, 1981. 419–41.

Greenblatt, Stephen. *Renaissance Self-Fashioning: From More to Shakespeare*. Chicago: U of Chicago P, 1980.

Guicharnaud, Jacques, ed. *Molière: A Collection of Critical Essays*. Englewood Cliffs: Prentice, 1964.

____. *Molière: Une aventure théâtrale*. Paris: Gallimard, 1963.

Gutwirth, Marcel. "*Dom Garcie de Navarre* et *Le misanthrope*: De la comédie héroïque au comique du héros." *PMLA* 83 (1968): 118–29.

_____. *Molière ou l'invention comique: La métamorphose des thèmes et la création des types.* Paris: Minard, 1966.

_____. "*Tartuffe* and the Mysteries." *PMLA* 92 (1977): 33–40.

Habermas, Jürgen. *Legitimation Crisis.* Trans. Thomas McCarthy. Boston: Beacon, 1975.

_____. *The Structural Transformation of the Public Sphere: An Inquiry into a Category of Bourgeois Society.* 1962. Trans. Thomas Burger with the assistance of Frederick Lawrence. Cambridge: MIT P, 1989.

Hagen, Uta. *Respect for Acting.* New York: Macmillan, 1973.

Hall, H. Gaston, ed. *The Seventeenth Century: Supplement.* Syracuse: Syracuse UP, 1983. Vol. 3A of *A Critical Bibliography of French Literature.* Ed. Richard A. Brooks.

Hémon, F. *Molière.* Paris: Delagrave, 1891. Vol. 6 of *Cours de littérature.*

Hobbes, Thomas. *Human Nature.* London: Bohn, 1840. Vol. 4 of *Works.* Ed. W. Molesworth.

Hollier, Denis, ed. *A New History of French Literature.* Cambridge: Harvard UP, 1989.

Hope, Quentin M. "Place and Setting in *Tartuffe.*" *PMLA* 89 (1974): 42–49.

Horowitz, Louise K. "Life in the Slow Lane: Molière's Marginal Men." *Papers in French Seventeenth Century Literature* 16 (1989): 65–76.

Hubert, J. D. *Molière and the Comedy of Intellect.* Berkeley: U of California P, 1962.

Jasinski, René. *Molière.* Paris: Hatier, 1969.

The Jerusalem Bible. Garden City: Doubleday, 1966.

Jurgens, Madeleine, and Elizabeth Maxfield-Miller. *Cents ans de recherches sur Molière.* Paris: Imprimerie Nationale, 1963.

Klapp, Otto. *Bibliographie der französischen Literaturwissenschaft.* Frankfurt: Klostermann, 1960– .

Knutson, Harold. *Molière: An Archetypal Approach.* Toronto: U of Toronto P, 1976.

Koppisch, Michael S. "'Partout la jalousie est un monstre odieux': Love and Jealousy in *Dom Garcie de Navarre.*" *Papers in French Seventeenth Century Literature* 12 (1985): 461–79.

La Grange, Charles Varlet de. *Le registre de La Grange, 1659–1685.* Ed. Bert E. Young and Grace P. Young. 2 vols. Geneva: Droz, 1947.

Lalanne, Ludovic. "Les rubans verts du *Misanthrope.*" *Bulletin de la Société de l'Histoire de Paris et de l'Ile-de-France* 18 (1891): 125–28.

Lancaster, Henry Carrington. *A History of French Dramatic Literature in the Seventeenth Century: The Period of Molière.* 2 vols. Baltimore: Johns Hopkins UP, 1936.

_____. *Le mémoire de Mahelot, Laurent et d'autres décorateurs de l'Hôtel de Bourgogne et de la Comédie-Française au XVIIᵉ siècle.* Paris: Champion, 1920.

Lawrenson, Tom. "The Wearing o' the Green: Yet Another Look at 'l'Homme aux Rubans Verts.'" *Molière: Stage and Study. Essays in Honour of W. G. Moore.* Ed. W. D. Howarth and Merlin Thomas. Oxford: Clarendon, 1973. 163–69.

Le Hardy, G. "Les Moliérophobes illustres." *Intermédiaire des chercheurs et curieux* 30 (1894): cols. 519, 632; 31 (1895): cols. 61, 211.

Liskin-Gasparro, Judith, and June Phillips. *Academic Preparation for Foreign Language: Teaching for Transition from High School to College.* New York: College Board, 1986.

Lonchampt, Jacques. "Ah! le grand médecin." *Le monde* 24 Mar. 1990.

Longhaye, le Père G. *Histoire de la littérature française.* vol. 2. Paris: Retaux, 1895. 4 vols.

Lougee, Carolyn C. *Le Paradis des Femmes: Women, Salons, and Social Stratification in Seventeenth-Century France.* Princeton: Princeton UP, 1976.

Lough, John. *An Introduction to Seventeenth Century France.* 1954. New York: McKay, 1966.

Lyons, John D. "Speaking in Pictures, Problems of Representation in the Seventeenth Century." *Mimesis, from Mirror to Method, Augustin to Descartes.* Ed. John D. Lyons et al. Hanover: UP of New England, 1982. 166–87.

Maclean, Ian. *Woman Triumphant: Feminism in French Literature 1610–1652.* Oxford: Clarendon, 1977.

Mallet, Francine. *Molière.* Paris: Grasset, 1986.

Marcabru, Pierre. "Une somptueuse contradiction." *Le Figaro* 24–25 Mar. 1990.

Marly, Diana de. *Louis XIV and Versailles.* London: Batsford, 1987.

Mauriac, François. "Molière le tragique." *Trois hommes devant Dieu.* Paris: Capitole, 1930. 15–51.

Mauron, Charles. *Des métaphores obsédantes au mythe personnel.* Paris: Corti, 1963.

Mélèse, Pierre. "Molière à la cour." *Dix-septième siècle* 98–99 (1973): 57–65.

Melzer, Sara. *Discourses of the Fall.* Berkeley: U of California P, 1986.

Merle, André. "*Tartuffe* mis en scène par Roger Planchon." *Travail théâtral* 17 (1974): 40–45.

Millon, Martine. "Regards indiscrets sur une famille en chemise." *Travail théâtral* 17 (1974): 46–49.

Molière. The Misanthrope *and* Tartuffe. Trans. Richard Wilbur. New York: Harcourt, 1965.

———. *Œuvres complètes.* Ed. Georges Couton. 2 vols. Paris: Gallimard, 1971.

———. The School for Husbands *and* Sganarelle; or, The Imaginary Cuckold. Trans. Richard Wilbur. San Diego: Harcourt, 1992.

———. The School for Wives *and* The Learned Ladies. Trans. Richard Wilbur. 1978. New York: Harcourt, 1991.

———. Tartuffe *and Other Plays by Molière.* Trans. Donald M. Frame. New York: NAL, 1967.

Molière d'Essertine, François de. *Polyxène*. Paris: Sommaville, 1644.

Mongrédien, Georges. *Recueil de textes et documents du 17ᵉ siècle relatifs à Molière*. 2 vols. Paris: CNRS, 1965.

Moore, Will G. *French Classical Literature*. London: Oxford UP, 1961.

———. *Molière: A New Criticism*. Oxford: Clarendon, 1949.

Mouret, Jean-Joseph. *Fanfares*. Jean-François Paillard Chamber Orchestra. New York: Musical Heritage Soc., n.d.

Nelson, Robert J. "The Unreconstructed Heroes of Molière." *Molière: A Collection of Critical Essays*. Twentieth-Century Views. Ed. Jacques Guicharnaud. Englewood Cliffs: Prentice, 1964. 111–35.

Nisard, D. *Histoire de la littérature française*. Paris: Firmin-Didot, 1849.

Nurse, Peter Hampshire. *Molière and the Comic Spirit*. Geneva: Droz, 1991.

Omaggio, Alice. *Teaching Language in Context: Proficiency-Oriented Instruction*. Boston: Heinle, 1986.

Ozouf, Jacques, and Mona Ozouf. *La république des instituteurs*. Paris: Gallimard, 1993.

Pascal, Blaise. *Pensées*. Trans. A. J. Krailsheimer. New York: Penguin, 1986.

———. *Pensées. Œuvres complètes*. Ed. L. Lafuma. Paris: Seuil, 1963.

Péguy, C. *Notre jeunesse*. Paris: Gallimard, 1959. Vol. 2 of *Œuvres en prose*. 2 vols.

Picard, Raymond. "*Tartuffe*: 'Production impie'?" *Mélanges offerts à Raymond Lebègue*. Paris: Nizet, 1969. 227–39.

Pierre-Petit. "Était-ce bien nécessaire?" *Le Figaro* 24–25 Mar. 1990.

Powell, John S. "Charpentier's Music for Molière's *Le malade imaginaire* and Its Revisions." *JAMS* 39 (1986): 87–142.

Powell, John S., and H. W. Hitchcock, eds. *Le livret du malade imaginaire*. Paris: Minkoff, 1990.

Pucciani, Oreste F., and Jacqueline Hamel. *Langue et langage: Le français par le français*. 5th ed. New York: Holt, Rinehart 1987.

Pure, Abbé Michel de. *La prétieuse ou le mystère des ruelles*. Paris: Droz, 1938.

Ranum, Patricia M. "Un portrait présumé de Marc-Antoine Charpentier." *Bulletin de la Société Marc-Antoine Charpentier* 4 (1991): 3–11.

Reiss, Timothy J. *The Discourse of Modernism*. Ithaca: Cornell UP, 1982.

Relyea, Suzanne. "Aggression, Enclosure, and the Caress: *L'honnête homme chez ses amies*." *Actes de New Orleans*. Biblio. 17. Ed. Francis L. Lawrence. Paris: Papers in French Seventeenth Century Literature, 1982. 125–52.

Rigal, Eugène. *Molière*. 2 vols. Paris: Hachette, 1908.

Riggs, Larry. *Molière and Plurality: Decomposition of the Classicist Self*. New York: Lang, 1989.

Romero, Laurence. "Molière's *Morale*: Debates in Criticism." *Molière and the Commonwealth of Letters: Patrimony and Posterity*. Ed. Roger Johnson, Jr., Editha S. Neumann, and Guy T. Trail. Jackson: U of Mississippi P, 1975. 706–27.

———. "Tropes of Scenic Writing: Aspects of Roger Planchon's Classical Stagings." Unpublished ms.

Rousseau, Jean-Jacques. *Lettre à Mr. D'Alembert sur les spectacles*. Ed. M. Fuchs. Geneva: Droz; Lille: Giard, 1948.

Ruppert, Jacques. *Le costume*. 5 vols. Paris: Flammarion, 1942–47.

Rybczynski, Witold. *Home: A Short History of an Idea*. New York: Penguin, 1986.

Sablayrolles, G. Notice. *L'écoles des femmes*. by Molière. Paris: Larousse, 1959. 7–15.

Sainte-Beuve, Ch.-A., ed. *Œuvres complètes de Molière*. Vol. 5. Paris: Calmann-Lévy, 1884.

Saintonge, Paul. "Thirty Years of Molière Studies: A Bibliography, 1942–71." *Molière and the Commonwealth of Letters: Patrimony and Posterity*. Ed. Roger Johnson, Jr., Editha S. Neumann, and Guy T. Trail. Jackson: UP of Mississippi, 1975. 747–826.

Saintonge, Paul, and Robert Wilson Christ. *Fifty Years of Molière Studies: A Bibliography, 1892–1941*. Baltimore: Johns Hopkins UP, 1942.

Schopenhauer, Arthur. *The World as Will and Idea*. Trans. R. B. Haldane and J. Kemp. London: Routledge, 1964.

Scudéry, Madeleine de. "De la tyrannie de l'usage." *Conversations sur divers sujets*. Amsterdam: Fresne, 1682. 63–79.

———. "Sapho à Erinne." *Les femmes illustres*. Rouen: Besongne and Ferrand, 1642.

Simon, Alfred. *Molière: Une vie*. Lyons: La Manufacture, 1988.

Somaize, Antoine de. *Dictionnaire des précieuses*. Paris: Jannet, 1861.

Stanton, Domna C. *The Aristocrat as Art*. New York: Columbia UP, 1980.

———. "The Fiction of *Préciosité* and the Fear of Women." *Yale French Studies* 62 (1981): 107–34.

Swaffar, Janet. "Learning Research Basis for a Process Approach: Distinguishing Learning Models from Teacher Methods." Workshop for Development of Foreign Language and Literature Programs, MLA convention. New York, 27 Dec. 1981.

Tobin, Ronald W. *Tarte à la crème: Comedy and Gastronomy in Molière's Theater*. Columbus: Ohio State UP, 1990.

———. "*Tartuffe*, texte sacré." *Mélanges pour Jacques Schérer: Dramaturgies, langages dramatiques*. Paris: Nizet, 1986. 375–86.

Vedvik, J. D., ed. *French 17: An Annual Descriptive Bibliography of French Seventeenth Century Studies*. Fort Collins: Dept. of Foreign Langs., Colorado State U, 1953–.

Vernet, Max. *Molière: Côté jardin, côté cour*. Paris: Nizet, 1991.

Veuillot, L. "Molière et Bourdaloue." *Revue du monde catholique* 5 (1863): 641–57; 7 (1865): 81–96.

Viala, Alain. "La formation des publics." *La naissance de l'écrivain*. Paris: Minuit, 1985. 132–50.

Voltz, Pierre. *La comédie*. Paris: Colin, 1964.

Walker, Hallam. *Molière: Updated Edition*. Boston: Twayne, 1990.

White, Hayden. "The Value of Narrativity in the Representation of Reality." *The Content of the Form: Narrative Discourse and Historical Representation*. Baltimore: Johns Hopkins UP, 1987. 1–25.

Wolf, John Baptist. *Louis XIV*. New York: Norton, 1968.

Woshinsky, Barbara. "The Discourse of Disbelief in Molière's *Dom Juan*." *Romanic Review* 72 (1981): 401–08.

INDEX

Modern Language Association of America
Approaches to Teaching World Literature
Joseph Gibaldi, series editor

Molière's Tartuffe *and Other Plays*. Ed. James F. Gaines and
    Michael S. Koppisch. 1995.
Momaday's The Way to Rainy Mountain. Ed. Kenneth M. Roemer. 1988.
Montaigne's Essays. Ed. Patrick Henry. 1994.
Murasaki Shikibu's The Tale of Genji. Ed. Edward Kamens. 1993.
Pope's Poetry. Ed. Wallace Jackson and R. Paul Yoder. 1993.
Shakespeare's King Lear. Ed. Robert H. Ray. 1986.
Shakespeare's The Tempest *and Other Late Romances*. Ed. Maurice Hunt. 1992.
Shelley's Frankenstein. Ed. Stephen C. Behrendt. 1990.
Shelley's Poetry. Ed. Spencer Hall. 1990.
Sir Gawain and the Green Knight. Ed. Miriam Youngerman Miller and
    Jane Chance. 1986.
Spenser's Faerie Queene. Ed. David Lee Miller and Alexander Dunlop. 1994.
Sterne's Tristram Shandy. Ed. Melvyn New. 1989.
Swift's Gulliver's Travels. Ed. Edward J. Rielly. 1988.
Voltaire's Candide. Ed. Renée Waldinger. 1987.
Whitman's Leaves of Grass. Ed. Donald D. Kummings. 1990.
Wordsworth's Poetry. Ed. Spencer Hall, with Jonathan Ramsey. 1986.